The Cinema of Michael Mann

Genre Film Auteurs

Series Editor

Eileen Jones, Dodge College of Film and Media Arts, Chapman University

Genre Film Auteurs is a new book series focusing on the transformation of film genres by contemporary directors working within them. Each monograph in the series will constitute an in-depth examination of the aesthetic points of intersection between the creative vision of a particular director and the enabling constraints of genre conventions. The result will illuminate the processes of genre construction and authorship that take place within, and shape, collaborative industry practices. The books in this series are intended for film scholars, film students, and anyone with a serious interest in film criticism, film genre, and film authorship.

The Cinema of Michael Mann

Steven Rybin

LEXINGTON BOOKS

A division of
ROWMAN & LITTLEFIELD PUBLISHERS, INC.
Lanham • Boulder • New York • Toronto • Plymouth, UK

LEXINGTON BOOKS

A division of Rowman & Littlefield Publishers, Inc.
A wholly owned subsidiary of The Rowman & Littlefield Publishing Group, Inc.
4501 Forbes Boulevard, Suite 200
Lanham, MD 20706

Estover Road
Plymouth PL6 7PY
United Kingdom

Copyright © 2007 by Lexington Books

All rights reserved. No part of this publication may be reproduced, stored in a retrieval system, or transmitted in any form or by any means, electronic, mechanical, photocopying, recording, or otherwise, without the prior permission of the publisher.

British Library Cataloguing in Publication Information Available

Library of Congress Cataloging-in-Publication Data

Rybin, Steven, 1979– The cinema of Michael Mann / Steven Rybin.
   p. cm. — (Genre film auteurs)
Includes bibliographical references and index.
ISBN-13: 978-0-7391-2042-2 (cloth : alk. paper)
ISBN-10: 0-7391-2042-5 (cloth : alk. paper)
ISBN-13: 978-0-7391-2043-9 (pbk. : alk. paper)
ISBN-10: 0-7391-2043-3 (pbk. : alk. paper)
  1. Mann, Michael (Michael Kenneth)—Criticism and interpretation. I. Title.
PN1998.3.M3645R93 2007
791.4302'33092—dc22   2007015987

Printed in the United States of America

∞™ The paper used in this publication meets the minimum requirements of American National Standard for Information Sciences—Permanence of Paper for Printed Library Materials, ANSI/NISO Z39.48-1992.

Contents

Acknowledgements		vii
Introduction		1
1	Beginnings in Television and *The Jericho Mile*	21
2	*Thief*	41
3	*The Keep*	59
4	*Manhunter*	75
5	*The Last of the Mohicans*	93
6	*Heat*	111
7	*The Insider*	131
8	*Ali*	151
9	*Collateral*	169
Conclusion: Michael Mann and *Miami Vice* in the Shadow of New Hollywood		187
Michael Mann Filmography		215
Bibliography		219
Index		225
About the Author		233

Acknowledgements

This book began as a master's thesis under the tutelage of David A. Cook at Emory University. His enthusiasm for and insight into the topic helped improve the content of what follows during its initial stages, and his encouragement also helped inspire my subsequent effort to shape the material into a full-length study. I would also like to thank the rest of the Film Studies faculty at Emory University—Matthew Bernstein, Nina K. Martin, Karla Oeler, and Evan Lieberman (now of Cleveland State University)—for two profitable years of education which substantially influenced and informed the best of what follows. Equal gratitude must go to the School of Interdisciplinary Arts at Ohio University, which has proven to be a stimulating and supportive community over the last two years. Thanks also to Eileen Jones, for her enthusiasm for the project as well as for her bringing it to the attention of Lexington Books, as well as to Joseph Parry and the rest of the editorial staff at Lexington for their wonderful support and guidance as the project neared completion.

A more personal note of thanks to my closest friends, Jason Roberts, Andrew Johnson, and Scott Hay, for their invaluable friendship and insight over the years; to Jerry Rybin, Terrie Rybin, and Amanda Rybin, for the unconditional love and support which they have generously bestowed upon me throughout my life; and to Jessica Belser, for her enrichment of my life with her wisdom, spirit, humor, and love, and for the apparently bottomless reservoirs of patience and understanding she possessed when I had to spend more time in Michael Mann's world than in hers.

Introduction

... [C]ritics have avoided this major American filmmaker of the last two decades, let him slip away.

Jean-Baptiste Thoret[1]

[*Heat*] ... gives off a blankness, an indeterminacy, that frustrates interpretation ... it's not easy to delve into, to find significance or resonance in its detail.

Richard Combs[2]

Events aren't consumable in the same way that narratives are because they tend to confuse and confound us by their very nature as blunt encounters, splintering experience and then meting it out to us in separate clusters rather than allowing it the kind of coherence that can only come from the continuity, logical progression, and cohesion of storytelling.

Jonathan Rosenbaum[3]

The shadow of a houseplant is cast across the corner of a ceiling; electronic music accompanies the image, while somewhere in another room a thief and the woman he has recently married make love. A story about the hunt for a serial killer opens with an overhead view of a police car's hood, an image which abstracts the roof lights from the rest of the vehicle as well as from the space surrounding it. A soundtrack drops to almost complete silence, save for the music of elegiac, yearning strings scoring the descent of an exhausted but determined cop rushing down a winding staircase. At the end of a story about corporate control of the media, an intrepid journalist quits his job at CBS and then leaves the corporation's building, walking away from the camera and disappearing into the bustle of a city street. A voice-over of Will Smith as Muhammad Ali (the central protagonist in a major Hollywood biopic) drops to an inaudible level, becoming just one sonic impression among many. A taxi cab's reflection shines back at us in the windows of an office building, creating a play of reflected red, yellow, and blue light as the shot's pulse is timed to a contemporary rhythm and blues tune.

This descriptive list of images and sounds, of visual and sonic moments from Michael Mann's films, hints at the compelling manner in which these movies extract small details from a world and then amplify them, marking certain images and sequences as stylistic events that suddenly ask for our attention in the midst of a story, rather than as the strictly economical, self-effacing vehicles of a narrative. Through such style Mann has not only positioned himself as a storyteller with flair but also as an implicative teller of his own telling, an illusionist who never forgets to move his audience by indicating, through the exactness of his compositions and the intermittent foregrounding of style over theme—or, perhaps more accurately, the intensification or the generation of themes through style—that what we are looking at is an image, composed in a particular way, with particular sounds accompanying them. If one were to follow this line of thinking, one might say that Mann's style avoids the "democracy," the viewer's sense of discovery, that André Bazin once argued was inherent in the deep-focus film image; after all, Mann once plainly stated that he is "just not interested in 'passive' filmmaking, in a film that's precious and small and where it's [entirely] up to the audience to bring themselves to the movie."[4] Of course, regardless of the approach of a filmmaker, attentive film critics always seek stylistic and thematic tropes. The only apparent difference in these films is that Michael Mann and his collaborators have made the job of discovering style and extracting its meaning a little easier.

Or have they? There are quite a few writers on the cinema who have had a hard time with Mann. Only a few, like Richard Combs in the second quote preceding this introduction, have come to terms with the challenge of talking about Mann's impressive and sometimes overwhelming style, and have made such difficulty an integral part of the criticism itself. How can one follow Combs's line of thought, which argues that Mann's style sometimes impedes a clear interpretation of the stories he tells, and at the same time remain open to another comment by a film critic, Manohla Dargis, which attributes to the high-definition digital-video style of *Collateral* (2004) "a kind of democracy of images, in which no object in the frame carries more weight than any other. . . . As a consequence, *Collateral* looks like it's capturing a completely unmediated image of the real world"?[5] The fact that Mann's cinema is for some critics monolithically stylized and closed, while for others generously open, points to the multiplicity of ways in which the experience of a Michael Mann film might be described and understood.

This study thus suggests an open-ended approach to the work of this important, and yet somehow unwieldy, director, one which focuses on both the pleasures and problems his film style presents and one which examines the ways in which that style intersects with issues such as genre, film criticism, historical context, and auteurism. This book will assist in filling an important void in current film criticism and scholarship, for academic (and smart journalistic) writing on Mann has been, until recently, almost nonexistent. Three book-length works, as I write this in 2006, have taken Mann as their subject. Mark Steensland's 2002 overview, *Michael Mann,* provides information on the production of the director's films alongside a brief thematic analysis and an evaluative, hierarchical ranking of the films; Mark E. Wildermuth's 2005 study, *Blood in the Moonlight: Michael Mann and Information Age Cinema,* traces in Mann's work the theme of the disappearance of productive symbolic exchange in modern society; and F. X. Feeney's *Michael Mann,* a 2006 entry in Taschen's series of lavishly produced coffee-table books on important filmmakers, provides an admirable chronicle of the director's career as well as many rare production photographs.[6] All of these analyses certainly have much to offer, and each has opened up an intelligent discussion about the director's themes, but what is finally missing in them is a thoroughgoing and methodical attention to the particulars of Mann's filmic style, and the way in which that style serves to generate both deeper shades of important thematic meanings and significant inflections upon and innovations within preexisting genre frameworks. Style is not only a path into the thematic weight of these films, but as I will explore, in Mann's cinema a consideration of style and theme is never extricable from the director's contribution to and innovations within genres. Each Mann film is locatable in a distinctive film-historical genre lineage; but regardless of the genre—whether it is the crime film, the journalism film, or the biopic—his inimitable film style serves as the conduit through which genre is inflected, innovated, and reformulated.

The avoidance of an investigation into the visual and aural style of Mann's films, coupled with the general lack of sustained critical attention paid to this director over the course of the last two decades, is on a certain level somewhat surprising, for there are few other American directors currently working who fit the bill of the "genre stylist" as well as some of the great auteurs in the history of the American cinema, including John Ford, Howard Hawks, and Alfred Hitchcock. For in the same sense that Ford the stylist made westerns (and occasionally crime films and historical dramas), Michael Mann the stylist makes crime films (and occasionally a western, or a biopic, or a journalism film). Just as Ford's, Hawks's, and Hitchcock's statures as auteurs ultimately contribute to our sense of genre filmmaking's expansive possibilities, Mann's rich approach to visual and sonic style also situates him as a filmmaker who chooses the iconographic backdrop of a genre less as a raison d'etre and more as a canvas upon which he can draw his own irreducible cinematic vision.

This study thus strives to find the right approach in communicating the striking qualities of Mann's aesthetic through critical prose, while at the same time painting an accurate picture of how the director's career develops in tandem with trends in genre production and how the films themselves foreground the intersection of style and genre. The issues I confront along the way include auteurism, historical context, ideas regarding mise-en-scène criticism and film form, and approaches to film criticism as both a tool to understand and describe films and as a material craft in and of itself. Before engaging with Mann's work directly, then, I want to use this introduction to explore the methodological underpinnings of this study. Such exploration involves a discussion of four distinct but closely intertwined issues. I will first consider the way in which the director's comments about his own work can function within a critical study, and what the inclusion of such comments in academic work can implicitly suggest about creative agency. I will then move on to a discussion regarding why some of the conventional approaches to formalism in academic film studies are inadequate for a consideration of the particular aesthetic experience Mann's cinema presents to viewers. This argument will then dovetail into the third section of the introduction, in which I posit an alternative film-critical poetics which is perhaps more suitable to an investigation into this auteur's style, themes, and deployment of and inflection upon preexisting genre frameworks (and the relationship between these three components of his films). I will then conclude the introduction by exploring the implications my critical approach contains for certain traditional and problematic notions of auteurism.

THE BIOGRAPHICAL LEGEND: AUTHORSHIP, READING STRATEGIES, AND FILM PRODUCTION

This exploration of Mann's oeuvre covers the director's entire career in chronological order. Each chapter in my study pivots around one of the following ten films: *The Jericho Mile* (1979), *Thief* (1981), *The Keep* (1983), *Manhunter* (1986), *The Last of the Mohicans* (1992), *Heat* (1995), *The Insider* (1999), *Ali* (2001), *Collateral* (2004), and, in the book's conclusion, *Miami Vice* (2006). I have avoided extensive discussion of Mann's television work, not because it is less worthy or less "artistic" than his cinema—anyone familiar with the pleasures of *Miami Vice* the television series (1984–1989) or a single episode of the engaging *Crime Story* (1986–1988) series surely knows otherwise—but rather because as the episodic product of a widely varying multitude of writers, directors, and producers (the particular combination of which can change on an episode-to-episode basis), Mann's televisual work often proves rather difficult to synthesize in terms of authorship, although certain background details from the television series are covered in this study in order to paint a comprehensive picture of Mann's career.

As I explore the shared stylistic touches and thematic tropes of these particular films, I practice a common auteurist approach: bundling the films together as the work of one director and exploring the consistencies across that body of work. However, I do not intend to blindly ascribe the effects of these films to a single biological entity known as "Michael Mann," since such a task is often ultimately beyond the possibilities of empirical research, most especially with a director such as Mann, who keeps the more personal details of his life story out of the publicity circuit, as Mark E. Wildermuth has also pointed out.[7] Rather, this study uses the idea of the "biographical legend" as a reading strategy in an investigation of Mann's work—which in this case situates Mann not as a director with a necessarily relevant personal biography but simply as a filmmaker who has made a number of useful and often quite articulate and stimulating comments about his own films and the industry in which he works.

David Bordwell's notion of the "biographical legend" allows the critic to construct, on the page, some idea of an author as, in the words of Russian formalist critic Boris Tomashevsky, "literary fact."[8] This means that the critic is not necessarily interested in the biological person as author, although every historical construction may contain traces of that person. My study constructs Mann's biographical legend, working through interviews, statements, testimony from colleagues, and other sources in order to suggest how one might think of him as an auteur with a (not necessarily "personal") public reputation and how this conception allows one a way into understanding the films. The biographical legend thus functions as a reading strategy in exploring the many meanings in film artworks. As Bordwell writes: "The biographical legend may justify production decisions and even create a spontaneous theory of the artist's practice. More important, the biographical legend is a way in which authorship significantly shapes our perception of the work."[9] In other words, viewers never come to films as "innocents"; inundated with knowledge about directors as both celebrity figures and artists, the critic's understanding of film is always colored by a peripheral, if sometimes unacknowledged, consideration of its authors. The biographical legend prizes—rather than rejects—this flood of information, and its inclusion in scholarly work allows for both a comprehensive construction of "the auteur" and a glimpse into the larger historical and collaborative background in which the filmmaker works.

In this way—and this is perhaps where I deviate slightly from the original intention of the "legend" as a critical method—such a reading strategy arrives at a rough, intermittent, but still inspiring makeshift theory of a personal vision through the "literary facts" which allow us to construct the biographical legend. This language may prick up the ears of those academics who run for the hills at even the slightest mention of such a "romantic" phrase as "personal vision," but a qualification is in order: While it is impossible to prove with empirically verifiable data that a personal vision exists (the very notion of such a possibility is itself rather strange), speculation upon such an idea allows us to retain and hold in our heads the perhaps liberating idea of the possibility of individual agency and individual acts within a proscribed, contingent history and context. Thus, a director's "vision" (which is a critical construct) and "intent" (which presumably exists, but is not open to the critic's research and not necessarily to the critic's sensibility) are marked by a significant inflection, since the critic's desire and drive to persuade an audience of the important meanings of one director's films becomes a crucial part of film theory and history. If the biographical legend, as historical narrative, also pays due attention to the influence of the environments in which the director and the director's collaborators act, then the study avoids becoming a polemical valorization of an individual vision or a distanced, isolated, and paralyzing consent to a stifling contextual determinism: Both individual agency and surrounding context are a crucial part of the web of authorship, and each assists in shaping the other.

This study of Mann, then, holds onto a certain optimism regarding the possibility for meaningful personal expression in filmmaking. In order to also arrive at a fuller understanding of the possibilities of social actions—an understanding crucial to this book, as the occasionally constricted possibilities of social actions of all sorts is an important, and often central, theme in Mann's cinema—one should strive to understand the possibilities of both individuals and the societies in which they act. Indeed, some scholars have not given up the larger implications of personal expressivity in the study of film and film authorship. As Janet Staiger has noted, "scholars have observed some authoring practices that they have claimed are methods for self-expression by authors with features of the self in minority categories"; one suspects that it is the very possibility of personal expression which at least in part inspires such scholarship and indeed all writing.[10] Although Michael Mann is in what critics might correspondingly call a "dominant category"—a white male filmmaker working in Hollywood, who possesses an industrial means of expression that far outstrips that of the mere film critic, not to mention that of the typical viewer or struggling independent filmmaker—the films he directs are not reducible to a single overarching ideology and will not yield their secrets when examined through an exclusively political lens. The stories and themes he explores through his style are hardly reducible to the insidious work of a dominant white male working in an industry: consider, for example, the subtle handling of corporate corruption in *The Insider* and the examination of institutional racism in *Ali*. Staiger points out the danger of automatically ascribing (and thus reducing) a member of a minority group to a single stance; likewise, scholars also needlessly limit our understanding of the cinema if a single member of a dominant group is reduced to a similarly narrowed definition. Where Mann's films fall short in their depiction of women (an issue this study will in part explore), they exceed in saying something meaningful and critical about certain men and their struggle in modern society (whereas most Hollywood films manage no part of that equation); so while a critical sensitivity to the flaws in Mann's work is required, no one single ideological theory is acceptable across the board. Spontaneous theories are more suitable to the work of a filmmaker whose films contain a style that is itself marked by seemingly spontaneous stylistic events.

FINDING THE RIGHT FORMALISM

I have suggested that in many ways the biographical construction of the film director can offer viewers an opportunity to hold the possibility of theoretical human agency in mind while considering films which are, without question, also a part of a massive commercial and industrial context known as Hollywood. However, criticism and spectatorship are themselves acts that may complicate or contradict the biographical construction. As Bordwell has written in his study of Carl-Theodor Dreyer, "there is . . . no simple congruence between legend and films . . . Not the least interesting aspect of Dryer for us today hangs upon the way the films *contradict* the biographical legend."[11] Part of the reason Bordwell is able to make this statement is because the critical language with which he chooses to discuss and interpret Dreyer's body of work foregrounds particular contradictions relative to the biographical legend construct which he crafts. Likewise, this study of Michael Mann requires a critical language appropriate to a discussion of the films, one which uses the director's legend not as the final word but rather as a piece of criticism in and of itself, an assertion of the particular value of a given film (from the point of view of one of its primary creative agents) which in turns forms an impetus for and generator of further contemplation, interpretation, and evaluation by the critic.

What critical approach, then, will best allow us to investigate the dense layer of visual and sonic style at work in Mann's cinema, which some have found impenetrable? This prompts some engagement with the dominant formalist theory presently at work in North American academic film studies, one which may ultimately be less than helpful in articulating the precise viewing experience posited by Michael Mann's film style. Bordwell applies a particular historical approach to exploring the effects and meanings of films, a method that takes as its main assumption the idea that artworks produce cues that can be cognitively understood. The particular way in which these cues are produced is engendered by the industrial context at the time the film was made, which determines the array of stylistic options, or norms, that are available to the filmmakers during production (or that provide the general basis from which a filmmaker may deviate, such as in the work of Dreyer and Yasujiro Ozu, to name just two of Bordwell's own examples).[12] Bordwell has also investigated how contemporary American cinema (up to 1985, the date of the book's publication) functions in terms of its relationship to the past forms of Hollywood cinema—and in relationship to the European art cinema that has heavily influenced many American films of the late 1960s and early 1970s—in the historical and critical study *The Classical Hollywood Cinema*:

> The classical premises of time and space remain powerfully in force, with only minor instrumental changes (e.g., multiple cameras to capture reverse angles, zooms doing duty for tracking shots). [Robert] Altman, probably the most interesting stylist to emerge in New Hollywood, none the less uses techniques which conform to the dominant paradigm. Secondly, even the most ambitious directors cannot escape genres . . . Classical film style and codified genres swallow up art-film borrowings, taming the (already limited) disruptiveness of the art cinema.[13]

For Bordwell, Robert Altman, the most aesthetically significant and against-the-mainstream Hollywood director of 1970s Hollywood cinema, essays a style which, while inflected by the more personal, auteur-based European art-cinema practice, is nonetheless bound to its particular industrial and historical context and ultimately conforms to an aesthetic unity which only borrows, in a pastiche form, from the modernist art cinema. Accepting Bordwell's argument on its own grounds, he makes a sound case; but at the same time one would not be mistaken in pointing out that, regardless of industrial norms, watching Altman's *The Long Goodbye* (1974) is nonetheless a markedly different aesthetic experience than viewing Howard Hawks's *The Big Sleep* (1941) or other prior instances in the categories of both the detective genre and Raymond Chandler adaptations. In a more global sense, there is some reason to be suspicious of a purely cognitive poetics which openly valorizes its own methodology as superior to others; as David A. Cook points out, "perceptual psychologists still understand very little about the neural and cognitive processes involved in the perception of motion," and limiting the methods by which we write and think about the cinema only succeeds in circumscribing how we might speak about it and understand it.[14]

With regard to the films of Altman, scholar Robert T. Self, incorporating certain aspects of Bordwell's work while at the same time implicitly refuting at least a part of that work, has convincingly argued that Altman consistently undermines the continuity of the classical cinematic paradigm through a modernist art-cinema narration.[15] Michael Mann's films, despite the considerable inflection of genre formed by their rich film style, do not radically deconstruct genre as do Altman's, and Mann's cause-and-effect narratives can be plausibly argued as fundamentally classical (with some important variations) in the light of Bordwell's paradigm. Nonetheless, I am not convinced that cataloging the effects of Mann's films according to cognitive theories of film is the best route for understanding how, in their particular aesthetics, they constitute a cinematic experience. Mann's work might be profitably read through the prism of Bordwell's useful conceptions of artistic, compositional, generic, and realistic narrative motivation, and even in certain cases through Bordwell's thorough discussion of parametric narration, but such a methodology would nonetheless conform to a particular style of classical academic writing on film which, in its assumptions about how we perceive and discuss film form and *in its own materiality* as criticism, represents only one of many possible formalisms.[16] It is not, as Robert B. Ray has observed, worth arguing (if one wanted to) with Bordwell and his coauthors on the terms they set for their study; their conceptualization of the classical Hollywood cinema is airtight not only because of their exhaustively impressive and persuasive empirical research, but also largely because the authors themselves are classicists. Ray characterizes Bordwell as the "Voltaire of North American film studies," and summarizes the implications of Bordwell's rejection of associative and metaphorical critical language in the study of cinema:

> Bordwell's work, like that of almost everyone designated by our culture as providing "knowledge," participates thoroughly in the apparatus that Nietzsche describes as Western civilization's last great religion: rational science. As a writer, Bordwell is classically clear. He eschews "excessive" metaphors and obviously bravura figures (the signs of his own desire) . . . Indeed, Bordwell's prose and format mime *CHC*'s subject: he and his coauthors produce the book equivalent of the widescreen, "invisible style," cause-and-effect linked Hollywood movie.[17]

For a writer such as Bordwell, the study of cause-and-effect structures in classical Hollywood cinema itself uses as its vehicle a writing style characterized by its own brand of classical continuity. This classical authorial signature is one of the most striking and consistent aspects of Bordwell's critical work. This style—couched with the impressive mass of empirical evidence which fuels it—allows the scholar to make meticulous causal connections across many decades of American film.

Mann, of course, cannot be rationalized as a modernist director. Regardless of the unique aesthetic experience his films offer, he and his collaborators, unlike Altman and his coauthors, tell stories motivated by cause-and-effect and occasionally employ well-worn genre conventions. If we as viewers and critics, then, are to get any sense of the manner in which Mann's cinema possesses an intriguing style which expands the limitations of past genre instances, we might discover it through a language different than that of classical academic prose. This does not mean that any writer who wants to talk about movies or film history in a different manner should reject Bordwell's methodology wholesale and retreat to an undisciplined, wholly impressionistic, free-associative writing style. A more open language, located in the history of expressive, evaluative film criticism as it has functioned both inside and outside of the academy, will prove effective.

MICHAEL MANN, FILM CRITICISM, AND FILM GENRE

Adrian Martin's important but mostly neglected article "Mise-en-scène is Dead, or The Expressive, The Excessive, The Technical and The Stylish," displays what I would characterize as a generous critical poetics, one which, as I will show throughout this study, is suitable for an exploration of Mann's films.[18] Martin's piece is an intervention into the history of mise-en-scène criticism: it maps the history of the critical approach and analyzes the assumptions behind instances of its practice over the last half-century while at the same time suggesting three categories of mise-en-scène style through which films can be perceived. Thomas Elsaesser and Warren Buckland have provided their own examination of Martin's article and summarize the assumptions behind traditional practices of this critical style and its eventual relationship to the New Hollywood cinema of the 1970s:

> *Mise-en-scène* critics dismiss the common-sense assumption that all a director needs to do is simply place the camera where the action can be seen best. Filming involves a productive relation between film style and subject matter, of style transforming the subject matter. This is where *mise-en-scène* criticism becomes evaluative, because its adherents evaluate films according to the skill and artistry in which subject matter is creatively transformed by the specifics of the

film medium. *Mise-en-scène* critics valorize classical Hollywood films (particularly those directed by *auteurs*) on the basis of their successful (economical and significant) transformation of the subject matter into film. But with the decline of the studio system and the ageing of Hollywood *auteurs* in the 1960s, a number of the most prominent *mise-en-scène* critics . . . detected in New Hollywood directors a decline in the creative use of *mise-en-scène*.[19]

I will discuss in later chapters how some critics of Michael Mann's films chastise the director for a lack of classical stylistic economy. Mann's first films come shortly after the demise of what is now historically known as the New Hollywood cinema of the 1960s and 1970s, and are thus roughly concomitant with the perceived "creative decline" in the new American auteurs.

Adrian Martin's article suggests that mise-en-scène, as a critical construct, is wide enough to allow for a descriptive and interpretive analysis of films with styles that do not function wholly as economical "vehicles" for the themes and story. He draws three broad categories of mise-en-scène: classical, expressive, and mannerist. Classical forms of mise-en-scène (which are, importantly, not found only in the "classical" period of the Hollywood cinema—before 1960—but also quite often in contemporary films) "are all works in which there is a definite stylistic restraint at work, and in which the modulations of stylistic devices across the film are keyed closely to its dramatic shifts and thematic developments."[20] Classical forms, for Martin, are then struck at a self-effacing, economical pitch, and their stylistic gestures come only as the themes demand them. In other words, as Elsaesser and Buckland write: "The scene remains intelligible whether or not the spectator is aware of the symbolism, since the credibility of the scene remains more important than the symbolism. But symbolism that can work within the boundaries of credibility becomes a valuable addition to the film."[21]

The two other stylistic forms are, in a way, thrown into relief against this classical style. Expressive mise-en-scène (not to be confused with "expressionism," although in given films the two may indeed overlap) exhibits what Martin calls a "textual economy . . . pitched more at the level of a broad fit between elements of style and elements of subject . . . general strategies of colour coding, camera viewpoint, sound design and so on enhance or reinforce the general 'feel' or meaning of the subject matter."[22] As Martin goes on to suggest, filmmakers such as Michael Mann, Robert Altman, Abel Ferrara, and Alan Rudolph exhibit this style, for, as Elsaesser and Buckland point out, "they use film style to enhance particular meanings in their subject matter."[23] In the last of the three forms, mannerist mise-en-scène, the style of a film "performs out of its own trajectories, no longer working unobtrusively at the behest of the fiction and its demands of meaningfulness."[24] This style justifies itself through nothing other than itself. This is the most critically disrespected of the three forms, as Elsaesser and Buckland write:

> It is in such mannerist films that the original critics of *Cahiers du cinéma*, as well as [classical mise-en-scène critics such as V. F. Perkins], see the concept of *mise-en-scène* being inoperative, precisely because the style does not serve the subject matter. Martin seems to be in partial agreement with these critics when he writes that, if post-classical Hollywood film "gains something interesting and novel, it seems to also lose a great deal that has been associated with the lofty concept of *mise-en-scène*. In particular, it loses the capacity for a more subtle kind of 'point-making'—the kind we associated with a certain critical distance installed between the director and the events he or she shows" . . . However, Martin, Perkins, and the *Cahiers du cinéma* critics are simply lamenting the demise of classical *mise-en-scène* in mannerist films, not *mise-en-scène* itself.[25]

Whatever Martin's own hesitations about "mannerist" style, his three-part critical construct allows for the critic to examine the style on its own terms, granting each category a validity that classical mise-en-scène adherents, always on the lookout for what is "excessive" in film style, reject.

In what way can a critic apply Martin's suggestive notions of mise-en-scène to a study of Michael Mann? Scholar Anna Dzenis, who has also commented on Martin's reference to Mann's style in her own article on the director, has suggested that Mann, at least in the wake of his later work, is best characterized as a director who shifts back and forth across the three different categories of style; however, I will concur with Martin in this study and place Mann's work mostly in the expressive category as his films generally eschew the other types of style, excepting some moments in films which can be seen as classical (*The Jericho Mile*) or mannerist (*The Keep*, *Ali*).[26]

Despite this insistence on developing a critical framework for describing and interpreting Mann's style, this focus on style must not occlude the simple fact that Mann's films continue to be enabled by the conventions of previous genre films. These categories of mise-en-scène style, far from constituting a concern separate from an exploration of genre, grant the viewer a window onto the manner in which Mann's work achieves its innovation within preexisting genre frameworks. Style is hardly ever extricable from genre in Mann's cinema; indeed, style can serve as a prime indicator of Mann's most salient contribution to the varying genre lineages and genre cycles of which his films are a part. In *Thief*, for example, stylistic gestures of both the film noir and the gangster crime film are interlocked in an expressive style, and the content generated by the film's stylistic approach gives us an altogether different—and highly contemporary—vision of the gangster as an antihero than that in classical Hollywood.

(The ideas about Mann's stylistic and thematic contributions to the crime film are introduced in the chapter on *Thief* and will be further developed in later chapters on Mann's subsequent crime films, *Heat*, *Collateral*, and, in the conclusion, *Miami Vice*). In *Manhunter*, meanwhile, *Thief*'s stylistic inflection upon neonoir and the crime film is developed in tandem with a stylistic reworking of certain tropes from the horror film. In *The Last of the Mohicans*, Mann delivers a surprisingly conventional western (and at the same time a rather unconventional James Fenimore Cooper adaptation) within an expressive style, whereas in *The Insider* he questions some of the fundamental assumptions of the journalism film genre and its characters through his intelligent and deeply felt rendering of a story about the impossibility of valuable communication in a world saturated by corporate-controlled media outlets. Finally, in *Ali* the use of contemporary covers of 1960s and 1970s pop songs on the soundtrack deviates from the approach of most traditional biopics, which tend to use pop songs from the time period covered in the film's diegesis in order to suture the viewer into an often nostalgic experience of a past moment in history. Mann avoids such nostalgia in *Ali* and instead offers us an experience of a historical biopic which foregrounds the importance of its social and political themes to our present-day situation, while at the same time combining the biographical genre with tropes from the boxing film in clever and innovative ways.

These examples of genre inflection will be explored throughout this study, in tandem with a more general focus on the powerful manner in which Mann's style communicates thematic meaning to audiences. However, Adrian Martin's article on film style has other implications for an investigation into these films, ones that complement my stylistic analysis of Mann's cinema with a focus on the particular type of critical language which is used in such a critique. Martin's article couches his survey of mise-en-scène criticism within a parallel argument which calls for a more open and expressive style of formalist criticism, one which explicitly (and, through Martin's own expressive verbal play, implicitly) rejects the stripped-down aspects of classical prose that serves as the stylistic vehicle through which some scholars construct and convey their critical methods and observations. Martin's essay thus addresses my concern with finding an alternative formalist language for describing the effects of films. Martin points out that the expressive, belle-lettristic writing of critic and scholar Jonathan Rosenbaum holds in common with Bordwell, Staiger, and Thompson a concern with "the power and affectivity of film form" and an appreciation for filmmakers such as Ozu, Dreyer, Bresson, and Tati; the crucial difference for Martin, and indeed for myself, is that Rosenbaum combines his formalism with more expressive appreciations.[27] Indeed, Martin suggests that a style of appreciative formalism might bridge the practices of the most sophisticated journalistic criticism and academic research. While reminding us that Bordwell's own

Making Meaning contains expressive appreciations of journalistic critics such as Manny Farber, Martin expresses his own ideal film criticism eloquently:

> Beyond his formidable contribution to cinema studies, I'm sure another reason for Bordwell's fondness for Farber in *Making Meaning* is because—and who would deny it—he is a great writer. But what does it really mean to say this? Why is the *materiality* of the writing of Farber—or Rosenbaum or David Thomson or Meaghan Morris—so often rendered immaterial, a wasteful luxury, mere surplus value? I believe this is an important question—and it is particularly addressed to those who (whether for empiricist, populist, or would-be policy-making reasons) at present issue disapproving pronouncements about "the unrestrained verbal play" characterizing several decades of cultural commentary . . . What about some sense of the *action* of critical writing, what it can conjure, perform, circulate, transform? In writing as much as in film, we must come to close terms with what is "at once mysterious and materialistic in matters of style."[28]

Martin's work as a film critic—and his vision for future film criticism—thus carefully holds and encourages, in a kind of productive harmony, the championing of a sensitive analysis of film style in tandem with an expressive critical language through which such a style can be described, appreciated, and understood. My criticism on Mann strives to achieve this balance.

MISE-EN-SCÈNE AND AUTEURISM

Martin's analysis of mise-en-scène criticism also opens the way for a broader conception of authorship. Auteurism and mise-en-scène criticism, of course, have a historical connection: the latter was employed in critical writing to suggest the "signature" of the film's "author," the director. It is important to note, as Buckland and Elsaesser do not, that Martin's article argues that mise-en-scène criticism of any sort need not be exclusively concerned with the auteur's mark; it may indeed offer a path through which to consider film style as the product of a collaboration, particularly in the way that Martin includes editing as a crucial part of what comprises mise-en-scène construction. Martin's historical mapping of the critical style finds that mise-en-scène was often defined, in journals such as the 1950s *Cahiers du cinéma*, as quasi-magical, inherently empirical evidence for the director's authorship, and it is "the reduction of direction—in a holistic sense—to the magic moment of shooting, the production phase (as distinct from pre- and post-production phases)" which Martin persuades the reader to leave behind.[29] Martin acknowledges in his article that the belief in the stylistic signature emerged from the historically important attempt to valorize the American director's role in the creation of artworks, but it is nonetheless a blind spot in the history of a particular type of mise-en-scène analysis which has, for too long, placed its overwhelming emphasis—at the expense of examining additional contributions—on what the director puts in front of the camera and how the director shoots those contents at the moment of the film's production. To progress beyond this narrow notion of mise-en-scène and its authorship, Martin cites a famous quote from Jean-Luc Godard: "If to direct is to glance, to edit is a beating of the heart . . . Editing, therefore, at the same that it denies, announces and prepares the way for directing; they are interdependent on each other. To direct is to plot, and one speaks of a plot as well- or poorly-knit."[30]

Martin, using this Godard quote as an introduction to his line of argument, believes that a mise-en-scène criticism which wants to proceed in tandem with a complex notion of cinematic authorship must also pay attention to choices of editing in order to properly inflect the typical concern with the placement of objects in front of the camera and the way the camera captures those objects with a consideration of editing. This is a significantly radical move in that it flies in the face of many academic definitions of mise-en-scène. However, Martin's concern is to find a critical language appropriate not only to his own proposed categories of film style (which, in their concern for the modulation of style across shots, involve a careful attention to the relationship between the placement of objects in individual shots and the subsequent editing-together of those shots) but also to a nuanced and expressive description of film form which includes a space for a consideration of its multiple authors. Martin cites Brian Henderson's 1971 argument, "The Long Take," to exemplify how editing must always broaden our understanding of mise-en-scène and move us beyond this type of criticism's traditional concern with the auteur's signature. As cited by Martin, Henderson writes:

> An entire category of long-take intrasequence cutting concerns the relation of camera to script and dialogue. A director may cut frequently, even on every line, and if he does so the result is a kind of montage, though one bound in its rhythm to the rhythm of the dialogue, not itself an independent rhythm. At the other extreme he may, as Mizoguchi often does, cut only once or twice within a long dialogue sequence. If he does the latter, then his cut must be carefully mediated and placed in relation to the dramatic progress of the scene, coming at just that point at which the relationships at stake in the scene have ripened into a qualitative change—a change reflected in the new or altered *mise-en-scène*.[31]

This passage, as Martin suggests, descriptively implies the web of decision-making which occurs at every point in the construction of a scene, from the modulation of the screenplay during the moment of filming and the further modulation of the filmed story through postproduction decisions regarding editing. (Henderson, it must be said, uses "Mizoguchi" and the word "director" here more as a figure of speech and less as a reference to a biological entity; "editor" could just well have been used.) In this way Martin's demands of a mise-en-scène analysis which pays due attention to the intricate, multilevel process of filmmaking appropriately complements my own approach to studying Mann's work, which places emphasis on not only the collaborators the director has worked with but also the "stylistic events" in his films in which the richness of the film itself precludes any simplistic notion of finding a signature somewhere in the frame.

I believe the methodologies of stylistic description and interpretation put forth in this introduction make challenges of a kind which can revitalize auteurism as a critical method, moving us away from attempts to prove an artist's evolving genius and toward a more complex critical sensitivity that inherently considers both the contributions of collaborators and the richness of an aesthetic design that sometimes overwhelms the critic adjusted to the shapes of classical films. For some, auteurism and classical decoupage were a perfect fit, because in such a style every frame was necessary: the efficient operation of the self-effacing attitude and the shot-by-shot modulations in the classical aesthetic invite us to analyze every single aspect of every single frame in a film for meaning. The director's signature was a part of this self-effacement, and it often evoked itself—at least in critical writing about the films—quite subtly. In an article about auteurism as a critical practice, William D. Routt suggests the following:

> These "old masters" are great because of the direct, uncomplicated nature of their work. They have achieved the highest places because they never evinced any ambition, they have been proclaimed the most wise because only they knew all along that they were not wise at all. There is a transvaluation of all values here which plays a crucial role in the iconoclasm of the auteurist position. Auteurism puts things on their feet again. It inverts the retinal image that is represented as real by the investigations of criticism practiced seriously, as science: we had thought that what appeared complex was complex, but we learn now that this is not so. What appears complex is merely complicated, needlessly elaborated like a doodle. True complexity is what calls to us from simple things, mundane details: a gesture, a face, a glance.[32]

But expressive or mannerist mise-en-scène does not necessarily welcome such analysis, and in mannered stylistic moments such attempts at analyzing the "excessively obvious," the phrase by which Bordwell describes much of the classical Hollywood cinema, are simply impossible.[33] Indeed, the aforementioned emphasis on editing and its place in constructing broadly expressive mise-en-scène complicates what Routt suggests is the auteurist's way of looking at cinema: "The auteurist must adopt an active relation with films. Close observation is required, and an 'open' looking that endeavours to 'see everything,' but also a way of looking that maintains the sensibility of director and of spectator simultaneously.... The perfect auteurist critic would enter into the presented and represented activity on the screen, observing closely and questioning each gesture, each shot, each cut, each sequence, discovering patterns both familiar and unfamiliar."[34]

In this book I make every effort *not* to "enter into the presented and represented activity on the screen"—at least not in every single moment of a given film. One who attempts in reading every single shot or, indeed, every single sound in Michael Mann's films—or the films of any expressive or mannerist filmmaker—in such fashion will end up not with a sense of the director's signature but in interpretive delirium, left only with a sense that Mann's work is a monolith of impenetrable style. Alternatively, of course, in the face of such frustration critics may simply come to consider expressive and (especially) mannerist styles as self-indulgent and excessive. But through seriously examining an auteur whose work almost never traffics in classical mise-en-scène, auteurism is challenged by the specter of its original formulation. Upon encountering Mann's cinema, one can no longer "prove" the signature of an auteur in a film by looking at a handful of closely knit images. At most, a Mann critic may be able to ascribe a broad aesthetic to the director, but one might instead relax the desire to identify such ultimately untraceable "signs" to a single individual and instead, at least to some degree, emphasize the contributions of collaborators. Agency in artistic creation is an idea then retained, but in a broader—and more collective—manner.

NOTES

1. Jean-Baptiste Thoret, "The Aquarium Syndrome: On the Films of Michael Mann," *Senses of Cinema*, http://www.sensesofcinema.com/contents/01/19/mann.html (accessed 15 November 2004).

2. Richard Combs, "Michael Mann: Becoming," *Film Comment* 32, no. 2 (March/April 1996): 10.

3. Jonathan Rosenbaum, "Death and Life: Landscapes of the Soul—The Cinema of Alexander Dovzhenko," in Rosenbaum, *Essential Cinema: On the Necessity of Film Canons* (Baltimore: The Johns Hopkins University Press, 2004), 400.

4. Harlan Kennedy, "Castle Keep," *Film Comment* 19, no. 6 (November/December 1983): 18.

5. Manohla Dargis and A. O. Scott, "The Directors, The Actors, The Issues, The Cameras. Discuss," *New York Times*, 16 December 2004, 20.

6. See Mark Steensland, *Michael Mann* (London: Pocket Essentials, 2001); Mark E. Wildermuth, *Blood in the Moonlight: Michael Mann and Information Age Cinema* (Jefferson: McFarland & Company, 2005); F. X. Feeney, *Michael Mann* (London: Taschen, 2006).

7. Wildermuth, *Blood in the Moonlight*, 2.

8. David Bordwell, *The Films of Carl-Theodor Dreyer* (Berkeley and Los Angeles: University of California Press, 1981), 9.
9. Bordwell, *Carl-Theodor Dreyer*, 9.
10. Janet Staiger, "Authorship Approaches," in *Authorship and Film*, eds. David A. Gernster and Janet Staiger (London: Routledge, 2003), 52.
11. Bordwell, *Carl-Theodor Dreyer*, 24.
12. See David Bordwell's chapter "The Bounds of Difference" in David Bordwell, Janet Staiger, and Kristin Thompson, *The Classical Hollywood Cinema: Film Style & Mode of Production to 1960* (New York: Columbia University Press, 1985), 70–84.
13. Bordwell, Staiger, and Thompson, *The Classical Hollywood Cinema*, 375.
14. David A. Cook, *A History of Narrative Film, 4th ed.* (New York: W. W. Norton & Co., 2004), 1.
15. Robert T. Self, *Robert Altman's Subliminal Reality* (Minneapolis: University of Minnesota Press, 2002).
16. For Bordwell, "artistic motivation," a concept borrowed from the Russian formalists, is a narrative style in which the viewer's attention is directed toward the forms and materials of the film; "compositional motivation" is a style which is used because of its necessity to the story; "realistic motivation" is a narrative which makes use of plausible, common-sense assessments of how the world works; "transtextual motivation" is the use of elements of narrative style which signify across groups of films (for example, in a gangster film, we expect to see mobsters shooting each other, even if the action is not plausibly explained in the narrative). See Bordwell, *Narration in the Fiction Film* (Madison: University of Wisconsin Press, 1985), 36. His notion of "parametric narration" accounts for stylistic patterns that occur outside the bounds of the demands of the story, but unlike Adrian Martin's notion of mannerist film style discussed later in this chapter, Bordwell sees this type of style as occurring only in clearly modernist filmmakers. See Bordwell, *Narration in the Fiction Film*, 274–310.
17. Robert B. Ray, *How a Film Theory Got Lost and Other Mysteries in Cultural Studies* (Bloomington and Indianapolis: Indiana University Press, 2001), 41.
18. Adrian Martin, "Mise-en-scène is Dead, or The Expressive, The Excessive, The Technical, and The Stylish," *Continuum: The Australian Journal of Media & Culture* 5, no. 2 (1990), 87–140.
19. Thomas Elsaesser and Warren Buckland, *Studying Contemporary American Film* (London: Arnold, 2002), 83.
20. Martin, "Mise-en-scène is Dead," 90.
21. Elsaesser and Buckland, *Contemporary American Film*, 85.
22. Martin, "Mise-en-scène is Dead is Dead," 90.
23. Elsaesser and Buckland, *Contemporary American Film*, 85.
24. Martin, "Mise-en-scène is Dead," 91.
25. Elsaesser and Buckland, *Contemporary American Film*, 85.
26. Anna Dzenis, "Michael Mann's Cinema of Images," *Screening the Past* http://www.latrobe.edu.au/screeningthepast/firstrelease/fr0902/adfr14b.html (accessed 11 January 2005).
27. Martin, "Mise-en-scène is Dead," 130.

28. Martin, "Mise-en-scène is Dead," 130–31.

29. Martin, "Mise-en-scène is Dead," 93.

30. Quoted in Martin, "Mise-en-scène is Dead," 94. It is important to note that Martin, for reasons of preference, eschews the standard English translation of this quote by Tom Milne in *Godard on Godard*, ed. Milne (London: Secker & Warburg, 1972), 39–41, and instead cites an older translation: Jean-Luc Godard, "Montage, Mon Beau Souci," in *Jean-Luc Godard*, ed. Toby Mussman (New York: E. P. Dutton, 1968), 47–49.

31. Quoted in Martin, "Mise-en-scène is Dead," 95. See Brian Henderson, *A Critique of Film Theory* (New York: E. P. Dutton, 1980), 55.

32. William D. Routt, "L'Evidence," *Continuum: The Australian Journal of Media & Culture* 5, no. 2 (1990). http://wwwmcc.murdoch.edu.au/ReadingRoom/5.2/Routt.html (accessed 15 November 2004).

33. Routt, "L'Evidence."

34. Routt, "L'Evidence."

Chapter One

Beginnings in Television and *The Jericho Mile*

As Anna Dzenis has written, the Michael Mann "biography spans nations, passions, and storytelling forms."[1] After graduating from the University of Wisconsin at Madison in 1965 with a bachelor's degree in English literature, Mann decided he wanted to learn the craft of filmmaking. His only production experience during his stay at Wisconsin resulted in an experimental, abstract, and now lost student film titled *Dead Birds, Dead Birds*, photographed in 8mm black-and-white.[2] Having studied the cinema as an undergraduate, he considered both UCLA and NYU for his graduate education, but eventually decided to attend the London Film School (which Mann attended from 1965 to his graduation in 1967, and which was later known as the London International Film School during the period of 1974 to 2001).[3] Mann then experienced, for the very first time, the relationship between a director's vision and the larger commercial and industrial context that inevitably always inflects and in some cases determines that vision. "The quality of the film school itself varied in indirect proportion to the state of the British film industry," Mann told an interviewer in 1979 shortly after the successful television broadcast of his first feature, the telefilm *The Jericho Mile*. Mann recalls that during the 1960s the London Film School's staff was populated by talented craftspeople who simply could not find work in commercial filmmaking at the time: "The worse the British film industry was, the better the school was."[4]

If the development of Mann's technical acumen benefited from this state of affairs, it is also true that he already knew what he was going to receive with an education in London: a chance to experiment. Many years later, Mann reflected upon his move to London in the middle of the 1960s and claimed that the impetus for shunning an education in film production in the United States was at least partially prompted by his belief that young filmmakers should "make two-and-a-half-minute, fully symbolic statements on the nature of reality that'll shame you 10 years later," instead of full-blown attempts in narrative, feature filmmaking which, to his mind, characterized the resulting student films of American production courses.[5] It could be simply that Mann wanted to experience life outside of the country in which he had spent all of his first twenty years; by the late 1970s he defined himself as a big believer in "injecting oneself into experiences . . . [of] injecting myself into a milieu and knowing it . . ."[6] And the factor of the Vietnam War was also important, for the University of Wisconsin at Madison was a politically radical campus in the 1960s, and Mann shared his fellow students' politically progressive consciousness; thus his move to London allowed him to avoid the draft.

In making this choice to study overseas, Mann became part of a group of important filmmakers who received their education at the London Film School during the mid-sixties, a graduating class that also included cinematographer Tax Fujimoto, Mike Leigh, and Ridley Scott. In terms of film aesthetics this education in London, as one might expect, significantly influenced Mann's later work. In a 1981 review of Mann's *Thief*, Richard Combs characterizes the director's style as similar to other British filmmakers of the time such as Scott and Hugh Hudson, suggesting that their "films always seem to break down into dramatic units like TV commercials, with a similar on-the-surface intensity."[7] These sleek surfaces, at least in Mann's and Scott's early films, may have been the result of an education in experimental aesthetics acclimating itself to commercial, narrative filmmaking, and Mann's predilection for an expressive or at times mannerist mise-en-scène likely derives at least in part from his early education and experience in London.

Mann was awarded prizes at the Cannes, Melbourne, Sydney, and Barcelona film festivals for his short abstract film *Janpuri* (1971), but this early period in his career was not wholly determined by experimental aesthetics. If there is a sharp edge of social criticism in much of Mann's work—sharp enough in the Hollywood context to rival even the controversial Oliver Stone, as David A. Cook has suggested[8]—it perhaps found its origin during his stay in Europe in the late 1960s. It was during this time that Mann signed an agreement with NBC to make a film about the 1968 Paris student riots, a move quite unusual for the American television company because their house filming crews nearly always shot the network's documentaries.[9] Mann's feelings about the resulting film, *Insurrection* (1968), articulated the awkward position in which he found himself at the time, in being both within a stone's throw of a career in the commercial film industry and at a close distance of a major political uprising: "I would make my own money on commercials and try to put it to use on my own projects. Some material I filmed on the Paris student riots wound up on NBC's 'First Tuesday' because NBC's own people couldn't get close to the radical leaders. You never resolve these contradictions."[10] One could read Mann's entire career as a series of films that hold such contradictions in an intriguing tension; his attraction to a liberal and at times radical politics has never swayed him from a commitment to cause-and-effect narrative forms and familiar Hollywood genres.

Mann's next documentary effort, the thirty-seven minute short *17 Days Down the Line* (1972), focused on "a *Newsweek* correspondent rediscovering his native land after five years abroad," closely paralleling the trajectory of the director's own life at the time, for in that same year Mann moved from Europe to Los Angeles to make his mark in television production.[11] He did not break into the industry right away, but soon found that writing for television was one way to make a living through creative work. His first scripts were written for Aaron Spelling's police show *Starsky and Hutch* (1975), an experience that taught Mann the basics of television screenplay structure.[12] Mann could later muse that his contribution to the series—including screenplays which became some of the first *Starsky* episodes to air on American television—was at least partly responsible for a "countercultural" tone in the show's early episodes that, in his view, paved the way for *Starsky*'s initial ratings success. In actuality, the series was, at best, superficially countercultural, and at worst politically reactionary. In many ways *Starsky* fed off the antiheroic portrayals of cops in such contemporaneous films as *Dirty Harry* (Don Siegel, 1972), an unreflective and uncritical celebration of fascist behavior that is a far cry from the politics of Mann's later films. And *Starsky* was certainly more "hip" and less grounded in a painstaking observance of realistic detail—at least on a narrative level—than *Police Story*, the show for which Mann wrote scripts during the late 1970s. Mann later claimed that his approach to the *Starsky* scripts was eventually diluted in the production process, of which he was not a part.[13] Indeed, *Starsky and Hutch*'s style, like much television at the time, restricts itself to conventional, character- and dialogue-motivated shot/reaction-shot setups, and only during action sequences are a larger variety of camera angles and rapid narrative pacing employed. Even in such instances the style serves only to punch up the expected resolution of each episode's central crime. On the other hand—and as I show throughout this book—in a Mann work, formal flourishes are not bracketed in such a way; style works broadly across the entire film. *Starsky* is, then, early evidence that Mann's genre-derived writing demanded the expressive formal textures of his later directorial work in order to fully convey the deeper thematic meaning that was only blueprinted, or hinted at, in his scripts.

These compromises notwithstanding, the four episodes of *Starsky and Hutch* that Mann wrote (three of which were broadcast in the first season, one of them in the third season) occasionally reveal interesting parallels with the thematic material of his later films. Investigating Mann's recurring themes in this apprentice television work has its limits in usefulness, of course, for his writing at this point in his career—or, at least, the trace of his writing that remained after the production process—is never very original or striking. At best, however, it affords us a look at the generic tropes to which Mann was most attracted during the early part of his career, those seemingly superficial narrative details which will become important strands in his film work. The first of these episodes, "Texas Longhorn" (originally aired on September 17, 1975) tells the story of a car salesman, Zack Tyler (Med Flory) whose wife is murdered and raped on the side of the road by two assailants.[14] One of these criminals, Chaco (George Loros) expresses dismay over the murder when he discovers that the woman was the car dealer's wife, and not merely a mistress or some "bimbo," an early manifestation of Mann's concern with the American family and the first sign of his criminals' characteristic desire to avoid "home invasions" (the disruption of the nuclear family and the realm of the private through criminal acts), an idea which feeds directly into the plot of *Thief* and more obliquely into the storyline of *Heat* and the film version of *Miami Vice*. These "professional" criminals in Mann's stories will often be contrasted with psychotic characters who willfully violate the criminal's ethical code; in "Texas Longhorn," Harris (Charles Napier) fills the villainous role, for he feels no regret over the woman's death and is thus the first in a long line of unfeeling psychotics populating Mann's films, characters which also include Leo in *Thief*, Dolarhyde in *Manhunter*, Magua in *The Last of the Mohicans*, and Waingro in *Heat*.

Subsequent episodes scripted by Mann—"Lady Blue" (originally aired on November 12, 1975), "Jo Jo" (February 18, 1976), and "The Psychic" (January 5, 1977)—also involve the home-invasion theme. In "Lady Blue," a psychotic serial killer has murdered Starsky's ex-lover, an invasion of the personal by the criminal that makes it difficult for the cop to keep his private life out of his professional existence. "Lady Blue" also marks the first appearance of a master thief in one of Mann's stories, in this case a man known only as Fifth Avenue (Ed Bakely), who provides information to the cops regarding the case. "Jo Jo," meanwhile, involves an ex-convict and rapist (Stephen Davies) who threatens a woman (Linda Scruggs) who has vowed to testify against him. And much of "The Psychic" is about the psychotic behavior of two kidnappers as opposed to other, more professional criminals; as Mann has Starsky say to the husband of a kidnapped girl, "You can make a deal with a professional thief. They stick to the rules. Kidnappers are usually . . . bent." In addition to possessing these themes, all four episodes set their climaxes against the backdrop of decaying industrial environments, such as scrapyards and old factories, landscapes which reappear in the films Mann would later direct. While this was a common feature in certain other episodes of *Starsky* in which Mann had no involvement, the presence of such settings in all of Mann's scripts is telling.[15]

Despite the show's lack of favor among critics and Mann's later claims that the series moved away from the vision of his first screenplays, *Starsky and*

Hutch boosted his commercial viability in the television world of the mid-seventies. *Starsky* also helped improve ABC's audience numbers in the fall season of 1975–1976, a major accomplishment for a network that had perennially placed third in the ratings battles.[16] As a result of this success, doors were opened for other projects. A short time after his *Starsky and Hutch* scripts went into production, Mann began developing a series titled *Bronk,* described sardonically by *New York Times* television critic John J. O'Connor as a transposition of *All in the Family*'s racial tensions to the world of detective shows (a comment with some relevance given that the producer of the show was the lead actor from *All in the Family*, Carroll O'Connor).[17] Mann's subsequent work on the show *Police Story* (1973–1977) proved to be an experience that offered a nurturing environment for his writing, since on this series, according to Mann himself, "the scripts were sacrosanct."[18] Mann's enthusiasm for so-called true stories is consistent across his career, and *Police Story* in many ways offered him, as a screenwriter, the first opportunity to "capture reality" in his creative work. In this *Police Story* was at somewhat of a remove from the sometimes glib hipness that characterized the early episodes of *Starsky and Hutch*. Mann says that each episode of *Police Story* "was based on a real event with real people. And you sit and talk with the policemen who lived *through* this event . . . and you asked them for some story . . . So the wealth of dealing with tactile, documentary reality and finding form and changing things and manipulating it around into dramatic structures is fascinating."[19] Although he would function only as a screenwriter on *Police Story*, Mann gained his first major directorial credit since *17 Days Down the Line* when he was called upon to helm a 1977 episode of the *Police Story* spinoff series *Police Woman*, starring Angie Dickinson, titled "The Buttercup Killer" (originally aired on December 13, 1977).

Clearly this early experience fueled Mann's interest in stories about the often blurry line between the law and criminality. He will often state in interviews that the cops-and-robbers, criminal underworld is one he has at least a superficial personal familiarity with, a claim perhaps boosted by the fact that the director was born in the inner city of Chicago during World War II. Nonetheless, he remained attracted by different kinds of material, in much the same way that some of his later films often break away from the crime genre. Mann attempted to move beyond the cop show by writing one episode of *Gibbsville* (1976), which David Marc and Robert J. Thompson describe as a "*Waltons* knockoff"; using John O'Hara's short stories as source material, *Gibbsville* was a short-lived series which portrayed the life of a reporter in a small town in Pennsylvania.[20] Unfortunately, it was cancelled after only seven weeks and six of its episodes never aired. Mann himself was responsible for the writing of only one episode, "All the Real Girls," (aired on December 16, 1976), which was broadcast shortly before the show was cancelled. Perhaps because of this setback, Mann returned to the somewhat more familiar thematic territory of the Las Vegas underworld in *Vega$* (1978), another project produced by Aaron Spelling. Although Mann was given credit as the writer of the show's pilot, *Vega$* ultimately diluted his original vision, for as Marc and Thompson point out, in this case "the stamp of the Spelling studio was dominant and indelible."[21] Once again frustrated by his experience with television producers, Mann decided to make a move to directing feature-length films, albeit within the mode of the telefilm.

The Jericho Mile (1979) is generally regarded as Mann's debut film proper, for it was shot on 35mm stock and, after a successful television premiere in America, released in theaters in the United Kingdom. It also gave him the opportunity to display a larger degree of authorial control over a project as a director. Nonetheless, the roots of *The Jericho Mile* extend farther back; the script was over ten years old, having been shopped around ABC some ten years earlier by its original writer, Patrick J. Nolan. Nolan, an English professor from Villanova University, collaborated on a rewrite with Mann and the resulting film won both of them an Emmy in the Outstanding Writing in a Limited Series or Special category of 1979.[22] The film also granted Mann with what were hitherto the kindest reviews of his career. *Films & Filming* noted that *Jericho* exhibited "Mann's ability as a director . . . to take street-bound situations and give them a powerful charge of heightened reality," and that Mann blended "a wry humanism with an extraordinary gift for technical resource"; the *New York Times* discussed the film's social themes, writing that its main character's "quest becomes a catalyst for adjusting the perceptions of the other prisoners. Tensions, primarily racial, are created and examined in frequently powerful close-up"; and the *Christian Science Monitor* praised the film as "a prison picture to rival such movie classics as 'The Big House' and 'Birds of Alcatraz.'"[23]

These positive notices were part and parcel with the growing critical respectability of the telefilm during the late 1970s as an alternative mode of film practice which avoided, at least in terms of subject matter if not aesthetics, some of the growing conservatism, and the need for reaching every possible demographic in the marketing of blockbusters, that had preoccupied Hollywood by the end of the decade.[24] *The Jericho Mile* was thus part of a larger phenomenon; in 1978, the year before the film's premiere on ABC, the major Hollywood studios had produced a greater number of films for television than they had for theatrical distribution.[25] This context helps explain how a writer and director such as Mann was able to vacillate between film and television production during the late 1970s and throughout the 1980s.

The Jericho Mile tells the story of Rain Murphy (Peter Strauss), a Folsom inmate convict whose running ability catches the attention of the prison's officials. A professional running coach from Sacramento State Prison, brought in to observe Murphy's talents, confirms that Murphy possesses the rare ability to run the four-minute mile, thus making him a possible competitor in the Olympics. Murphy's desire to achieve this Olympic dream is predicated on an endorsement from a private benefactor, however, who demands that Murphy state unequivocally that he would not commit again the crime which sent him to prison: murder (specifically, the murder of his malevolent father). Murphy, however, refuses to compromise, believing that prison is where he belongs and that the murder he committed against his violent father was justified. He is thus denied attendance at the Olympics in the penultimate sequence in the film, in which his bid for athletic stardom is rejected by his potential corporate sponsors, who fear he has not adequately reformed himself. The final scenes depict him running the four-minute mile on the prison's racetrack, a feat timed to a radio broadcast of the actual Olympic event. Murphy, in what is partially a vicarious triumph, completes the race before the eventual Olympic winner does. Mann uses this story to sketch a backdrop of prison culture in which racial tensions are highlighted; somewhat unbelievably, the ending of the film seems to solidify the prison's populations, as they rally to support Murphy in his transcendent climactic run.

The "Jericho walls come tumbling down" in this sentimental finale, but more subtle touches are on display elsewhere in the film. If Patrick J. Nolan's original screenplay employed heavy religious symbolism that was largely the product of the screenwriter's Catholicism, Mann's rewrite emphasizes a street-tough sensibility and a greater focus on the sense of athletic (and personal) competition between fragmented groups in the real-life Folsom Prison where *The Jericho Mile* was filmed.[26] The film's depiction of racial and ethnic divisions and athleticism, according to Mann, was in part inspired by the real sports pages in Folsom's prison newspaper, reflecting Mann's recurring concern for the way individuals are represented in the media, a theme that is echoed in later films such as *Manhunter*, *The Insider*, and *Ali*.[27] In some scenes prisoners are presented congregating around the television set, asking each other what they're watching that evening; Murphy's only friend in the prison, Stiles (Richard Lawson), talks in a slang reminiscent of the character played by Jimmie Walker on *Good Times* (which completed its final season the same year *The Jericho Mile* first aired); and the radio broadcast of the Olympic race at the end of the film allows Murphy to vicariously participate in the running of the mile. One then gets a sense of the prisoners as aware of—and perhaps defining their identity through—the media, which both represents the outside world to them and represents them to the outside world. Indeed, the way in which the extras—actual prisoners from Folsom—often gaze into Mann's camera while walking past it suggests the extent to which the inmates are aware of the media apparatus, and their glances contribute a self-reflexivity to the film that surely Mann must have prized.

If the director was inspired by Folsom's real prisoner newspaper, his production methods—an approach made possible through the permission granted Mann and his crew to film the story in the living environment of Folsom State Penitentiary—were geared toward capturing a certain reality. In so doing Mann was keen to immerse his professional actors in the prison lifestyle as much as was practically possible. He claimed that the white actors began congregating with the white prisoners while the black actors began to spend most of their time with the black prisoners, an adaptation to the real, preexisting fragmentary environment on the part of the actors.[28] Mann manipulates this realism with a formal style that broadly generates its theme through set design and lens filters; the sea-blue tonalities associated with Murphy's prison cell, for example, form a stylistic precedent for the way Mann often links blue and gray color schemes to the existential crises of his characters in later films, such as Frank in *Thief*, McCauley in *Heat*, Bergman and Wigand in *The Insider*, Sonny Crockett in the film version of *Miami Vice*, and Muhammad Ali after he hears of the death of Malcolm X in *Ali*.

This combination of fiction and documentary, as well as the particular way in which the film represents the relationship between the prisoners and popular media, are two of the major contributions *The Jericho Mile* makes to the genre of the prison film and one of its striking subgenres: the prison film about athletes, a category which also includes *The Loneliness of the Long Distance Runner* (Tony Richardson, 1962), *The Longest Yard* (Robert Aldrich, 1974), and *The Glasshouse* (Tom Gries, 1972, a film which also uses real prisoners as actors). In his 1989 study of the prison film, Bruce Crowther places *The Jericho Mile* in a lineage of prison-set movies about the social reform of individuals whose socially limited mobility contextualizes their past histories (although in retrospect the film would have just as easily fit into the author's chapter on "true stories" set in prisons, given the documentary tinge present through the use of real prisoners as actors).[29] Crowther's motivation for placing the film in this category seems rather unclear, for unlike social-problem prison films such as *The Defiant Ones* (Stanley Kramer, 1958) and *Sounder* (Martin Ritt, 1972), the viewer of *The Jericho Mile* gets little sense of Murphy's socioeconomic background; the only information we learn about his previous life outside of prison is in regards to his relationship with his abusive father (whose murder Murphy has frankly and unapologetically admitted committing). *The Jericho Mile*, at least in its rough outline, is in some ways more similar to *Cool Hand Luke* (Stuart Rosenberg, 1967), with its emphasis on a solitary protagonist who, as Crowther writes, "can redeem himself by drawing upon his own inner resources."[30] But Mann's film goes beyond even this, for *The Jericho Mile* suggests that "inner resources" and reliance upon the solitary self can only advance the prisoner's cause in limited ways. Rather than highlight the strength one can find in solitude, Mann's film emphasizes the symbiotic relationship between the constructed social world outside the prison walls and the constructed social world within them. For the majority of these prisoners, social identity is not solely a product of internal fortitude; as is the case with Mann films to come, *The Jericho Mile* both admires and laments its staunchly individualistic protagonist. Indeed, Murphy is the most solitary figure in the film, and is depicted as alienated rather than liberated. His loneliness is precisely his problem. It is not through inner strength alone that Murphy and the other prisoners achieve what they do, but also through an intriguing relationship with various forms of media such as radio, music, and television. It is in the creative appropriation of these media by the prisoners that the construction of social groups and of expansive individual identities manifests itself in *The Jericho Mile*, and this is, as we will see, an idea that Mann builds through the film's style.

A closer look at the form and themes of *The Jericho Mile*—and the point in television's aesthetic history in which its forms and themes appear—reveals the film not only as a significant contribution to its genre but also as an achievement far beyond the mere apprentice work of Mann's early television writing. Although *The Jericho Mile* can be adequately categorized as one of Michael Mann's minor films, it nonetheless captures the director at an important point of transition in his career, for his stylistic approach in *Jericho* has more in common with the aesthetics of his later films than it does with the stylistics of many earlier television series and telefilms produced in the 1970s. The significance of this fact is crucial, for while the symbiotic (and occasionally contentious) relationship between cinema and television aesthetics has been a given in one way or another since the 1950s, Mann's debut feature is unique in that it functions as an intervention into the conservative stylistics of telefilms prevalent during the 1970s. Before exploring the specific styles and meanings present in *The Jericho Mile*, then, I would like to take a very brief look at the history of the relationship between television and cinema up to the late 1970s, which will help place Mann's film in a wider context.

As John Thornton Caldwell has pointed out, the very first telefilms in America, produced by the Walt Disney Company, imported to the new medium of television the narrative-motivated classical style associated with classical Hollywood cinema:

> Thirty-minute telefilms made for television were now joined by big-budget feature films aired nationally on the small screen. The stylistic impact of these changes cannot be overestimated. Cinema did not just import programs, it imported a way of seeing narrative and a distinctive way of constructing images. Although many telefilms were bland, expressive lighting and choreographed

cinematography were not uncommon in late 1950s television. Along with the telefilms and features came practitioners and crafts people; 35mm Mitchell cameras and Mole Richardson lights; art direction and upright Moviolas; and the controlled stylistic world of the film-studio soundstage.[31]

Beyond "expressive lighting" and "choreographed cinematography," stylistic flourishes which might be deemed in some way excessive in comparison to a self-effacing classical style were always bracketed as such in these early television programs, and in the end were always generated by the needs of the narrative. For example, Caldwell points out that certain episodes of *77 Sunset Strip*, and even a particular episode of *Father Knows Best*, employed stylistics from film noir in ways that were motivated by the demands placed on style by the particular story being told in that episode.[32] And while what Caldwell calls "extended and arty montages" often provided a formal exception to the established standard aesthetic in 1960s television (in, for example, the series *The Mod Squad*), for the most part such stylistic license was ultimately reigned in by a narrative approach that was still fundamentally classical and story arcs that were generally conservative.

Interestingly, Caldwell suggests that the most aesthetically distinguished stylistic works on television were those that were in some way concerned with representations of race and ethnicity, and here he points to series like *Julia* and *Kung Fu* as examples.[33] The more mainstream exception of *Rowan and Martin's Laugh-In*, in turn, often sacrificed star performance to a rapid montage style of editing.[34] By the 1970s, however, even politically progressive television programs, such as the Norman Lear–produced *All in the Family*, *The Jeffersons*, and *Maude*, retreated to a kind of "zero degree," three-camera classical style that rejected the flourishes of exceptional 1960s television. This stylistic regression extended to the telefilm:

> Even movies of the week, originally envisioned as an alternative to importing feature films for broadcast on television, began to look exactly like episodic television. Both had roots, after all, in the same production mode. If visual flash *was* needed, these shows achieved it through props, action, and anatomy, rather than through tonal control, narrative manipulation, or visual stylization.[35]

As Caldwell also points out, there is a certain irony about historians and critics who regard this 1970s period in television as a "second Golden age," particularly because it betrays most mainstream commentators' fundamental lack of interest (at the very best, it is only a secondary interest before which comes the value of narrative) in the possibilities of artful and distinctive visual style on television. This critical attitude anticipates many of the negative critical responses that have characterized Michael Mann's career, responses which often suggest he is more concerned with superficial style over narrative substance. *The Jericho Mile*, though, is interesting even outside the context of Mann's career because it does not conform to a conservative and purely narrative-motivated style of production: while abundant, perhaps predominant, traces of the classical style are evident (much of the film is structured through typical shot/reaction-shot structures) the most intriguing parts of the film remain those that challenge us to derive meaning from an expressive construction of mise-en-scène. In this regard, the film's most stylistically distinguished scenes gesture toward what Caldwell calls the "emergence of a self-conscious aesthetic pose" which arose in the 1980s as a response to the regressive stylistic conservatism of 1970s television (indeed, an aesthetic emergence in which Mann's popular television production *Miami Vice* is an important part).[36]

This fresh aesthetic is perhaps most evident in *The Jericho Mile*'s opening montage, which prefigures the stylish introductions (which often take the form of a montage) to Mann's subsequent films. Considering that Mann's film deals with issues of race and class, one might categorize the televisual "stylistic flourish" of this montage with the aforementioned socially conscious stylistics of earlier television products such as *Julia* or *Kung Fu*. But to an extent greater than most televisual aesthetics, this opening montage in *The Jericho Mile* demands that we pay attention to its careful juxtapositions and compositions. To begin with, there is nothing close to an establishing shot of the prison in this introductory sequence: Mann plunges us into an abstract space which only the viewer's perception—of both image and sound—can help unify. This montage begins with a shot of an inmate—a black man—listening to music on a pair of headphones and dancing; the song he plays, a cover of the Rolling Stones' "Sympathy for the Devil," also plays on the film's soundtrack. That this "unofficial" version of a popular song should be used in the opening credits parallels the ways in which we will later see the prisoners use and appropriate popular culture, from Stiles's evocation of the Jimmie Walker character from *Good Times* to the radio broadcast of the Olympic race which takes on an entirely unintended and unique meaning when it underscores Murphy's own triumphant run within the walls of the prison.

In this scene, the music clearly comes from a single diegetic source—the prisoner's headphones—but the tune also has a commanding presence which sounds nothing close to what true diegetic source music should properly sound like. Instead, the music from the headphones is amplified on the film's own soundtrack. In other words, the audience does not literally hear the music coming from the inmate's headphones as if they were standing right next to him; Mann's aural technique draws the viewer/listener into this world (in a sonically voyeuristic fashion, given that headphones are normally a private space for listening to music), while at the same time pointing to the film's visual and sonic aesthetic as a construction, or as (quite literally speaking in this case) a slightly and self-consciously amplified representation of reality, a key trait of so many Mann images and sounds to come. The reflexive nature of the music's diegetic source is also indicated in the fact that the inmate seen with the headphones (and, in later scenes, with boomboxes and radios) is never pictured without his music and never seen as part of another group within the story. This "character"—who functions as something close to a subtle Greek chorus, indirectly commenting upon the story through the music and radio broadcasts he plays on his equipment—is almost totally outside of the film's narrative, and certainly at the margins of its diegesis. Indeed, at one point in the opening montage, he stares straight into the camera, as if explicitly inviting the film's audience to share in his grooves. His presence rationalizes the choice of a cover of "Sympathy for the Devil" as the opening score to the montage: like the band responsible for the tribute to the Rolling Stones, this inmate uses other artists' work to express his own thoughts and desires. The presence of the textual poacher in Mann, a director who often uses music in ways that blur the difference between diegetic and nondiegetic sound, is also found in important scenes in *Ali* and *Collateral* (in many of these cases the "poacher" in question is an African American, perhaps suggesting that Mann's cinema has sensed the cultural trend found in hip-hop music's creative appropriation of preexisting pop songs).[37] The man with the music is also an oblique parallel to Murphy in that he is the only other character in the film who seeks solitude, but whereas Murphy's solitary nature initially separates him, in a negative fashion, from potential friendships with others, this unnamed prisoner assists in driving the flow of images and the story itself through the sounds emanating from his radio. Thus in *The Jericho Mile* Mann does not reduce possibilities of productive human agency to notions of pure collectivism; individuals, as well as groups, can accomplish a great deal that is valuable in Mann's world. Indeed, there is no clean division between individuality and collective action in the productive agency figured in Mann's cinema, for the individual *as* an individual is never unequivocally separate from groups, as the increasingly public nature of this prisoner's music-playing devices would seem to indicate. He moves from the private realm of headphones to the public performance of the boombox later in the film, while never wholly capitulating to any of the numerous, fragmentary collectives within the prison.

A faithful portrayal of reality, which nonetheless points to the artificiality of an aesthetic construction of that reality, remains an important idea throughout *The Jericho Mile*. The film's mix of professional actors with real prison convicts from Folsom is a case in point. Occasionally prisoners seem to be performing for the camera and the camera alone, giving the film a certain documentary quality, and yet the camerawork is never wholly static: it either assists in the meticulous composition of interesting and dynamic shots, arranging the "real" into a clearly artificial aesthetic, or it is on the move, greeting the living, breathing prisoners not as an indifferent recording device but almost as another moving body. Interesting aesthetic interventions are also found in the film's editing. The music rhythmically drives the introductory montage, generating juxtapositions that serve to connect the various games and sports the inmates play. And yet the men nonetheless remain apart, even within groups: the editing functions to cleave all of these men (and all of the various racial groups of which they are part) from one another and into separate spaces.

Music further inflects our sense of composition and cutting. The first sonic appearance of an electric guitar in this cover of "Sympathy for the Devil" matches the first visual appearance of a graffiti painting of a decoratively garbed Grim Reaper on the prison walls. As more portions of this painting are slowly revealed across a number of fragmented shots, more musical aspects are introduced into the tune: when the Reaper painting next appears, for example, a dynamic burst of piano is cued on the soundtrack. It seems somewhat ironic that the most energetic sounds in this music should be timed to a painting which evokes an aura of death and murder, and yet such a juxtaposition reveals an important Mann theme: the co-presence of both productive and destructive agency and creativity in single instances, and the relativity upon which definitions of each rest. The painting of the Reaper itself gestures toward this meaning, for as a work of art it is both a creative act (by the inmates, who release productive tension through crafting it) and an act pointing toward violence and decay in the specter of Death which it represents (the end of creativity). That the Reaper painting has been introduced to us in fragments in much the same manner that the various racial and ethnic groups have been introduced is also important, for the approach suggests that the painting's meaning is relative to the particular point of view from which it is seen. An individual viewer's reaction to a painting of Death is likely to be different than that of the individual who created the work, especially when that individual is a prisoner. By including images of the Reaper in the context of a rhythmic montage which also intertwines fragmented images of individuals and racial groups, Mann and his editing team suggest that the painting's meaning is determined by one's particular position in society (or within a microcosmic society, like a prison) and one's own individual point-of-view (which is always related to, if never wholly determined by, issues of race).

Given the initially equivocal nature of both the viewer's relationship to the visual and sonic abstractions in the film (especially in the opening montage) and the real social fragmentations which make relationships more difficult for characters to achieve within the film's diegetic world, any alliances which develop between individuals figured within the abstracted space of Mann's Folsom become doubly important, for they provide not only the concrete solidarity of human connection for the characters within the film, but they also at the same time ground the audience in a dynamic, dramatic storyline which helps the viewer adjust to a perhaps unexpected televisual aesthetic. This does not mean that Mann's film simply inscribes a conservative or clichéd storyline into an otherwise interesting stylistic concoction; rather, this dichotomy points to his attempt—one that will continue throughout his career—of portraying dramatic human problems while also stylistically generating a sense of the sometimes foreboding and decaying environments in which these conflicts are found. In Mann's best work to come, an understanding of this drama becomes increasingly inextricable from a simultaneous understanding of the world that intersects and grounds the story. The one reason why *The Jericho Mile* remains a minor work in comparison to a later film such as *Heat* is that the content (the preexisting script) of *Jericho* seems to generate much of the style found in the film, while in later films the relationship between story and aesthetic will become far more complex. The montage at the beginning of *The Jericho Mile*, for example, seems entirely appropriate for a story that is already about fragmentation between individuals and groups. In subsequent Mann films the given dramatic situations will continue to motivate stylistic choices, of course; it is only that as Mann's aesthetic becomes increasingly richer and more complex in the later films, the viewer develops a greater sense of the ways in which style also generates additional layers of meaning which considerably expand the preexisting dramatic concerns of the script.

At a number of important junctures, however, visuals in *The Jericho Mile* speak powerfully. The recurring images of Rain Murphy and his friend Stiles running around the race track in the opening montage indicate their emerging friendship. Their relationship is the one form of human contact, above all the others depicted in the film, which guides *The Jericho Mile*'s narrative development. Amidst all of these images of games and sports, the actions of Murphy and Stiles are at first not particularly distinctive, except for the fact that their friendship signals an obvious mixing of race whereas relationships between members of the other groups do not (an idea complicated later in the film when one of the African American convicts reveals himself to also be part Mexican American, suggesting that racial prejudices within this prison community are quite literally superficial). This opening sequence marks the only moment in the film wherein Stiles is seen racing alongside Murphy, suggesting (and later scenes will support this idea) that there is more to their friendship than that which is immediately visible, and complicating assumptions that the only thing that these two men might have in common is athleticism.

Most of *The Jericho Mile*, at least in relation to this opening burst of energy in the montage, proceeds at a somewhat more reserved pace. The balance of the film's style corresponds for the most part to what a viewer might expect of a classical telefilm (the frequent use of standard and largely undistinguished shot/reaction-shot structures being a key trait), but Mann's generation of meaning through expressive mise-en-scène is nonetheless present in a number of compelling scenes. *The Jericho Mile*'s most meaningful stylistic touches often occur during interaction between Murphy and Stiles as each sits in his own respective jail cell; the compositions and juxtapositions in these sequences suggest aspects of the relationship between Murphy and Stiles that otherwise go unsaid. The two live in adjacent cells—referred to as "houses" by the inmates in the film—and talk to each other through the walls, although during the first depicted conversation between them it is Stiles who does most of the talking. Murphy spends most of his time cooling down from his most recent run, while Stiles talks about the birth of his new baby daughter. Murphy is reticent and withdrawn; he is framed in close-up shots more often than Stiles during this first dialogue between the two, suggesting that Murphy's attempts to remove all chance and contingency from his very narrow view of existence are in contrast to Stiles's more open, social style of living. Indeed, in this sequence Murphy is not figured in a long shot which inscribes a larger social space around him until Stiles walks outside of his cell to Murphy's to show off the photograph of his new baby daughter, a clever kind of character-motivated screen movement which beautifully reveals in a single shot the profound, socially expansive impact Stiles will eventually have on Murphy's life. And while most of this scene is shot from outside the cells, emphasizing the prison bars (the kind of vertical lines which Mann will favor throughout his career), occasionally Mann juxtaposes closer shots of both characters to suggest that there is a potential bond between them—yet to be discovered *by* them—which will allow them, at least momentarily, to transcend their material situation in the same manner that the camera traverses material boundaries like the prison cell.

The second scene depicting Murphy and Stiles in their cells takes place during the evening. No words are exchanged in this sequence: the form implies everything. In the first shot of a row of prison cells, taken from a side angle, the only light in the frame emanates from the two houses in which Murphy and Stiles live, suggesting that these two characters are loners (Stiles, while a highly socialized individual, does not belong to any particular group within the prison) and once again stylistically figuring a potential friendship which has yet to be fully developed in the narrative. The scene subsequently cuts in on close-ups of both Murphy and Stiles, each of them focused on their own particular obsession: Murphy is stretching his muscles, while Stiles is plaintively looking at the photograph of his wife and daughter. Once again the camera here transcends the prison bars and intimately links the two characters through montage. Stiles shuts his light out first, while Murphy stays up and works out—in the final shot of the sequence we can see that his cell light is now the only one still on—implying that there are varying levels of solitude desired by each particular character.

One of the crucial differences between Stiles and Murphy is that the former, as he himself puts it, "needs things," whereas Murphy "doesn't need anybody." Stiles desires human contact, and to that end he arranges for an early conjugal visit with his wife through a deal he makes with one of the prison's gang leaders, Dr. D (Brian Dennehy). During a conversation between the two of them in the cafeteria, Murphy seems close to warning Stiles about the dangers of dealing with Dr. D, but hesitates. In a later scene, Murphy and Stiles are confronted by a group of African Americans who accuse Stiles, because of his friendship with Murphy, of "jiving with whitey" and dealing drugs with Dr. D's racist compatriots. After this encounter—which is ironically the most intimate human contact either Murphy or Stiles experience up to this point in the narrative—the two retreat to their cells for their last conversation. The camera captures and juxtaposes each of them in a close-up, and although they are separated by the wall of the cell, in terms of screen direction they nonetheless face one another, suggesting that for the first time Murphy is attempting to break out of his solitude and engage in a productive human interaction. The cool, melancholy blue tones which code Murphy's cell, as well as his own disavowals of social contracts—"I am into nothing, that is how I do my time"—subtly contradict the fact that for the first time he has shown concern for another human being, emotions that only rise to the surface once Stiles is murdered by Dr. D's crew at the halfway point of the film.

If the growing relationship between Murphy and Stiles is perhaps the key narrative through-line in the first half of the film, the attention Murphy's skilled running draws from the prison warden, Earl Gulliver (Billy Green Bush) and the prison psychologist Dr. Bill Janowski (Geoffrey Lewis) is thematically equal in importance, for it provides the film with an analysis of class to complement its racial themes, in addition to providing the appropriate psychological motivation for Murphy's eventual triumph. Every time one of these characters appears, an implication about their position in a social hierarchy is never too far away. When we first meet Dr. Janowski, it is during a scene in which Murphy's skills are brought to his attention by the sports reporter for the prison newspaper; Dr. Janowski and the reporter are clearly demarcated by dress, and Janowski is seen as the boss in the situation when he orders the reporter to unearth more facts on Murphy despite the writer's lack of interest (the reporter refers to Murphy as a "goof that runs around in circles," an attempt to secure his own place within the prison hierarchy by denigrating another). The character blocking, in which the reporter stands above the psychologist, thus seems slightly ironic. In another scene, the viewer sees Gulliver wearing fancy blue suits which separate him from Dr. Janowski, but the suit's significance later points to an inversion of Gulliver's place in the food chain when he meets a running coach from Sacramento State who has come to time Murphy's run. The running coach's judgment of Murphy's ability—and the coach being the expert, it is a judgment only he can make—gives him a power in this social situation that eclipses Gulliver's. In turn, the runners who the coach brings from Sacramento State prison regard Murphy's makeshift track—"four laps around the trashcans is a mile"—as beneath them.

Mann's formal style seems somewhat removed from many of these meanings; conversations between characters mostly unfold in simple shot/reaction-shots without much stylistic commentary on the prison's social order. Additionally, the characters seem totally innocent of the ways in which they make use of the particular power they wield at the multiple positions on the social hierarchy they hold, unlike Frank and Leo in *Thief* or Bergman and Wigand in *The Insider*. And unlike those in *Thief*, the characters in *The Jericho Mile* ultimately work together to collectively achieve goals. The running coach, for example, provides Murphy with better running shoes with which to train (such class-transcending collective effort seems to succeed at least until the end of the film, at which point Murphy is once again denied access to the power structures which allow for such achievement). *The Jericho Mile*, then, anticipates the more intricate and formally affective analyses of social hierarchies in nearly all of Mann's subsequent films. Perhaps because of this ultimately incomplete and naïve attitude toward class hierarchies, and despite the mixed emotional tone of the film's ending—which emphasizes both Murphy's personal accomplishment in successfully running the four-minute mile in the prison yard and his ultimate failure to successfully run in the Olympic race—*The Jericho Mile* remains the most sentimental (and perhaps the most optimistic) of Mann's films.

One of the most interesting images in the final scene of the film occurs right before Murphy is about to run his final triumphant mile in the prison. Just as Murphy approaches the track, the camera locates the aforementioned music-playing inmate who from time to time has reappeared to comment on the story through the music he plays. A zoom-in captures this man and his boombox (which will provide the diegetic broadcast of the Olympic race to which Murphy runs his own mile) and the shot once again suggests the productive manner in which these prisoners appropriate popular texts from the outside for their own positive uses in the prison. The desire for a kind of transcendental freedom in *The Jericho Mile* is fueled by these appropriations of artifice, and the extent to which Mann himself remains intent on portraying the reality of prison life through an aesthetic construction intensifies the similar accomplishment of his characters at the end of the film.

Sadly, in the case of *The Jericho Mile*, Mann's commitment to the realistic depiction of a society had certain unintended consequences. Mann spoke of "a lot of Pirandelloesque things that went on" during the filming of *The Jericho Mile* at Folsom Prison, not the least of which was the actors being able to closely identify with real convicts simply because of their close proximity to them.[38] The situation was also clearly a very dangerous one, and posed an ethical conundrum, reflected in Mann's observation that whatever reality Folsom and the real convicts contributed to the film, the film in turn left a profound mark on the psychology of the convicts:

> The irony of it is that one of the guys who "stabbed" Stiles, the man with the swastika tattoo on his stomach . . . he *was* the character. Except the character magnified his real personality and when the film was over *he* magnified the *character*'s personality. Now he's jumped a whole magnitude! Before he was an aggressive guy, he used to have a reputation of "coming up into people's face," right? But he kept it fairly under check. He kept going at his film role until four weeks after we wrapped and were out of prison . . . and three Mexicans just took him out.[39]

This sad postscript to the film (its sadness lost or at least mitigated in Mann's somewhat macho relaying of the event in the quote above) suggests that the transcendent optimism on display in the film's ending is only temporary, and perhaps in the end entirely fictional. The Peter Strauss character in *The Jericho Mile* may engender a sense of political camaraderie among the inmates through his spirited athleticism and his refusal to capitulate to the demands of corporate culture, but the fragility of such a triumph is plainly evident, especially considering that Mann's subsequent films will emerge as relatively pessimistic about the possibility of productive individual and collective agency in contemporary America.

NOTES

1. Anna Dzenis, "Great Directors: Michael Mann," *Senses of Cinema*, http://www.sensesofcinema.com/contents/directors/02/mann.html (accessed 11 January 2005).

2. Julian Fox, "Four Minute Mile," *Films & Filming* 26, no. 4 (January 1980): 19.

3. F. X. Feeney provides the dates of Mann's attendance at the London Film School in *Michael Mann* (London: Taschen, 2006), 10.

4. Fox, "Four Minute Mile," 19.

5. Michael Sragow, "Mann Among Men," *Salon.com*, http://www.salon.com/bc/1999/02/02bc.html (accessed November 14, 2004).

6. Fox, "Four Minute Mile," 24.

7. Richard Combs, "Violent Streets," *Monthly Film Bulletin* 33, no. 569 (June 1981): 121.

8. David A. Cook, *A History of Narrative Film, 4th ed.* (New York: W. W. Norton & Co., 2004), 878.

9. Fox, "Four Minute Mile," 19.

10. Sragow, "Mann Among Men."

11. Quoted in Fox, "Four Minute Mile," 25.

12. David Marc and Robert J. Thompson, *Prime Time, Prime Movers* (Boston: Little, Brown & Co., 1992), 233.

13. Fox, "Four Minute Mile," 25

14. My information on the original airdates of television episodes mentioned in this chapter are from Paul Taylor, "Castles in Romania," *Monthly Film Bulletin* 52, no. 615 (April 1985).

15. These "post-industrial landscapes" and their affect on Mann's characters have been explored in an essay on Mann's films by Christopher Sharrett. See Sharrett, "Michael Mann: Elegies on the Post-Industrial Landscape," *Fifty Contemporary Filmmakers*, ed. Yvonne Tasker (London: Routledge, 2002), 255.

16. Leonard Sloane, "ABC On Its Way Out of the Cellar," *New York Times*, 9 November 1975, F1.

17. John J. O'Connor, "'Matt Helm,' 'Bronk' in Detective Ranks," *New York Times*, 20 September 1975, 59.

18. Fox, "Four Minute Mile," 25.

19. Fox, "Four Minute Mile," 25.

20. Marc and Thompson, *Prime Time*, 233.

21. Marc and Thompson, *Prime Time*, 234.

22. See the Internet Move Database, http://pro.imdb.com/name/nm0634338/awards (accessed October 12, 2004).

23. See Fox, "Four Minute Mile," 19; Fox, "The Jericho Mile," *Films & Filming* 26, no. 2 (November 1979), 39; John J. O'Connor, "TV Weekend: Natalie Wood Sparks ABC's 'Cracker Factory,'" *New York Times*, 16 March 1979, C31; and Arthur Unger, "'Jericho Mile' Bids to Become a Minor TV Classic," in *Christian Science Monitor*, 17 March 1979, 19.

24. For a larger discussion of the relationship between the rise of the telefilm and the American film industry during the 1970s see David A. Cook, *Lost Illusions: American Cinema in the Shadow of Watergate and Vietnam, 1970–1979* (New York: Charles Scribner's Sons, 2000), 22. See also Kirk Honeycutt, "Made-for-TV Films—Hollywood's Stepchild Comes of Age," *New York Times*, 19 August 1979, D1.

25. See Cook, *Lost Illusions*, 22.

26. Fox, "Four Minute Mile," 20.
27. Fox, "Four Minute Mile," 20.
28. Fox, "Four Minute Mile," 20.
29. Bruce Crowther, *Captured on Film: The Prison Movie* (London: B. T. Batsford Ltd., 1989), 34–35.
30. Crowther, *Captured on Film*, 33–34.
31. John Thornton Caldwell, *Televisuality: Style, Crisis, and Authority in American Television* (New Brunswick, NJ: Rutgers University Press, 1995), 50.
32. Caldwell, *Televisuality*, 50.
33. Caldwell, *Televisuality*, 53–54.
34. Caldwell, *Televisuality*, 53–54.
35. Caldwell, *Televisuality*, 58.
36. Caldwell, *Televisuality*, 59.
37. I borrow the term "textual poacher" from Henry Jenkins' work on fan culture and television. See Jenkins, *Textual Poachers: Television Fans and Participatory Culture* (London: Routledge, 1992).
38. Fox, "Four Minute Mile," 22.
39. Fox, "Four Minute Mile," 22.

Chapter Two

Thief

The success of *The Jericho Mile* on American television, as well as the unexpected theatrical run the film received in Britain, paved the way for Mann's second feature, *Thief* (1981). James Caan, chosen to play the film's lead character, a professional jewel thief, was fresh from the experience of directing *Hide in Plain Sight* (1980), in which he also acted in the role of an embittered working-class man. After this experience in directing, Caan was happy to be in front of the camera again: he spoke bitterly of studio heads interfering with his final cut of *Hide in Plain Sight*, adding intrusive music to a film that the actor-director had envisioned as a mix of fiction and cinema-verité.[1] *Thief*, on the other hand, would involve a commitment to a realism of a very different nature. At Mann's behest, Caan learned gun handling and target practice with a professional gunman in Arizona, a man who, according to Caan, had known many thieves throughout his life.[2] In supporting roles, meanwhile, Mann creatively inverted the real-life experience of his actors. For example, an ex-convict and former thief, John Santucci, plays a cop in the film and served as Mann's technical advisor.[3] One of the mob's thugs is played by Dennis Farina, who also appears in later Mann projects such as *Manhunter* and *Crime Story*; Farina had once been a cop for the Chicago police department. In the very casting of these roles Mann suggests the fragile line between the enforcer and the transgressor of the law, a notion developed in greater depth in *Manhunter*, *Heat*, and the film version of *Miami Vice*. Also at Mann's disposal in this quest for realistic detail was the most sophisticated and cosmopolitan film crew he had worked with to date. Donald E. Thorin was chosen as cinematographer; after a career as a camera operator on films by John Cassavetes, Woody Allen, and Hal Ashby, this was his first job in the role of director of photography. Dov Hoenig, a veteran of collaborations with directors such as Jean Rouch and Moshé Mizrahi, edited. The musical score, by the band Tangerine Dream, gave the film a distinctive soundtrack (which will be discussed at greater length later in the chapter).

Thief concerns Frank (Caan), a master thief who aims to perform enough "scores," or heists, of highly prized jewelry and large amounts of cash, to allow himself to spend the rest of his days comfortably raising a family. His own picture-perfect conception of the American dream is represented by a photo collage he keeps in his wallet, complete with mostly generic images from magazines of children and women, alongside one specific photograph of a father-figure, Okla (Willie Nelson), a friend from prison who mentored him in the tricks of the thieving trade. As Frank pursues his ideal mate, a café cashier named Jessie (Tuesday Weld), he sticks closely to his principles of working without the burden of a contract. Apart from a single partner, Barry (Jim Belushi), Frank's only contacts with the criminal underworld are with individual dealers who purchase the items he steals. These buyers have the air of businessmen; Frank carefully avoids interaction with buyers on the street. Ironically, the film's release title in Britain was *Violent Streets*, evoking *Mean Streets* (1973), but unlike the rough and tumble gangsters of Martin Scorsese's early film, Mann's Frank does business conservatively: his business dealings occur in public spaces such as restaurants, office buildings, and even Frank's own used-car shop. Frank desires these enclosed spaces for his business transactions in order to avoid unexpected contingencies and to prevent his professional life from interfering with his personal one. "I am Joe-the-boss of my own body," Frank says, asserting his right to capitalize upon the fruits of his own labor. It is an individualistic ethos developed in prison, derived from the honing of an attitude for survival in confinement that is not dissimilar from Rain Murphy's in *The Jericho Mile*. As Frank says: "You gotta get to where nothin' means nothin' . . . I don't care about me, I don't care about nothing . . . I know that I survived because I achieved that mental attitude." Frank, though—who speaks of his thievery as a "magic act" through which he can regain the time he lost in prison and achieve the dream represented in his collage of images—eventually makes the seemingly inevitable decision of signing a contract with a mob boss, Leo (Robert Prosky), who will be able to secure the largest, highest-paying scores in the business, enabling Frank to speed up his acquisition of the American dream through a corporate arrangement.

The screenplay is based on a novel by Frank Hohimer titled *The Home Invaders: Confessions of a Cat Burglar* (1975), penned while the author was behind bars in Fort Madison, Iowa. The precise relationship between *Thief* and *The Home Invaders* is rather loose, given that Mann himself is credited with a new screen story in addition to the screenplay, resulting in a number of changes from book to film. Unlike Hohimer, Caan's character in the film clearly states that he doesn't perform home invasions, a statement which is consistent with his general respect for comfortable living with a home and a family, goals that provide the basis of his professional activities. Unfortunately the fulfillment of these goals is inextricable from the way in which Frank's own home is invaded. This point is further emphasized in *Thief* after Frank finds the tapped phone lines the police have rigged in his house, and through the way in which Leo's corporate mob is able to infiltrate every aspect of Frank's private life. Invasions of Frank's home occur in subtle ways: Jesse cannot birth children, so the adoption of Frank's and Jessie's child is arranged through Leo, and the purchase of a house is made possible through the money Frank is promised by the gangster.

Hohimer himself—who was in prison at the time *Thief* was produced—is now somewhat less famous for the string of cat burglaries he performed for the mob and more renown in legal circles for once being accused of the murder of Valerie Percy, a crime in which Hohimer denies involvement.[4] (Hohimer was eventually cleared of the murder charges, and the case remains unsolved). Apart from a few ambiguous lines of dialogue in the film during which Frank tells Jesse about a "manslaughter beef" he incurred while in prison, *Thief* doesn't make reference to homicide as a part of its main character's history. Nonetheless, Caan's way of speaking in the film seems influenced by Hohimer's abrasive, to-the-point manner of writing, and some elements of backstory and certain lines of Hohimer's novel—such as "I changed cars and women like most people change socks"—are lifted into Mann's screenplay with only the slightest of revisions.[5]

The manner of address in the novel is also strikingly different than the generally more omniscient point of view of the film. One gets the sense from reading *The Home Invaders* that Hohimer is addressing his narrative to the very wealthy people he once robbed:

> You name the State and the Mob will give you . . . the names of the millionaires and their addresses . . . Those of you that have already been ripped off know the score. Those still on the list don't be alarmed if someone shines a light in your face around two or three in the morning . . . It is just a burglar the mob sent to pay you a visit.[6]

Later, in explaining how he arrived at prison in the first place, Hohimer points an accusatory finger at the reader: "Fifteen lousy . . . years back and forth between two of the most brutal, lousiest prison systems in the State of Illinois. For a goddam $40 robbery you are more guilty of than I was."[7] *Thief* makes no such direct address, preferring to immerse its audience in the accrual of sometimes unexplained details of criminal life. For example, Mann depicts Caan and Belushi staking out an insurance company early in the film not so much to allow the audience to learn the intricacies of the heist they will later execute, but more to simply allow us to observe the characters in the act of observing. This point may seem obvious, but in many ways it is at the heart of Mann's attempt to capture his idea of reality primarily through a heightened visual expression and attention to atmospheric detail rather than through only narrative information or psychological verisimilitude. Mann's realism in *Thief* often works on this purely visual level, even if his sense of narrative and psychological realism is perhaps, at least in *Thief*, occasionally a little out of step; as Vincent Canby observed in his review of the film, Frank is established as a little too street-smart to make his eventual agreement with Leo entirely dramatically valid.[8] Regardless, the emphasis on an attentive visual style is further evidence of Mann's concern with the process of capturing "tactile, documentary reality and finding form and changing things and manipulating it around into dramatic structures . . ."[9]

It is in this way that *Thief* is clearly the work of an expressive stylist moving away from the economical precision of Hohimer's sentences and, indeed, the generally classical style of *The Jericho Mile*. Some critics of Mann considered such a formal approach as one that generates superficial style rather than substance. David Sterritt, writing in *Christian Science Monitor*, implied that the film was at fault for failing to conform to a classical Hollywood tone by claiming that "the livid language and vicious violence of the '80s pack *less* punch than the subtler shades that were used in the '40s"; Canby himself detected a similar lack in subtle filmmaking when he criticized the film's aesthetics as "pretty enough to be framed and hung on a wall, where, of course, good movies don't belong."[10] Despite such criticism, for the most part *Thief* eschews pure mannerism. Mann is much less concerned with making thematic points in very carefully modulated moments of framing and arrangement (in a way that a critic such as Sterritt might prefer) than he is with drawing connections across the film, creating a style which develops and accumulates meaning over the course of two hours rather than revealing meaning through form at those points which are exclusively determined by narrative. *Thief* is thus the first feature-length exemplar in Mann's directorial career of the broad fit between style and theme that Adrian Martin suggests is characteristic of expressive mise-en-scène.

Toward the end of the chapter I will examine more closely how the film's style, and the thematic material generated out of its style, relate to its genre, the crime film. But I first want to explore in greater depth the expressive style of *Thief* that I have hinted at above. An example of how Mann employs such an aesthetic can be ascertained by describing and interpreting the first sequence of the film, in which Frank and two of his cohorts perform a jewel heist. It is a three-person job: Frank will break into the safe and lift the jewels, Barry will disconnect the wires to the alarm system, and an unidentified third man (seen again in the film only during the second heist scene) will remain in a getaway car with a police radio, closely watching for cops. There is no exposition in this prologue: apart from establishing a dark, noirlike setting on the wet urban streets of what we later learn is Chicago, the depiction of this heist is concerned exclusively with the body and the technology which enables the human body to perform what Frank later describes as his "magic act." But the Chicago in *Thief*—at least during this opening sequence—could be any American urban city on a cold, rainy, dark night. As in the opening montage of *The Jericho Mile*, Mann again establishes very little surrounding visual space in individual shots for the development of economical stylistic modulations within scenes; he is instead creating a cinematic, stylistic "event" in place of an analytical découpage of character interaction in space. The viewer gets little sense of the job as a whole, as in a meticulously arranged classical heist picture like *Rififi* (Jules Dassin, 1954). Instead, each character is somewhat abstracted from his environment; our perception of character in *Thief* begins with the fact that each individual seen on-screen is connected to the concrete space around him only through a particular technological or mechanical device.

In a review of the film that appeared upon its release, Al Auster and Leonard Quart qualified *Thief* as "partially a high-tech film noir, filled with innumerable Bressonian close-ups of welding tools creating golden showers of sparks as they burn through reinforced steel doors."[11] This opening sequence is perhaps the best evidence for their observation. Mann alternates between several types of shots in his portrayal of Frank's jewel heist. Long medium shots establish at least a fragment of the space to which Frank and his crew connect in their use of technological instruments. Closer medium shots enable us to see Frank's face and hands as he manipulates the tools. Close-ups of Frank's hands follow his gestures as he manipulates the hydraulic drill that will allow him to crack the safe. Finally, we see close-ups of the tools themselves and further extreme close-ups of the tools that use the camera's zoom lens to show the inner workings of Frank's technology, a sight that the human eye alone could not capture. "Stanley Kubrick. Eisenstein. Dziga Vertov. And 'Kino Eye,'" Michael Mann once starkly said when asked of his influences.[12] The reference to the second Russian director mentioned in this quote seems particularly apt, for Mann's aesthetic, in an overt manner, moves beyond what his characters themselves can see and understand in much the same way that Vertov sought to extend humankind's ability to see beyond itself through cinematic technology. If Mann's technical precision in a sense mirrors the virtuosic technical ability Caan's character displays, Mann's ultimately goes far beyond and sees much more than Frank, and in doing so points to the limitations of the protagonist's own agency—his "magic act"—and thus to his eventual downfall.

In *Thief* there is another melancholic aspect to this broad interaction of theme and style. While sequences such as the first heist prove Mann to be a professionally adept director, Frank's technical acumen leads to nothing but the destruction of everything he works for, so much so that the only technical proficiency and meticulousness that means anything to Frank during *Thief*'s devastating climax is the character's cold ability to manipulate firepower in killing the corporate mobster bosses who have sealed his fate. Indeed, the close-ups of men brandishing guns during the film's violent final scenes suggest an intimate material relationship between man and technological device which is similar to that suggested in the film's opening sequences. Thus for Mann there seems to be a kind of *potential* equivalence between Frank's work as an individual agent and the work of the violent, corporate criminals who eventually tear Frank's life apart. Any single human action possesses no intrinsic meaning when such acts are foregrounded by the filmmaker as material events in and of themselves, such as in these close-up shots of Frank wielding his tools (whether that tool be a hydraulic drill or a gun), shots which sheave away the surrounding environment to focus on the acts only. As in the Reaper painting figured in *The Jericho Mile*, every action in *Thief*—especially those which Mann aesthetically highlights as singular stylistic events not demanded out of narrative necessity, and which are depicted, to again quote Canby, in frames and shots "pretty enough to be framed and hung on a wall"—possesses a relative meaning, the value of which changes according to the individual who happens to be performing those acts, as well as according to *for* whomever the acts in question are being performed. Thus, Frank's actions are, at varying points in the film, both for himself and for the benefit of the corporate gangsters who co-opt his work.

Frank's ability to act meaningfully is thus related in part to the particular implements of his trade. The heist sequences (of which there are two in the film) and the violent gunfight (of which there is one, during the film's climax) foreground the material relationship between Frank and his tools and as the most obviously bravura, spectacular scenes they serve to anchor the film's narrative. Intervening scenes, meanwhile, complicate and inflect our understanding of Frank and his relationship to the mob. Frank's tools represent the control he has over the means of his production in the beginning of the film; they are the material that will be co-opted by Leo's corporation later on. And yet Frank is not simply an innocent character who is corrupted by institutional forces. He is, after all and most obviously, a thief, a fact that places the character in a morally and ethically ambiguous position. The relationship between Frank and Leo is not a simple dramatic dichotomy between a pure, self-serving, individualistic labor ("good") and a faceless corporate conglomerate ("evil"). Frank sits in a complicated place on the scale of social hierarchies. While he may well intend to be "Joe-the-boss of my own body," Frank is also a boss himself. He owns a used-car lot and a bar, and is in a clearly dominant position to his employees (which include mechanics, his secretary, and the bartender). One early scene in particular demonstrates Frank's own alienation of others' labor quite well. Frank walks out of his office and toward the front of the car lot. The camera is placed inside the lot's garage, frontally presenting the work of the mechanics on two automobiles in a medium shot as we see Frank move away from them in the background. The sound of drills and other mechanical tools are heard on the soundtrack while the mechanics talk to one another; one shouts out to Frank: "What's doin', bossman?" Another, searching for a device, declares, "I can't work without my tools!" But no true dialogue between Frank and his employees is generated: Frank walks away from them, not acknowledging their presence, and the tools they use do not belong to these mechanics after all: they belong to Frank, and their labor is a source of his capital. Granted, the fact that Frank is a jewel thief might suggest that the used-car lot and the bar are nothing but fronts, superficially legitimate businesses that serve as a cover for his criminal activities. Mann never makes this clear: did Frank own these establishments before he pulled his greatest heists, or were they the products of such labor? It is not possible to know, but in either case the businesses, like all sources of capital, serve their owner more than they serve their employees.

Given the quality of Frank's position as described above—one of mitigated agency at best, absolute ineffectuality at worst—Mann avoids characterizing his protagonist as an antihero in the Dirty Harry mode, and in doing so he moves beyond the conservatism of his early television scripts for *Starsky and Hutch*. *Thief* is not so much a celebration of the violence which Frank, at film's end, resorts to in order to disentangle himself from institutions (two of these being the corporate criminals represented by Frank and Frank's own used-car business, which generates capital out of the labor of others) but is rather an analysis and lament of such a situation. The influence of Vertov in Mann's cinema is found in the director's ability to generate social and political meaning above and beyond the comprehension of any particular character in *Thief* (who remain the victims of the very society Mann is critiquing). Vertov's influence is never present in Mann as an already articulated political or theoretical position; it is generated through the quality of Mann's aesthetic designs and the ensuing attitude and understanding he brings to his characters and their predicaments.

In the shot following the one described earlier in front of Frank's business, the protagonist sits against a blue fence and reads a letter from his prison buddy Okla. It is an intimate moment visually: Frank is blocked off from society both by the fence and his reading of the letter. But on the soundtrack we continue to hear the mechanical tools from the garage, a sound which evokes a presence not available visually at this juncture—perhaps the truest Bressonian touch in the entire film—obliquely suggesting that this personal moment has been made possible by the very impersonal labor of others. By complicating Frank's place on the social food chain in this manner, Mann continues to develop one of his important recurring themes: the increasing difficulty of defining oneself as outside the influence of corporate capitalism, an idea which will find further development in later Mann films such as *The Insider*, *Ali*, and *Collateral*. Frank will repeatedly assert that he is an individual and that he and only he is in control of his destiny. And yet Mann has made clear in the opening sequence that all actions are wholly contingent on the context in which they take place (thus making them ripe for corporate co-option) and, in the first scenes depicting Frank on his car lot, it is also clear that Frank himself has already co-opted the labor of others without being fully aware of it. Try as he might, Frank cannot move outside the corporate forces that mitigate his individual agency.

If the opening sequence in the film suggests a master thief working in a kind of abstract time and space, the second heist sequence, with Frank now under the corporate auspices of Leo, carries an entirely different inflection. The first sequence emphasizes each individual member performing his contribution to the heist in separate frames; conversely, this bigger, more dangerous second score is clearly presented as a collective effort. The scene begins with Frank, Barry, and an unidentified third member of the crew sawing a hole into the elevator shaft from atop the roof and tapping the alarm system. This moment between Frank and Barry is one of the longest they share for one uninterrupted sequence in the entire film; when Leo murders Barry later in *Thief*, much of its resonance may indeed derive from this scene, in which the separate contributions of Frank and Barry's labor are clearly and closely intertwined. What is seen here is a collective effort, but one that is ultimately under the auspices of a corporate arrangement, which thus mitigates each member's own individual agency.

Mann does emphasize individual action later in the sequence in order to more clearly display how that action is now qualitatively different from the heist at the beginning of the film. Once Frank is inside the building, he begins slowly pulling out large screws from a heavy steel door, a movement depicted by a single shot: a high-angle close-up of Frank's hands, his tool, and the giant steel door he is breaking into—a door which, in terms of shot volume, takes up nearly half of the frame, emphasizing its heaviness. This door is clearly not a barricade that will yield to the simple hydraulic drill of the film's first heist; this corporate job demands a higher-grade industrial tool (not the sort of item that Frank or Barry has lying around). Up to this point, the scene has been scored to Tangerine Dream's pulsing electronic music, but as this shot begins—as Frank brings his industrial-sized screwdriver to the door— the music drops out just as the sound of metal twisting on metal (combined with the sound of leather as Frank's gloved hand turns the screws) is mixed in on the soundtrack. The visual and aural sensations of Frank's labor in this shot carry a truly Bressonian quality to them, "a small but indelible smudge of vibrant, present-tense aliveness . . . A rarity in film: it's a scene that involves the actual tasks and materials of a job," as Kent Jones writes of Bresson's own *L'Argent* (1983).[13] For Frank, the tasks and materials of this corporate job are far beyond anything that he alone can muster.

A close-up gives way to a long shot as Frank steps inside the safe room. Mann pans to follow Frank as he moves into the room and walks farther away from the camera, and in doing so emphasizes a sense of space which is beyond and (literally) above Frank's own vision. In the intimate mise-en-scène of the first heist sequence, the viewer never sees Frank alone in this kind of long shot, but in this second heist sequence there is no questioning that this is maybe the most beautiful safe in the world, looking as it does like an elegant hotel lobby. This shot gives the viewer a much larger sense of surrounding space than anything conveyed in the dark, moonlit close-ups of the first sequences, and it continues to suggest, like the earlier shots in the sequence, that while the heist's success is still dependent on the meticulous nature of Frank's own "magic act," it is no longer a personal job. Frank's now narrowed vision is confirmed as he talks to Barry on his two-way radio: "Come on, we own it," he says, referring to the safe as their property after this successful curbing of the alarm system's activation. But everything they lift from the safe now belongs to someone else—in this case, Leo, the mob boss.

If these two heist sequences are primarily concerned with the cold and unemotional tasks and materials of Frank's jobs (in these qualities they are even more similar to shots from a Bresson film), their objective correlative (and from Frank's perspective, their purpose) are the domestic scenes in which Frank slowly begins to construct his dream of a family. Every step of the way, however, it is clear that Frank is not pursuing this dream as an autonomous agent: his home is bought and paid for with the assurance that the money to pay for it will come through his next heist, and the adoption of the baby— which Frank cannot accomplish on his own due to his standing as an ex-convict—is arranged by Leo. The film's aesthetic representation of private, domestic spheres evokes all of these themes. In contrast to the nondiegetic electronic music which scores most of the film, the organic instruments of jazz, rock, and blues are heard (as diegetic source music) in two important scenes with Jesse: first at the café when she and Frank make their date for later in the evening and again in the bar when Frank arrives late to pick her up. After Frank and Jessie subsequently develop an emotional bond in the café scene, Tangerine Dream's music reappears on the soundtrack, which in comparison to the previous two instances of the blues music is a slightly odd juxtaposition that perhaps prefigures the eventual downturn in their relationship. Montages of images also reveal the extent to which Frank's relationship with Jesse is contingent on his business dealings with Leo. After a scene in which Frank, Barry, and Leo scope out the next heist, the film jumps to Frank and Jessie standing together in their home, a home which has been made possible through Frank's business dealings with Leo. This scene between the two lovers is not fully developed, but its partially perfunctory nature seems appropriate given that their relationship is ultimately little more than an interstice between shots of industrial and commercial landscapes (indeed, it is made wholly possible by the men who control these landscapes, which in this case is Leo and his mob). Frank's private life, in the construction and arrangement of these images, is quite literally sandwiched in between representations of the contingent reality that will constantly threaten his desire for autonomy.

Expressive use of sound and image juxtapositions generate further commentary about the collapsing distinction between the private and public realms in Frank's life. In the beach scene after the second successful heist, the Tangerine Dream music on the film's soundtrack, which up until now has been paired with images of urban Chicago, seems out of place compared to the natural environment visible on-screen. But then this incongruity becomes even more unsettling. The music continues to play on the soundtrack as the film cuts to a scene inside Frank's home. Frank and Jessie put their baby to bed and then retreat to the bedroom to make love; the sequence is accompanied by a shot in which the camera pans across the family home, autonomous in that its gaze is not motivated by narrative or character movement, in which we see a stereo playing music that is plausibly also the music we as an audience hear on the soundtrack. If Tangerine Dream's electronic music, alongside the autonomous movement of the camera, is ultimately associated with the kind of technology which both makes Frank's dream of a family possible and wrenches that dream away from him, then this is the scene in which such technology finally appears once and for all to have invaded Frank's own home, scoring as it does intimate scenes of lovemaking and child rearing. This idea is further emphasized when these images of Frank's home are in turn immediately followed by images of Leo's house (a juxtaposition which is bridged by the music, which bleeds into the next scene before it fades out).

Natural environments, Frank's private life, and Leo's domain are all bridged in a subtle montage scored to (and linked together by) the same music, indicating that it is impossible for us (or Frank) to fully apprehend any of these spaces as wholly apart from the other. Mann seems to avoid analyzing space in the manner of classical découpage because in his universe the differences between various spaces in society have been leveled out and homogenized, and even nature has been tainted by the traces of an alien technology.

What makes this musical meaning particularly difficult to perceive in Mann's work is the way in which he and his collaborators refuse to bracket self-reflexivity as such in the form of the film. As in certain scenes in *Manhunter*, in which still photographs and video images become important to the story and are in turn an important aspect of the film's aesthetic, or in *The Jericho Mile*, *Heat*, *The Insider*, and *Ali*, which all reflect upon the use of media by stylistically commenting upon its presence in a story, Mann's use of cinematic reflexivity is implicit rather than explicit, and the audience is drawn to it through its function as a curiously engaging stylistic event. The use of sound and music in *Thief*'s climactic scene, in which Frank murders Leo in the gangster's home, is again expressive in a manner similar to the visual aesthetic of the film. Mann rarely uses music as it might be used in a music video, that is, exclusively for purposes of rhythm. Although his musical choices are flexible enough to work on one level as the kind of glossy patina characteristic of advertisements or other empty stylizations, Mann's musical choices also mean something, and their meaning comes across more powerfully and emotionally for its *not* being purely cerebral or distantly self-reflexive: that is, Mann never gives up the affect which conventional uses of Hollywood film music provide (in much the same way that he refuses to give up the expectations that the use of genre frameworks engender), but he will always qualify such use, or simply add something irreducibly singular or intriguingly complex to the preexisting Hollywood formula. Much of *Thief* is scored to Tangerine Dream, and the electronic soundscape provided by that band's music, as suggested in the previous paragraph, occasionally accentuates the industrial and technological elements of the mise-en-scène. Unlike a lot of anachronistic uses of film music—for example, the use of both modern orchestra and electronic music to score the ancient story world of Ridley Scott's *Gladiator* (2000), and the intentional and meaningful use of cover versions of period songs in Mann's later *Ali*, which I will discuss in chapter 9—the music heard on *Thief*'s soundtrack might plausibly be produced in the world on display in the film's frame. Thus the score is suitable for depicting Frank's environment, for just as the emotional life of the character and his goals for creating a comfortable domestic life are contingent on the technology and industry of capitalistic society, the emotions are conveyed to the audience through a musical-technological apparatus that is very much of the film's time period (which, in 1981, was more or less "the present"). The general types of melodies, however, do not really change and they remain fairly conventional in nature: the film's score opens on an ominous low note, corresponding to the mysterious noir environment in which its characters will first be found; and when Frank and Barry take their girlfriends to the beach to celebrate their second successful heist, the music grows appropriately triumphant.

What has changed in *Thief* is the manner of the score, and for Mann manner truly does matter, perhaps even more than the notes actually played. As previously suggested, the beach scene is indeed the first sign of a kind of disjunction between Frank's world and the world signified by the music: in a mise-en-scène wholly devoid of industrial or technological objects (unlike the contingency figured in the cityscapes present in the rest of the film, this beach is close to Frank's stable American Dream in that it is free of all impending societal obligations and wholly "natural"), Tangerine Dream's electronic music feels oddly out of place despite the fact that it corresponds to the narrative's demands for triumphant music in this instance. This intriguing stylistic rift between the manner of the music and the depicted event gains special resonance later in *Thief*. When Frank murders Leo and his crew at the end of the film, an instrumental rock tune appears (one which is also scored by Tangerine Dream but that is largely free of the electronic dabbling audible in most of their score). What this music generates is an unabashedly rebellious and emotional release for Caan's character: the rock music rejects the cold technology of electronic music in much the same way that Frank implicitly rejects everything the music might have stood for or been associated with up to this point in the film, including not only Leo but his now tainted relationship with Jessie. These final scenes offer a reflexive moment: we as an audience are in turn asked to consider the multiple responses such variations in the sonic aesthetic engender. A simple idea, maybe, but in large part the charge of the scene is in its character's return to a zero degree of gangster behavior, a return to his *own* simplicity: his direct, instantaneous gunfire dispatches with the situation in a remarkably economical way that Leo himself (who makes Barry's death a complicated, vengeful spectacle, truly the trappings of a bureaucratic, corporate gangster culture) and his underlings (who wield larger guns that are not substantially more efficient) are incapable of. Even the violence in *Thief*, then, and the manner of its stylization, carries thematic weight.

Mann's crafting of sound inflects the scene even further. As Dennis Farina's bodyguard raises his automatic rifle, Mann cuts in on a slow-motion close-up of his weapon. The sound which follows—the harsh, efficient blast of Frank's pistol, which appears when Mann next cuts immediately to a shot of Frank lying on the ground—is perhaps not what the audience expects to hear, for Mann cues us to anticipate the sounds of Farina's more technologically advanced weapon (heard earlier in the scene) through the preceding close-up. Sound then becomes a crucial aspect of the aesthetic generation of meaning, and in addition to providing the requisite suspense and surprise in this case, it also alerts us to the *sonic* difference between Frank and the corporate criminals (who benefit from more advanced weaponry). Later, before Caan walks off into the distance and away from the audience, Mann focuses on Frank kneeling on the ground for a few seconds as he rips off his tattered shirt to reveal a bulletproof vest underneath. The soundtrack carefully captures the fabric of shirt and vest ripping as Frank investigates his wound (apart from the music it is now the only other audible sound) as if to suggest Frank is something of an outmoded artisan or warrior whose way of battle is no longer fashionable; shades of Kurosawa are present here. Frank is, regardless, a uniquely individualistic antihero in Mann's oeuvre, especially given that in Mann's next major heist film, *Heat*, the gangsters—who otherwise share certain aspects of Frank's solitary personality—more or less acclimate themselves to the corporate world of machine guns and surveillance systems, and their exploits are in turn scored to subtler rock-electronic hybrids which reject the relatively crude dichotomy of electronic and rock in *Thief*. But none of that business for Frank: as he walks out of *Thief*'s final frames to blistering rock n' roll, he truly becomes extinct. This nihilism, which is found on the level of both character (Frank rejects a meaningful existence with Jessie) and the film's stylization (which revels in the aesthetic affect which generates our sense of Frank as a now nihilistic character, made so partially because of the brutality of corporate capitalism) is the only moment in Mann's oeuvre when a major character explicitly and violently rejects, and literally turns his back on, humanity.

This use of expressive mise-en-scène and sound, through which Mann essays a broad fit between style and theme, then allows the filmmaker to portray both the intimate nature of Frank's work and its eventual corporate co-option. As a style, however, it has historical precedent and intersects with Mann's distinctive genre construction. *Thief* is most directly related to the gangster genre, but at least in terms of some aspects of its stylistic approach it is also in part an early example of a cycle of "neonoir" films of the 1980s which also includes Lawrence Kasdan's *Body Heat* (1981), Bob Rafelson's *Black Widow* (1986), Alan Parker's *Angel Heart* (1987), and Mann's own *Manhunter* (1986).[14] *Thief* is most clearly a noir picture, stylistically, when Frank first encounters the mob boss Leo, who offers Frank an opportunity for bigger and higher-paying scores. James Naremore, in linking this new cycle to films noir of the past, points out that "because color has been normalized, the conventional effects of black-and-white lighting can also be integrated smoothly into recent films that have no retrospective or nostalgic intent."[15] Naremore goes on to discuss the particular effects of *Thief*:

> Consider Michael Mann's *Thief*, photographed by Donald Thorin, which was released in the same year as the deliberately retro *Body Heat*. *Thief* begins with a night-for-night shot in which the camera drifts slowly down between two buildings to reveal a black car sitting in an alleyway during a rainstorm; backlit rain falls through a dramatically silhouetted network of fire escapes and gathers in shiny puddles on the asphalt. This sort of tried-and-true "mystery" imagery soon gives way to quite a different style: daytime scenes in windowed offices are photographed with tungsten filters, so that the world outside becomes a bluish haze; lighting in diners and various institutional settings is unremittingly flat; and in most of the intimate sequences, telephoto close-ups reduce the backgrounds to a blur. But whenever the protagonist . . . holds a meeting with his sinister employer . . . everything once again becomes shadowy and atmospheric . . . to make the moral perspective clear, every close-up of [Leo] is lit from below, whereas every close-up of [Frank] is lit from slightly above.[16]

Thief is not an out-and-out noir picture, and nor is it a nostalgic tribute to the genre as *Body Heat* clearly is. What is most interesting in the sequences described by Naremore is that Mann is adapting expressive noir stylistics to the gangster genre; the emergence of Leo, the mob boss, is the first sign that Frank, the simple thief, is being woven into a larger corporate structure which promises much but delivers little. As Naremore suggests, the director is able to short-hand a moralistic worldview through noir lighting. And yet the simplistic moral division between Frank and Leo evinced in this scene is constantly complicated by the film's portrayal of Frank, which sees him as complicit with the mechanisms of corporate capitalism (although to a degree less obviously brutal than Leo's involvement). Indeed, the blocking and framing of the first conversation between Frank and Leo offers a kind of counterpoint to the black-and-white moralistic design of the lighting: while at the beginning of the conversation Frank is figured against old relics of American industry (including a steel bridge and old warehouses), Leo and his thugs stand against a backdrop of the vibrant city skyline. As the conversation progresses, however, the backdrop behind Frank changes so that he is eventually depicted against the city lights initially figured behind Leo, suggesting that Frank is a part of the contemporary capitalistic machine—and always being drawn further into such structures—more than he is aware of or willing to acknowledge. So while the film has no qualms about portraying Leo as insidiously evil, it strikes a more ambiguous tone in the figure of Frank, whose place on the social hierarchy seems much more equivocal and complex. Like Murphy in *The Jericho Mile*, Frank seems at times to possess a kind of honesty that only a productive human relationship might be able to nurture; this is perhaps the meaning of the scene with the fisherman early in the film, whose relationship with Frank, while unlike any other human bond evinced in the film (they sit together and simply appreciate nature in a rare moment in which Frank is not driven to do anything in particular), is also short lived and never fully developed, much like his eventual relationship with Jessie. That Frank initially seems to value a certain kind of humanity, a quality not at all present in Leo and his thugs, renders his naïveté about his own ultimate complicity with the system that much more tragic. Indeed, it is this potential for productive human agency that makes Frank's murderous, nihilistic behavior at the end of *Thief* particularly wrenching.

Robert Warshow, one of the earliest commentators on the gangster genre, wrote eloquently on the troubling paradox behind the gangster figure:

> No convention of the gangster film is more strongly established than this: it is dangerous to be alone. And yet the very conditions of success make it impossible not to be alone, for success is always the establishment of an *individual* preeminence that must be imposed on others, in whom it automatically arouses hatred; the successful man is an outlaw. The gangster's whole life is an effort to assert himself as an individual, to draw himself out of the crowd, and he dies *because* he is an individual.[17]

Frank himself does not fit the mode of the classical conventional gangster. He expresses a need for assimilation into the mainstream of American culture, in his desire for a family and a comfortable life. Indeed, to a certain degree he is already assimilated, in that he operates his own businesses and profits from the alienated labor of others. Warshow observed that the gangster's activity — whether it be running numbers or selling liquor — is often kept in the background of these films, so that his transgressive behavior becomes "a kind of pure criminality."[18] Frank's activities, meanwhile — whether they be pulling heists, selling used cars (perhaps as a front), unknowingly oppressing his own staff, or selling off his diamonds to black-market buyers — are meticulously outlined in *Thief*'s narrative and visuals. Frank, too, announces to Jessie that he's a thief; he comes out in the open. It is Leo, rather, the mob boss, whose criminality is invisible; his wheelings and dealings are kept offscreen, and he comes across as pure evil as he tracks down and kills Barry and threatens Frank near the end of the film. The gangster has become corporate, and like corporations, his activities are no longer individual, but are still invisible. It is the pact that Frank signs with Leo's corporation that seals his doom, for at that point his complicity with the system becomes irrevocable. Frank, in the end, risks death not because he is ostentatiously individualistic, as in the early gangster films, but because he has turned over his individual rights to a faceless corporate structure. He destroys his business, sends his wife and adopted child away, and murders his mobster employers. In an inversion of the classical gangster trope, an inversion largely accomplished by Mann and his collaborators through the stylistic generation of the film's themes, Frank can only survive alone.

It is this sense of loneliness—specifically male loneliness—which most academic critics have pinpointed as the source of Mann's most acute social and political observations and it seems to find embryonic expression in *Thief* before becoming more fully and subtly developed on the larger canvases of *Heat*, *The Insider*, and *Ali*. As Christopher Sharrett notes, Mann's representations of "ineffectual protagonists overwhelmed by circumstance" are linked to the despairing environments in which these characters are found; if Mann's audience gets a sense of Frank as alienated from his own labor in the opening stanza of *Thief*, the portrayal of his loneliness in that instance corresponds to a general visual approach throughout the film (and indeed throughout much of Mann's work). Sharrett writes:

> Mann's bleak vision is shared with, say, the horror films of the 1970s, which saw civilization as a dead end but could not posit any alternative vision. Mann's representation of crisis is not nearly as visceral though; his sense of the postmodern *cul de sac* comes across in the delineation of his cinematic landscapes. Like Antonioni—especially *The Eclipse* (1962), *Red Desert* (1964), and *Zabriskie Point* (1969)—Mann sets humdrum stories (rooted very much in genre) against carefully constructed backdrops that emphasize his characters' alienation. Images recall the paintings of David Hockney, Eric Fischl, Robert Longo or Gilbert and George, with lonely subjects framed by cityscapes, industrial wastelands, bodies of water, or large bay windows, with images often photographed with heavy blue or amber casts to convey an icy or autumnal effect.[19]

The bleakness of Mann's overall vision is perhaps slightly exaggerated by Sharrett, as Mann's codas tend to be ambiguous; they often emphasize both despair and triumph simultaneously, most noticeably in the finales of *The Insider* and *Collateral*. Mann seems just as concerned with the potential existence of a productive and successful human agency as he is with the individual's frequent incapability to overcome circumstance. *Thief*, of course, which ends with Frank sending his wife and child away, burning his home and his used-car dealership to the ground, and murdering his mobster employers, is perhaps the best evidence in Mann's oeuvre for Sharrett's intriguing observations. Alienation and ineffectuality play a central role in the film, perhaps most obviously in its ending but also in, as Sharrett suggests, Mann's framings, which often emphasize decaying, postindustrial environments abstracted from a larger sense of their surrounding geography. Such images contribute to our visual understanding of the constrictions the director's characters face in their attempts to transcend their socially inscribed situations.

NOTES

1. Chris Chase, "At the Movies," *New York Times*, April 3, 1981, C6.
2. Chase, "At the Movies."
3. Mark Steensland, *Michael Mann* (London: Pocket Essentials, 2002), 26.
4. The Percy case, tossed aside as an unimportant detail in the "true story" of *Thief*, is still open, despite the fact that Hohimer's name has been cleared. Details of the crime can be found at http://www.crimelibrary.com/notorious_murders/famous/valerie_percy/ (accessed January 17, 2005).
5. Frank Hohimer, *The Home Invaders: Confessions of a Cat Burglar* (Chicago: Chicago Review Press, 1975), xvii.
6. Hohimer, *Home Invaders*, xviii.
7. Hohimer, *Home Invaders*, 1.
8. Vincent Canby, "Screen: 'Thief,' With Caan and Tuesday Weld," *New York Times*, March 27, 1981, C12.
9. Julian Fox, "Four Minute Mile," *Films & Filming* 26, no. 4 (January 1980): 25.
10. David Sterritt, "Short Takes," *Christian Science Monitor* 16 April 1981, and Canby, "Screen."
11. Al Auster and Leonard Quart, "Thief," *Cineaste* 11, no. 3 (1981): 38.
12. Fox, "Four Minute Mile," 20.
13. Kent Jones, *L'Argent: BFI Modern Classics* (London: British Film Institute, 1999), 46.
14. For a longer list of neonoir films (extending into the 1990s) see David A. Cook, *A History of Narrative Film, 4th ed.* (New York: W. W. Norton & Co., 2004), 873–74.
15. James Naremore, *More Than Night: Film Noir in its Contexts* (Berkeley and Los Angeles: University of California Press, 1998), 193.
16. Naremore, *More Than Night*, 193.
17. Robert Warshow, *The Immediate Experience: Movies, Comics, Theatre, and Other Aspects of Popular Culture* (Cambridge, MA: Harvard University Press, 2001), 102–3.
18. Warshow, *The Immediate Experience*, 101.
19. Christopher Sharrett, "Michael Mann: Elegies on the Post-Industrial Landscape," *Fifty Contemporary Filmmakers*, ed. Yvonne Tasker (London: Routledge, 2002), 255.

Chapter Three

The Keep

Thief was not a major success at the box office, grossing only $4.3 million in its United States theatrical run, but such a relatively minor disappointment could not foreshadow the overwhelming commercial failure of Mann's next film, *The Keep*, a genre hybrid of fantasy and horror.[1] Budgeted at $6 million, *The Keep* managed to recoup only 1.2 million, and bad timing might have had something to do with its anemic performance in theaters.[2] Released in December 1983 at the height of the holiday film season, *The Keep* was unable to compete with a crowded field of popular releases such as *Scarface* (Brian DePalma), *Terms of Endearment* (James L. Brooks), and *Sudden Impact* (Clint Eastwood). *The Keep* was originally scheduled for a summer release, and was delayed only by the sudden death of its visual-effects supervisor, Wally Veevers, whose previous work included *2001: A Space Odyssey* (Stanley Kubrick, 1968), *Superman* (Richard Donner, 1978), *Saturn 3* (Stanley Donen, 1980) and *Excalibur* (John Boorman, 1981); his unexpected passing postponed the film's production for six months, as new visual effects had to be created in order to match both the footage he had already helped to create during the film's production and the specifications he left for the postproduction effects.[3]

A number of market mechanisms and trends in genre production allowed for the production and release of *The Keep*. Producers Howard Koch Jr. and Gene Kirkwood purchased the rights to the film's source novel as part of a package deal that also included the race-horse film *The Pope of Greenwich Village* (Stuart Rosenberg, 1984).[4] *The Keep* fits (albeit rather awkwardly) within genre cycles prevalent during the 1980s: fantasy films including *The Dark Crystal* (Jim Henson, 1982) and *E.T. the Extra-Terrestrial* (Steven Spielberg, 1982); sword-and-sorcery films (a stylistic parallel evoked in *The Keep*'s nearly medieval atmosphere) such as *Dragonslayer* (Matthew Robbins, 1981), *Krull* (Peter Yates, 1983), and *LadyHawke* (Richard Donner, 1985); and mainstream horror productions, such as *Poltergeist* (Tobe Hooper, 1985), *The Hunger* (Tony Scott, 1983), *Firestarter* (Mark L. Lester, 1984), and *Poltergeist II* (Brian Gibson, 1986).[5] Mann, for his part, recognized another mechanism for the potential success of his fantasy-horror film, and his comments are somewhat ironic given his move back to television after *The Keep*: "Now people see moving pictures six hours a day. So, what's the motivation to go to the cinema? It has to be a different order of experience. Otherwise, stay home and watch the idiot box."[6]

The Keep is a different sort of experience, without question; it is the most stylistically excessive of Michael Mann's films, and its occasional lapses in narrative logic pose challenges for critics more interested in describing and interpreting its effects than in prescribing its flaws. Based on F. Paul Wilson's novel of the same name, the film's story—one difficult to synopsize only because in actuality the narrative arc, while clear in the novel, is often either opaque or convoluted in the film—is set in a tiny village in Romania during World War II. Detachments of Wehrmacht soldiers are sent to guard a large mountain pass, thought to be a crucial area of land for the eventual concentration camps planned for Romania. To their surprise, they find a castle keep there, built at the outskirts of a small village. Many of the German soldiers are attracted by the silver crosses they find on the keep's walls, but in their attempts to steal them they begin to unleash the mysterious power of a monster—later referred to as Molasar—who murders them. This awakening of an evil spirit somehow triggers the senses of a mysterious man named Glaeken (Scott Glenn), Molasar's ambiguous foe, who heads for the keep. Meanwhile, the head of the Wehrmacht, Captain Klaus Woermann (Jürgen Prochnow) sends for reinforcements to help find the source of the murders, leading to the arrival of a more malevolent SS superior, Major Kaempffer (Gabriel Byrne). The Nazi Kaempffer, trusting the advice of the villager Fonescu (Robert Prosky), sends for an ailing Jewish professor, Dr. Theodore Cuza (Ian McKellen), who can supposedly explain the source of the keep's evil, although in truth this is a ruse performed by Fonescu in order to free Cuza and his daughter Eva (Alberta Watson) from the concentration camps. Cuza employs some clever lies of his own in his dealings with both Kaempffer and the relatively more sympathetic and antifascist Woermann, pretending to study the keep and the writings found within it in order to protract his and his daughter's freedom; eventually, however, Cuza encounters Molasar, who grants the ailing old man eternal life in exchange for his assistance in helping release the demon from the keep. Shortly thereafter, Glaeken—called upon, it turns out, to deliver Molasar back into the keep before his evil can spread across the world—arrives at the keep to do battle with the monster, while at the same time developing an intimate relationship with Eva, revealing a human side that Molasar does not possess. Glaeken, though, must become, more or less, the "good" figure to Molasar's "evil," and in the end sacrifices himself so that the evil can be contained. As in the finales to most of Mann's films, the protagonist's journey ends on a note that is not purely heroic: Glaeken has defeated Molasar, but has lost Eva, a denouement that recalls the cop Vincent Hanna's ambiguous abandonment of his wife at the end of *Heat*; in becoming the "good" force necessary to oppose Molasar's evil, Glaeken has lost the one part of his being which rendered him human.

On the one hand, *The Keep* is similar to *The Jericho Mile* and *Thief* in that its director desired realistic detail, which in the case of *The Keep* led to a representation of the stylization of the Nazis themselves. As Mann has said, "When you're dealing with the authenticity of the haircuts, the underwear, the shaving gear, the packs, you find yourself in an area that looks totally stylized, simply because it's real, which is very convenient for me."[8] But in this film Mann has shrouded these marks of concrete verisimilitude in evocative and ethereal visual designs that are as far away from strict cinematic realism as possible. A conscious move on its director's part to break from the "street movie," *The Keep* also marked Mann's first conscious attempt to "go beyond traditional, three-act narrative into something more expressionistic, something with more enchantment."[9] In this respect the film has left its mark on Mann's career, for its dreamlike atmosphere and its opaque narrative logic (if not its occasional abandonment of narrative coherence) prefigures a response Mann would give in an interview with Joel Engel in 1995:

JE: Does something that goes bump in act one have to crash in act three?

MM: Not necessarily. There are no rules. That's rule one. It's context. Because the whole of a screenplay, the whole of a motion picture, if it works, is a consensual dream. It's a relativistic universe that you create. It's a good idea, when you're creating that universe, to invent some consistent laws by which it operates; and to be cognizant of the fact that this motion picture is going to move through time, approximately two hours of it. There are certain rhythms by which we perceive a flow of events and a story. So it's a fairly good idea to have four acts or three acts.[10]

As Kristin Thompson points out, Mann is one of the rare Hollywood filmmakers who has proposed a four-act structure for film, and as I will show in a consideration of *Manhunter* in the next chapter, approaching his films as four-act constructions occasionally offers a productive reading strategy.[11] While *The Keep* does not offer as clear a sense of a four-act structure, it does offer an ephemeral, atmospheric imagery that functions as evidence of the director's intention to craft a "consensual dream," and as an early indication of his desire to move beyond the strictures of classical construction.

Interviews with Mann around the time of *The Keep* reflect his enthusiasm for creating a filmic world bound only by the spatial and temporal logic its creators infuse within it and not by the rules of screenplay structure or preexisting literary conceits. The director also suggests the manner in which viewers might draw a connection between the heightened realism of *Thief* and the less plausible "realism" of *The Keep*, which exudes an entirely different sense of the accurate capturing of reality, in that fantasy films strive to portray the details of a wholly *invented* reality:

> The starting point really preceded the book. I'd just done a street movie, *Thief*. A very stylized street movie, but nevertheless stylized *realism*. You can make it wet, you make it dry, but you're still on the "street." And I had a need, a big desire, to do something almost similar to Gabriel Garcia Marquez's *One Hundred Years of Solitude*, where I could deal with something that was non-realistic and create the reality. There's an effect in the film whereby Molasar accrues to himself particles of matter from living organisms. Now what is the logic of that? What does it look like? How does it happen? What is the sound of it? . . . You have to be consistent. You're not rendering objective reality, you're making up reality.[12]

The form of Mann's Molasar is slowly revealed to the audience as the film unfolds; this technique itself communicates not only the appearance of the creature but also the very self-reflexive, temporal act of the cinematic "putting-together" of such an artificial being. Perhaps to the detriment of the film's narrative thrust, Molasar comes across as less a powerful force in and of himself and as more of an aesthetic curiosity through the way he is visually depicted. The character is like a sculpture in time, with aspects of both his corporeal and intangible existence slowly shaped over the course of the film.

In addition to reflecting the director's stated intent in crafting a "consensual dream," such an approach is also interesting for what it suggests about Mann's attitude toward adaptation. *The Keep*, like *Thief*, is based on a book, but like *Thief* relative to Frank Hohimer's *The Home Invaders*, *The Keep* abandons the logical structure and causal explanations that characterize F. Paul Wilson's novel. Critic Kim Newman, in a review of *The Keep* for *Monthly Film Bulletin*, suggests that *The Keep* was "a novel almost entirely dependent upon cinematic effects" with its "ease and urgency of John Carpenter during his low-budget days. . . . As a novel, *The Keep* is already a great, traditional horror movie. Michael Mann, however, has not made that film . . . As with Stanley Kubrick's *The Shining,* Mann has chosen not so much to adapt Wilson's novel as to prune it drastically."[13] Newman faults the film for its gradually cumbersome accrual of inexplicable narrative and visual details, most of which are explained in the novel, such as the silver crosses which are mounted on the walls of the keep, which do not figure, as one might reasonably assume, as Christian symbols, but as "representations of the talismanic sword hilt which Glaeken needs to complete his weapon[.]"[14] In the film, this weapon appears less as a sword and more as a kind of supernatural vacuum machine, which literally sucks up Molasar's evil at the end of the film. The viewer is left to wonder, quite simply, "what is this object?" Mann invents a fantasy world with its own internal logic, while at the same time demanding that his audience immerse itself in the surface qualities such logic produces.

Pulling off this kind of fantastical gambit—especially in a world in which most film critics are obstinately literary minded—is certainly not easy, and it is debatable whether or not *The Keep* fully succeeds in its attempt. It is important to point out that a number of the film's narrative potholes—especially regarding the romantic subplot between Glaeken and Eva—were not consciously designed but were rather the result of substantial and apparently haphazard trimming which occurred after unsuccessful test screenings.[15] Some of these jarring trims are most evident in the final half-hour of the film, which features a number of awkward (but no less interesting for that) editing strategies, including cuts that interrupt pieces of nondiegetic music (a phenomenon which does not mark the editing approach in the first two acts of the film). Other plot points which are left unexplained—such as the backstory behind Glaeken's supernatural relationship to Molasar, which is elaborately detailed in the book—seem plausible only in light of Mann's desire to create an atmospheric visual world whose causality, in turn, can only be inferred by the visual evocations which are on the screen, and not by a type of literary explanation which can, it must be said, only truly be found in Wilson's source novel. Mann was aware that a straight adaptation would damage the film's ability to construct its own spatio-temporal universe, but in his clear attempt to distance himself from the film's source material—and in his association of his own desire to make the film with the more "respectable" novel by Marquez—the director can be placed in a lineage of filmmakers (including the aforementioned Kubrick) who intentionally disregard their own source material in order to elevate, on a purely rhetorical level, their "personal vision" to grander heights. As James Naremore has pointed out, this was the approach of another meticulous director, Alfred Hitchcock, who always claimed he liked to "read a story only once, and if I like the basic idea, I just forget about the book and start to create cinema."[16]

But Mann has not removed details from the novel simply for the sake of removing them. One passage in Wilson's book suggests the direction that Mann ultimately takes in constructing his film (which at the same also implicitly points out the direction that Wilson does not take in his novel). Wilson's Dr. Cuza is explaining to Woermann and Kaempffer that the books found in the keep describe a kind of evil which is almost ineffable in its gruesomeness:

> "What could possibly be so awful?" Woermann said, pulling the leatherbound, iron-hasped copy of *Unaussprechlichen Kulten* toward him. "Look. This one's in German." He opened the cover and flipped through the pages, finally stopping near the middle and reading . . . Magda [Eva in the film] was tempted to warn him but decided against it. She owed these Germans nothing. She saw the captain's face blanch, saw his throat working in spasms as he slammed the book shut. . . . "What kind of sick, demented mind is responsible for this sort of thing? It's—It's—" He could not seem to find the words to express what he felt.[17]

Wilson here describes the ambiguous effects of Molasar's evil rather than the specific visible manifestation of the evil itself, making this passage one of the more intriguing parts of the novel, and it is an approach subsequently abandoned by Wilson, who, in the writing of a psychologically driven bestseller, must more or less describe everything in explicable—if appropriately fantastic—terms. Mann's film version, at its most interesting, avoids describing events through exposition and instead evokes their meaning through intricate aesthetic designs. Part of what some critics read as the failure of *The Keep* occurs when the film abandons literal explanation entirely, charging ahead with its aesthetic even when the narrative seems frustratingly opaque.

In other words, rather than transforming the content of the adapted novel into an altogether different statement—such as Stanley Kubrick did in *The Shining* when he focused squarely on the subject of the American family rather than on the gruesome, horrific detail of Stephen King's rambling novel—Mann leaves *The Keep*'s explanations behind wherever he can, indulging his interest in creating a relativistic universe of evocative images rather than a literal translation of a very plot-driven novel. If anything, it is this approach to the cinema, specifically to the genre of fantasy cinema, which, in and of itself, is the director's statement in *The Keep*. Mann has said:

> Initially, I didn't care much for the book, but then realized it contained something fantastic. I rewrote, and then took the screenplay in a direction the book doesn't go, with the idea of doing a fable. It's a fascinating form—you don't have to deal with the origins of things in terms of natural phenomena or natural causes. If there's a wolf dressed up as granny to eat Little Red Riding Hood, you don't have to explain how or why; it's all accepted. You can just channel the characters into metaphor.[18]

Mann's mention of a popular fairy tale is meaningful. In another interview before the release of the film, the director stressed his interest in Bruno Bettelheim's *The Uses of Enchantment: The Meaning and Importance of Fairy Tales*, and much of what Bettelheim says about the nature of our engagement with fairy tales is useful when attempting to understand what Mann seeks to achieve in *The Keep*.

Bettelheim, for instance, suggested that part of the pleasure of reading about the monsters and goblins in fairy tales derives from our ability to generate the imagery of such creatures in our own heads, rather than have every detail depicted for us in an accompanying illustration. Bettelheim agrees with J. R. R. Tolkien that "However good in themselves, illustrations do little good to fairy stories." Bettelheim goes on to observe:

> Asking children, for example, what a monster they have heard about in a story looks like, elicits the widest variations of embodiment . . . On the other hand, seeing the monster as painted by the artist in a particular way, conforming to *his* imagination, which is so much more complete as compared to our own vague and shifting image, robs us of this meaning. The idea of the monster may leave us entirely cold, having nothing of importance to tell us, or may scare us without evoking any deeper meaning beyond anxiety.[19]

Mann and his collaborators, like all filmmakers, begin one step behind Bettelheim's game, for film as narrative art demands visualization of story elements. Little Red Riding Hood and the Big Bad Wolf must be shown; for a visual storytelling art, there is no way around this fact. But narrative films do not necessarily require a literary explanation to exactly coincide with a visual depiction of that explanation; perceiving meaning in pictures and sounds which constantly progress in time and space grants the medium an elasticity that far outstrips the description-alongside-picture pairings found in illustrated fairy-tale storybooks. Mann has explored this very property of cinema in *The Keep* by placing his evocative images one step—sometimes several steps—ahead of the film's exposition. This distinctive approach is in contrast to that of another fantasy genre film (and many others like it), Steven Spielberg's *E.T.: The Extra-Terrestrial*, which has at its thematic center, like many of Spielberg's films, the theme of the family. Although Spielberg's alien remains fundamentally mysterious, his behavior becomes more or less understandable to the viewer in clear human terms as the creature becomes more and more "psychologically" involved with his adoptive human family.

Rather than asking his audience to visualize a monster described only through words—an impossibility for the film director—and instead of explicating the monster's behavior in roughly human psychological terms, Mann inverts the formula, inviting his viewers to indulge themselves in a gallery of evocative, atmospheric images which, in their rich pictorial detail (and in the corresponding and similarly rich meaning generated out of the juxtaposition of the various frames), often willfully abandon the kind of literary conceits and themes which we so often expect of narrative cinema. By placing visual design as a priority ahead of narrative explanation—and, indeed, when the exposition in *The Keep* does arise, it is often clunky and far less graceful than the purely formal elements of the film—Mann invites our exploration of the visual and sonic tapestry of his aesthetic for meaning; thus, the imagination is once again prompted as in a fairy tale, the only difference being that in Mann's cinema viewers must imagine what the fantastic visual details the director has given us amount to. Indeed, much of the pleasure derived from viewing the film is in perceiving the way in which *The Keep*'s style implicitly sketches themes in beautifully expressive aesthetic designs. Likewise, the film remains aesthetically interesting in a mannered way when shots and scenes fail to move the story forward. In a sense, then, with *The Keep* Mann has come full circle from *The Jericho Mile*. While theme and narrative, with some very important exceptions explored in chapter one, determine the classical mise-en-scène style of *The Jericho Mile*, and whereas in *Thief* a balance is struck between expressive mise-en-scène and theme so as to make form and content seem ultimately inextricable (much in the manner of Mann's later, and most successful, films), *The Keep* tips the balance in favor of a mannerist sound and vision at the occasional expense of narrative logic, an approach that is appropriate given Mann's interest in creating an adult fairy-tale fantasy in the cinema.

The ideas that *The Keep* does generate out of its form are, ultimately, mostly aesthetic ones that do not ultimately dovetail with a richly designed story (much of which has at any rate already been left behind in the process of Mann's adaptation). In the end, *The Keep* has only one significant (and perhaps clichéd) theme and it is one the form of the film reiterates throughout: the clash between, on the one side, a flawed humanity with its historical contingencies and complexities, and on the other, everlasting spirits of monolithic evil. The film thus marks one of the few moments in Mann's feature-film oeuvre in which a character in the narrative (the demon Molasar) appears as unequivocally, absolutely evil. Mann has suggested that he intended to make both Glaeken and Molasar ambiguous, but fully succeeds in doing this only with the former. In Glaeken, Mann (at least until the final climatic battle of the film, which as a typical fantasy-film dénouement requires a force of good pitted against a force of evil) refuses to indulge in the obvious heroic or villainous qualities such a character might hold, and this is to his credit. The character commits deeds at various parts of the film which are ambiguous in their intent, and his journey is finally neither wholly heroic nor wholly tragic. By only "presenting" Glaeken and refusing to dissect him as a character, Mann withholds (in a frustrating fashion according to some critics) important information from his audience, rerouting his role as a storyteller into the formal depiction of Glaeken's characteristic ambiguity; and, as we will see, many of the gaps are never filled with a logical explanation. As I hope my scene-specific argument in the next section of this chapter demonstrates, *The Keep* is less an intrinsically successful fantasy film than an intriguing example of a young director trying to figure out how to craft a relativistic, purely formal visual experience, and one that only dabbles, without full commitment, in expressing some of the themes common to his other films. All films, of course, are finally in some way "about the cinema," but not all of them—and certainly not very many Hollywood films—thoughtfully render this quality as such a salient attribute—or, in the case of *The Keep*, as a raison d'etre.

I suggested above that *The Keep* features one dominant theme (the clash between a contingent and variable human history and an unchanging and monolithic evil), as well as some intriguing subthemes which are, for the most part, abandoned shortly after they are introduced. The excess present in the film—comprised of those moments which don't communicate any sort of form-generated content to the audience—are instead mannered aesthetic designs which function only to further immerse us in the immediacy of Mann's foreign fantasy world. Interpreting *The Keep*'s stylistic construction thus forces one to consider both the expressive and the mannerist mise-en-scène approaches that the film exhibits.

The Keep opens with a montage that works on a number of levels and is in many ways the most interesting sequence in the film. It finds Mann and the cinematographer, Alex Thomson, at their most omniscient: the camera begins its downward descent from, quite literally, above the clouds, as a tilting shot vertically scans the sky. As the camera moves closer to earth the sky gets darker and clouds begin to appear. The camera pans past the outline of a forest. Thunder is heard on the soundtrack and the low rumble of Tangerine Dream's score is introduced, offering a sort of non-diegetic harmony to the natural diegetic sound of the storm. Raindrops fall right in front of the camera and appear out of focus in this telephoto shot (the storm seems to have passed the area of land which is at the deepest point in the image's perspective; it is now raining only at the closest plane in front of the camera). Mann and Thomson accomplish two rather breathtaking feats with this opening tilt: they establish the spectator at a privileged position in the narrative (the viewer, given a privileged view through the camera's mid-air position, can literally see more than the earth-bound characters will ever be able to) but at the same time they also disorient and qualify our perspective through the creative use of the telephoto lens (which makes it difficult to tell exactly what we're seeing the first time this shot is viewed). The use of Tangerine Dream's ominous music contributes to this sense of disorientation; the score introduces an artificial, technological soundscape alongside a shot that is otherwise comprised of a wholly natural environment.

At first, Tangerine Dream's score seems merely ambient, but its volume and its rhythmic thrust increases as the shot continues. As the camera tilts down the forest, there is no longer harmony between the thunder (a spatially dispersive sound not generated in discrete units of time) and the score (one that now moves through a specific temporality, given that the rhythmic beats in the music have now overtaken its ambient properties).[20] This change in the aesthetic greets the first human characters seen in the film. A German army detachment heads toward an overpass in the Carpathian Mountains in Romania. The faces of tired soldiers are matched with cuts of the vehicles traversing the mountainside, their weariness associated with the brutal effects of war-making technology. A close-up of Woermann's blue eyes seems to associate this weariness directly with him; no other character in the sequence is focused upon in such a manner. In a creative way, these match cuts almost seem to wear out Woermann, whose eyes are constantly juxtaposed with circular images of the army's mechanized vehicles, such as wheels and mirrors; this is a quick and tidy expression by Mann of the dehumanizing nature of war (one which accumulates more meaning as the film proceeds, since Woermann is by far the most humane of the military figures featured in the film). The sequence, at the same time, introduces one of the jarring aspects of the film's mise-en-scène through parallel editing: the contrast between the materiality of modern technology—the Nazi jeeps, guns, and dress—and the almost medieval atmosphere evoked in the villagers and their mountainous surroundings.

Mann and editor Dov Hoenig also use match cuts to emphasize the contrast between natural elements and modern technology in very specific terms. As he rides in one of the vehicles, Woermann lights a cigarette; the tip of the light is matched to an out-of-focus shot of another truck's outside mirror. Until the camera brings the object into sharp focus the light and the mirror, each already abstracted from space, look, at the level of abstract shape, the same. This match cut is also the earliest sign of the film's occasional strategy of crafting unexpected visual and thematic inversions and reflections, also seen in the reflection of the mountains in a pool of water in this opening montage, the association between the pure evil of the monster Molasar and the Nazis later in the film, and the way the keep itself functions; as Gavin Smith suggests, "the central setting of *The Keep* is a fortress that has been built backwards—not to keep people out, but *to keep something in*."[21] As the viewer of *The Keep* will soon discover, this "something" also exists outside of contingent, historical time: as the trucks drive into the village, the fog dissipates and we seem to enter an ahistorical time as well as an anachronistic space. The music follows suit, as the beats fade out and the music becomes more spatially dispersive and ethereal. At the end of the opening titles sequence, with a long shot of Dinju Pass and the village surrounding it, titles tell us we are in the Carpathian Mountains in Romania in 1941, but otherwise this is an environment which exists only through editing and shot composition; with no establishing shots through which to ground our visual experience in this sequence, everything becomes atmosphere.

Mann has implicitly introduced a dominant theme in the opening montage of *The Keep*, and it is one which will be inflected and modified in various ways throughout the fable: the encounter between a temporalized, and therefore wholly contingent, form of destruction (signified by the Nazis and the German army) and one which exists outside of human time and space as a kind of purely eternal spirit (figured in the evil of Molasar). In between these two poles exists Glaeken, who possesses both human attributes and a power that far outstrips the agency of mere mortals. In this opening sequence, Mann has introduced the theme of contingent existence and monolithic control in terms of both visual and sonic information. The idea is evident in the contrast between the appearance of the German soldiers and their mechanized technology, which belongs to only one historical epoch, and the eternal natural environment, which Mann grants an autonomous existence within the context of the introduction by presenting it in separate shots; trees, water, rain, and the small village town maintain their own material essence. Thus a great deal of drama is evoked in any shot that throws the historical and ahistorical into contact with one another (which is sometimes figured in simple intrashot montage such as the rolling of a vehicle's tire through the mud). Sonically, Tangerine Dream's score strikes a balance between music which moves forward in time (through beats), a quality which often coincides with the appearance of the German soldiers, and other pieces of music which exist almost entirely in space (the ambient parts of the score are most often associated with the keep and Molasar). Mann plays with these aesthetic configurations throughout the film, and as a result the most moving and intriguing conflict in *The Keep* derives from the clash of contrapuntal aesthetic elements rather than from narrative developments. When the film settles into typical shot/reaction-shot structures it is mostly to cue the presence of an expository scene, and these are arguably the least interesting moments in *The Keep*.

Furthermore, Mann infuses this tense relationship between the eternal and the ethereal with a kind of dream-logic that sustains itself across the entire film. While the relationship between temporal visual elements such as costume design and technology will continue to form a contrapuntal relationship to elements of nature, Mann also suggests that the eternal, the natural, and the mysterious has the upper hand, enshrouding historical detail in an atmospheric fog (which in *The Keep* is sometimes literally fog). Mann introduces this idea toward the end of the opening montage, as the Wehrmacht detachment proceeds into the village; the rhythm of the montage slows as shots linger to capture elements of nature such as stones and bodies of water. The camera first cuts to an extreme close-up of the tired Woermann, his eyes closed, as he appears to sleep. In the following shot of a lake next to a mountain, we see the reflection of the same mountain in the water. As a reflection, the mountain seen in the water exists only in immaterial light, but in the serene stillness of the lake at this moment the inverted image seems to possess a kind of tangibility (so much so that this shot, for some viewers, may be difficult to perceive accurately as a reflection on first viewing). In the next shot, Woermann opens his eyes, and it is as if everything he now sees (including the small village, which is pictured for the first time in the fourth, foggy shot of this sequence) exists in a similar immaterial but tangible dream, an inversion of the real world. In the relativistic, self-sustaining, creatively designed universe of *The Keep*, the laws have now changed; everything Woermann now sees (and, by extension, everything that we see, for we experience each of these shots with a Vertovian immediacy that eclipses that of any character's point of view) is an inextricable and imperceptible mix of the concrete (such as the German army dress and machinery, replicated through Mann's typical attention to realistic detail) and the abstract (such as foggy or dark atmospheres, and imprecise geography—most evocatively figured as the keep itself). These shots also suggest that the narrative that follows in the film depicts a kind of eternal and subconscious battle that haunts humanity regardless of particular historical contingencies.

The Nazis, *The Keep* suggests, have designed a worldview that desires a monolithic control much in the manner of Molasar, but as a temporal, historical human endeavor their plans are open to failure. As the film soon makes clear, Woermann himself is one of those unpredictable contingencies that threaten the balance of the Nazi psyche: he is a man who does not totally acquiesce to the human system of warfare of which he is nonetheless ineluctably a part. Although he has the appearance of the ideal Nazi—striking blue eyes and blond hair—he is not an official member of the fascist organization, but rather a captain in the German army who will often protest the brutal procedures of his Nazi associates. His first dialogue in the film might first strike the viewer as typical speech for a German officer (or at least a German officer from the movies) at this time in history: "We are all done fighting. Now we are the masters of the world. Does that enthrall you?" Jürgen Prochnow, however, delivers these lines in a slightly ironic tone, suggesting that his character himself is something less than fully enthralled with the Nazi project. The character seems to engage in most of his activity as a soldier with a kind of rote sense of duty, and only becomes a dynamic figure in opposition to the more obviously sinister Nazi Sergeant Kampffer, who arrives on the scene later in the first act, and whose acts of destruction are eventually associated with the eternally evil behavior of the demon Molasar.

As Woermann walks into the keep, Mann disorients our sense of space by presenting only slices of the fortress's geography to us at a time, and by avoiding at all times establishing shots which would allow us a greater sense of the keep's space. As Mark E. Wildermuth has pointed out, the first shot of the keep's interior, although eventually revealed to be an overhead shot when a human figure enters the frame, could alternately be viewed as a depiction of a floor, a ceiling, or walls; as a piece of architecture depicted through cinema, its true structural materiality is rendered imperceptible.[22] Mann uses this first scene inside the keep not only to disorient our perceptions of the setting's surrounding geography but also to forcefully indicate the role of the subconscious in his story. In a conversation with the guardian of the keep, Alexandru, Woermann is told that it is dreams which always drive away those travelers who dare to stay at the keep overnight. "Nightmares?" Woermann replies, Prochnow delivering his dialogue sardonically. Despite his skepticism, Woermann nonetheless foreshadows the relationship between the keep's evil spirits and the human destruction of the Nazis when he says that the real nightmares are the war man has made upon other men.

This line in the film is important; it makes clear that *The Keep* does not construct a view of the world in which simple and unambiguous forces such as good and evil do battle. Mann clearly finds human evil in the failure of systems, and not in individuals: it is economic gain which prompts the German soldiers to remove the crosses from the wall (thereby releasing the spirit Molasar), thus, in their actions, they are no more or less despicable than the professional thieves in *Thief* and *Heat*; the Nazi sergeant Kaempffer, while certainly villainous, is more clearly marked by the Nazi swastika on his sleeve than he is by any idiosyncratic psychological traits which might account for his violent behavior; and even Glaeken himself, ostensibly the "hero" who fights and defeats Molasar at the end of the film, is marked by an ambiguity which resists any simple heroic definition of his character. Whereas Molasar is nearly always associated with the dark, both white and dark aesthetic designs accompany Glaeken. In one scene, for example, he dispatches with two Iron Guard soldiers in order to pass through a forest in his journey to the keep; after doing so, he hops on his motorcycle and the entire frame darkens through the use of blue filters, marking a strange shift in the scene's previous daytime setting. And while dispersive, ambient music helps capture the eternal, always-present nature of Molasar's evil, no such score definitively characterizes Glaeken. Indeed, Glaeken is most often depicted in scenes which are scored to a mix of both rhythmic and ambient musical textures, suggesting that he moves through a distinctly human history while waging his eternal battle with Molasar and that he possesses human qualities, most evident in his eventual relationship with Eva. And in some of the music tracks accompanying his journey, Tangerine Dream's soundscape electronically mimes humanlike voices with a device known as a vocoder, which refigures choir music as a kind of semihuman vocalization (vocalization which seems to struggle to be heard amidst the colder techno backdrop of the group's music), suggesting that *The Keep*'s hero, and his endeavor to define his goodness against the eternal evil of the keep's spirit, relies upon at least an oblique sense of humanity in order to vanquish his foe.

Glaeken's humanity is the source of his ambiguity, for it is his humanity, in all its flaws and historical contingencies, which prevents him from being either wholly good or wholly evil. This idea is thrown into relief through the behavior of other characters in the film, such as the ailing Dr. Cuza, who is tempted by the monster Molasar after the spirit grants him eternal youth. Glaeken's human side is suggested through his need to experience love and human contact—most visibly rendered in the sex scene between him and Eva, a moment in the narrative which seems to derive only from the needs these two people have to touch and to be touched, and not from any other psychological motivations (their love story is missing all of the rich development an audience might demand in depictions of relationship in the cinema, which for some viewers will render their tryst as gratuitous or even quasi-pornographic). The film's aesthetic associates their lovemaking with blue and white colors, suggesting the basic innocence of their coupling against the dark, moody atmospheres that characterize the rest of the film. This need for contact, a desire for messy and dialogic human relationships, defines the basic difference between Glaeken and Molasar; similar distinction can be found between Rain Murphy and Stiles in *The Jericho Mile*, Will Graham and Dolarhyde in *Manhunter*, and Max and Vincent in *Collateral*.

Mann's tale concludes with Glaeken casting Molasar back into the keep. In doing so the character has prevented the spirit from spreading its evil across the world, but he has not succeeded, of course, in saving the world from Nazi terror (a goal which was never part of the character's design in the first place). The only attribute in Molasar which might strike the viewer as a good deed—the elimination of the brutal Nazi sergeant Kaempffer—suggests a significant theme in Mann's story which nonetheless remains underdeveloped: the relationship between the anarchic evil of Molasar and the human-designed, systematically controlled evil of the Nazi regime. On the one hand, *The Keep* suggests that once systems initiate a psychological propensity for accepting murder as a form of rule, such action becomes wholly ungovernable. Mann, ultimately, is more interested in crafting his visual and sonic fairy tale than he is in truly exploring this theme, which is developed only in purely expository scenes (such as nearly all of the dialogue exchanged between Woermann and Kaempffer, in which Woermann questions the distinction between the force which is murdering the German and Nazi soldiers and the evil of the Nazis themselves). While Mann has not yet returned to exploring World War II in his subsequent films, the theme of intricate human plans and systems—and the contingency in modern society which always threatens to disrupt and overturn them—will be fleshed out in Mann films after *Thief* and *The Keep*: in films such as *Heat*, for example, the best laid plans of both cops and robbers violently intersect with one another, and in *Collateral*, the audience sees the highly temporalized life of a Los Angeles cab driver thrown out of its usual routine. Without the satisfactory development of this intriguing theme, the main interest of *The Keep* remains an aesthetic one, but in this regard the film is more than fitfully successful.

NOTES

1. Figure is from the Internet Movie Database, http://www.imdb.com/title/tt0083190/business (accessed February 15, 2005).
2. The Internet Movie Database, http://www.imdb.com/title/tt0085780/business (accessed February 15, 2005).
3. Paul Taylor, "Castles in Romania," *Monthly Film Bulletin* 52, no. 615 (April 1985), 130.
4. Taylor, "Castles," 129.
5. For a further list of films see David A. Cook, *A History of Narrative Film*, 4th ed. (New York: W. W. Norton, 2004), 869–70.
6. Harlan Kennedy, "Castle 'Keep,'" *Film Comment* 19, no. 6 (November–December 1983), 19.
7. F. Paul Wilson, *The Keep* (New York: William, Morrow & Co., 1981).
8. Taylor, "Castles," 129.
9. Taylor, "Castles," 129.
10. Quoted in Kristin Thompson, *Storytelling in the New Hollywood* (Cambridge, MA: Harvard University Press, 1999), 212. This interview can be found in its original context in Joel Engel, *Screenwriters on Screenwriting: The Best in the Business Discuss Their Craft* (New York: Hyperion, 1995), 176–77.
11. Thompson, *New Hollywood*, 212.
12. Kennedy, "Castle 'Keep,'" 16.
13. Kim Newman, "The Keep," *Monthly Film Bulletin* 52, no. 615 (April 1985): 127–28.
14. Newman, "The Keep," 128.

15. Newman, "The Keep," 128. Stéphane Piter, whose website, http://www.the Keep.ath.cx/default_en.htm (accessed January 29, 2005), details his obsession with Mann's film, has screen captures from the film's "director's cut"—the source of which is apparently extended television versions of the film—which remains otherwise unavailable in any format.

16. Quoted in James Naremore, ed., *Film Adaptation* (New Brunswick, NJ: Rutgers University Press, 2000), 7. Hitchcock's quote is from François Truffaut, *Hitchcock*, rev. ed. (New York: Simon & Schuster, 1985), 71.

17. Wilson, *The Keep*, 129.

18. Taylor, "Castles," 129.

19. Bruno Bettelheim, *The Uses of Enchantment: The Meaning and Importance of Fairy Tales* (New York: Vintage, 1989), 60.

20. Philip Brophy goes into more detail about the sonic landscape of *The Keep* in his masterful chapter on the film in *100 Modern Soundtracks: BFI Screen Guides* (London: British Film Institute, 2004), 149–50.

21. Gavin Smith, "Mann Hunters," in *Film Comment* 28, no. 6 (November–December 1992): 75.

22. Mark E. Wildermuth, *Blood in the Moonlight: Michael Mann and Information Age Cinema* (Jefferson, NC: McFarland & Company, 2005), 82.

Chapter Four

Manhunter

The commercial failure of *The Keep* certainly changed the course of Michael Mann's career, but as Margy Rochlin has pointed out, the notion that the popular television police drama *Miami Vice* propelled Mann back into the world of feature filmmaking after the disastrous commercial and critical reception of *The Keep* is a false one.[1] Although another planned Mann project, *Stringers*—described by Paul Taylor as "a comedy about freelance video journalists in New York," a script that had been previously attached to Michael Cimino[2]—languished in turn-around, Mann began writing the screenplay for *Manhunter* and had a development deal in place for the project before he was offered the role of producer on *Miami Vice*. Nonetheless, the series, titled *Goldcoast* when it was offered to him in 1984, prevented Mann from filming *Manhunter* until *Vice* was into its second season.[3]

Analyzing the television series *Miami Vice*, and connecting its themes and aesthetics to Mann's directorial film work, is especially problematic for a study such as this one, not only because of the many directors and writers who worked on the series, but also because of the publicly contested nature of its authorship. *Miami Vice*'s initial teleplay, and thus its created by signature, is attributed to Anthony Yerkovich, whose previous credits included writing and supervisory work on the series *Hill Street Blues* (1981–1987), but in interviews with the press certain comments, supposedly made by Mann himself, suggested that many of the series' thematic and aesthetic qualities were Mann's. One particularly controversial article appeared in *Rolling Stone*; in the article, Mann takes credit for the show's contemporary pop-rock soundtrack (according to the article the original plan had been to include country-western songs). In the same article Mann also takes credit for the choice of the Miami setting. However, Mann later claimed that *Rolling Stone* published comments that he never made.[4] The *Los Angeles Times*, meanwhile, which had followed *Rolling Stone*'s lead in declaring Mann the auteur of the newly successful series, ran apologies for the mistakes at the behest of both Mann's and Yerkovich's representatives. "It's a tough enough business without somebody grabbing at your by-line," Yerkovich stated in a letter to the *Times*.[5] Nonetheless, in later interviews Mann still takes a good deal of post-production credit for the *Miami Vice* television series. In response to a query about why he avoided directing individual episodes, Mann said, "I didn't want to. I had to maintain my distance: the directing of an individual episode is not my point of work on the show. The work I did was not so different from what I would do on a feature film if I was directing it—I was involved in the writing, I determined the casting, determined the shape and scope of the rhythms and the patterns."[6] The February 2005 DVD release of *Miami Vice: Season One*, meanwhile, in what appears a calculated attempt to appeal to fans of the director's films, credits Mann as the creator of the show, although the 2006 film version of *Vice*, directed by Mann, credits Yerkovich with the creation of the original series.

Shortly after production began on the second season of *Miami Vice* in 1985, Mann took a break from his executive-producer duties on the series to film *Manhunter*, based on the Thomas Harris novel *Red Dragon* and the first of several films based on the stories surrounding the Hannibal Lecter character (subsequent versions include *The Silence of the Lambs* [Jonathan Demme, 1991], *Hannibal* [Ridley Scott, 2001], and the second adaptation of *Red Dragon* [Brett Ratner, 2002]). Mann's effort remains the most intriguing and stylistically sophisticated of this subgenre of Lecter films; as scholar Tony Williams has written, *Manhunter* "is far more subtle" in comparison to *The Silence of the Lambs* "a visually impoverished, redundant text" according to Williams.[7]

The story in *Manhunter*, as adapted from the novel, concerns a former FBI investigator, Will Graham (William Petersen), who explores his own psyche in order to understand the minds of the killers whose crimes he investigates. Graham, however, has retired because of the disturbing mental stress caused by such activity, and at the beginning of the film must be persuaded by FBI Chief Jack Crawford (Dennis Farina) to return to the bureau in order to explore the case of the "Tooth Fairy" (a killer revealed later as a man named Dolarhyde, played by Tom Noonan) who has murdered families in Atlanta and Birmingham. Graham agrees, and in order to recover the mindset that he needs to explore the darker regions of his own mind and thus tap into the psyche of the killer, he visits the imprisoned serial killer Hannibal Lecktor (played marvelously by Brian Cox; the standard spelling of "Lecter" in both the book and the three other films mentioned above is changed, inexplicably, to this variation in *Manhunter*).

Mann's film is structurally similar to the Harris novel, but it also removes a good deal of backstory from our understanding of Dolarhyde, as well as from our knowledge of Graham's wife, Molly (Kim Greist); visual aesthetics often replaces and always augments a literal understanding of character in this evocative film. *Manhunter*'s narrative provides the first strong evidence of a four-act structure (as discussed in the previous chapter) in a Michael Mann film. Beginning with the first act (roughly thirty-five minutes), we follow Graham as he becomes initially involved in the case; the second act (approximately twenty-five minutes) explores both Graham's own psyche after his initial meeting with Lecktor and also details aspects of the police procedures behind the case; the third act (roughly forty minutes) spends a good portion of its running time portraying Dolarhyde and in some ways folds back upon the motifs associated with Graham in the first half of the film; and the fourth act (approximately twenty minutes) leads to the climactic meeting between Graham and Dolarhyde.

In addition to this structural approach, *Manhunter* also achieves something like a synthesis of all the films Mann had hitherto directed: not only does it continue to develop his expressive mise-en-scène aesthetic, but the film itself is primarily concerned both thematically and aesthetically with ideas regarding vision and acts of seeing. In the book, while sight still plays a key role, Graham relies on all of his senses to capture Dolarhyde. Vision, meanwhile, is Graham's salient weapon in the screen story. There is perhaps no other film in the Mann oeuvre that more masterfully asserts and comments on the power of seeing through its own highly expressive mise-en-scène. No shot in *Manhunter* can be classified as mannerist because the entire dynamic range of compositions, no matter how excessive (a common critique of the film by reviewers), ultimately ties into the motifs of seeing present in the work.[8] And the film's cinematographer, Dante Spinotti, was well aware that the film was a significant departure from classical film aesthetics. Asked to compare his collaboration with Mann on the first Thomas Harris adaptation to his later work on Ratner's *Red Dragon* shortly before the release of the latter film, he claimed that the strengths of Mann's version were "based on the language of the film—the use of camera and the style of the movie. The movie that Brett had in mind, however, took a more realistic approach; it was less formal in a way, yet more classic. The strength of this movie [Ratner's version] is derived from a very good script, a more accurately worked-out adaptation of the novel."[9]

One trait *Manhunter* does share with its Thomas Harris-Hannibal Lecter brethren is its place in a genre lineage, although Mann's film traverses genres in a more complicated manner than the other Lecter movies. The film deftly combines elements of the horror film (particularly the serial-killer subgenre), the neonoir (in its self-conscious stylization of an often morally ambiguous detective story), and the police procedural (with its attention to the minute detail of Graham's investigation, which in addition to the focus on Graham's mental affinities with the murderers also includes other rather more quotidian details such as meetings with his boss and the help he receives from other cops and detectives during the case). But it is Mann's deployment of the horror genre in *Manhunter* that has been a main point of interest in scholarly writing about the film. For Tony Williams, the presence of Dolarhyde signals an examination in the film of the instability of the social identity of the secure American family, a recurring theme in scholarship on the horror genre: "*Manhunter* develops psychic parallels between pursuer and pursued. For Graham his encounter with Lecter [sic] and obsessive pursuit of Dolarhyde represent the recognition of his fragile social identity."[10] In *Manhunter* Graham's social identity is in large part stabilized by his role as husband and father in his own family, an institution that the film's serial killers (Dolarhyde and Lecktor) directly target. But Graham himself, as Williams suggests, eventually becomes complicit in this destabilization. The protagonist's identification with some component of the life or personality of his ostensible antagonist is a consistent Mann theme prior to *Manhunter*. It is present in Frank's suffering under the debilitating effects of postindustrial capitalism (which he can also be seen to engender in his own status as the owner of capital) in *Thief* and through Woermann's inability to act outside Nazi imperatives in *The Keep*. For Philip L. Simpson, meanwhile, "*Manhunter* is a profoundly ambiguous and destabilizing film. The dialectical tensions between binary oppositions are quite pronounced, creating uncomfortable affinities between protagonist and antagonist(s), especially the ways in which they are threatened and exploited by others."[11] Simpson's tentative plural in the preceding quote suggests both the obvious and the oblique natures of Graham's foes in the narrative. Dolarhyde is the obvious social deviant, in that he commits murder and thus destroys what is stable, but he is also a victim of an abusive childhood (a past explained in detail in the novel, but only hinted at in the film, although Graham himself seems almost preternaturally aware of the killer's past). The FBI itself, as Simpson points out, becomes both protagonist and antagonist in its relationship to Graham and Dolarhyde, as it draws the former back into the dangers of detective work, at the expense of Graham's familial stability, and as it ruthlessly pursues the killer, with the intent to destroy him.[12]

In my analysis of the film's style that follows, I do not oppose the general theses or main points proposed by Williams or Simpson in their separate inquiries into the film. I should point out, however, that as in my analysis of Mann's work in the first three chapters, my interest in *Manhunter* is in teasing out layers of thematic meaning from Mann's formal style, meaning which may not necessarily find articulation through analyses primarily concerned with narrative and the horror genre alone. Mann's expressive style in *Manhunter*—and the manner in which that style weaves together genre elements apart from the horror film, such as neonoir and the crime film—expands and complicates some of the assertions Williams and Simpson occasionally make. Williams, for example, suggests that "Dolarhyde's condition pathologically reenacts Lacan's mirror stage. Sexually abused by his mother, Dolarhyde has not successfully entered the oedipal stage. He cannot distinguish himself from mother's body and gaze to constitute himself as a separate being."[13] Simpson, on a slightly different note, remarks that *Manhunter* explores the dangerous implications of the male gaze in cinema, in that "the murderous use of technology in combination with the predatory male gaze is demonstrated."[14] Both of these arguments are accurate, in so far as they go, but in the following analysis I wish to move away from a primarily psychoanalytic reading of the film not only because Williams and Simpson have already admirably covered this ground, but also because it is ultimately impossible to reconcile the various contradictions which arise when these writers' studies of the film are compared. In other words, another psychoanalytic study of *Manhunter* can take us no farther. In the quotes above, for example, Williams positions Dolarhyde as victim (of the suffocating mother), while Simpson presents him as antagonist (through his "predatory male gaze," although this trait is of course something Graham himself possesses). No doubt Dolarhyde, and indeed Graham, function as both antagonist and victim at once, as Williams and Simpson (and indeed the film itself, in its rich ambiguities) recognize. In my reading of the film, then, I want to focus on *Manhunter*'s theme of ways of seeing on a more general level, one which includes, but is not limited to, vision's relationship to the unconscious and the male gaze. In doing so I hope to show that the various ambiguities present in the film's treatment of vision—both unadorned and technologically mediated vision—can be dealt with on the interrelated levels of narrative, genre, and style.

Manhunter begins with a stylistic event: a shot positioned from a high angle, gazing down at the top of a motor vehicle. (The viewer will not know for sure until nearly halfway through the film that we are looking at the top of Dolarhyde's van). This abstraction is notable for its color scheme: In the foreground the vehicle's lights are a sickly burnt-orange color; the green brick wall on the upper left side of the frame is reflected on the straight surfaces of the van's roof. Suddenly, the camera moves to the left, as if in search of the answers to a number of pertinent questions: Who is in the van? Who is standing in front of it? In addition to this inquisitive camera movement, the opaque sunroof at the top of the van intensifies and simultaneously blocks our desire to discover and see something. A similar block occurs in the middle of this camera movement, for just as the camera moves us closer to the object in question, the shot abruptly ends. Mann and cinematographer Dante Spinotti here suggest the cinema's power to reveal and conceal, and its related power to both present a stylized reality, and to limit or cut short our vision of that reality when and how the filmmakers see fit.

The next shot inflects the thematic motif of searching and investigation, and as in the first image our own gaze becomes implicated in the proceedings. The image is a roughly first-person shot of someone walking up the steps of a home, the path illuminated by a flashlight. In fact, given that we learn later in the film that Dolarhyde uses various types of media to vicariously re-experience his killings, it is reasonable to consider this shot as equivalent to what the killer himself would be filming with a hand-held camera as he walks up the steps. As the shot continues we begin scanning the screen for information, coming across a handful of objects—a child's shoes, and then a stuffed toy penguin—before startlingly realizing that our experience of analyzing the frame is parallel to the serial killer's own act of seeing. The music used in these opening frames, with its single synthesizer chord, suggests a stopped heartbeat; it serves as a framing device to the film itself, which ends with a song titled "Heartbeat." On one level, this second shot in the film portrays the murderous male gaze at work, but on another more general level the shot destabilizes the gaze itself, in much the same way that social identity will be destabilized throughout the narrative. To what degree are our own desires and curiosities implicating us in the voyeurism present onscreen? And to what degree are such qualities being manipulated by the filmmakers? Is the killer videotaping this murder, or is this a stylistic rendition of the murderer's gaze, made to look like a hand-held home video by Mann and his cofilmmakers?

The third shot in the sequence is, upon reflection, perhaps the most disturbing in the film: it is a slow-motion, left-to-right camera pan across the doorway leading into a child's bedroom. The villainous acts of seeing committed by the hitherto unseen Dolarhyde in this sequence are chillingly paralleled with the telescope in the corner of the child's bedroom in this shot, which implies in a three-second image that a potential murderer lies within any young child, and effectively digesting, in a single shot, the many pages Thomas Harris devotes in the novel to exploring the upbringing of Dolarhyde and connecting that history to his acts of violence. The subtle slow-motion visual technique used here, in a manner more overt than the painterly composition of color in the first frame, also indicates that this is a visual experience that has been modified from its original form, for in its slow motion it bears the traces of a postproduction process; the viewer is, in a sense, "reseeing" these visions. Thus, given the central presence of the motif of vicarious experiencing and mediated reexperiencing through the image in *Manhunter*, the shot becomes richer than initially expected on repeat viewings.

The final shot of this sequence, still portrayed to us in what we can roughly label a first-person perspective, depicts a woman slowly waking and sitting up in bed, a flashlight shining on her face. It is women, then, that will be the object of looking for both killer and investigator in *Manhunter*. Furthermore, as she wakes up, slow motion is employed once more, again suggesting that what we are seeing has been modified, and is thus being "reseen" by us and by the killer (some time after the event of the murder itself) who is possibly filming or taping it. But then a stylistic event occurs which owes nothing to the potential media manipulations of a character in the film. Mann, composer Michel Rubini, and editor Dov Hoenig avoid showing us the murder on-screen, and instead evoke it stylistically: as the woman wakes up, percussion, suggesting a human heartbeat, is mixed into the single-chord ambient score, and then this beat is eradicated by a sudden cut to black and the subsequent main titles. Mann, through style, resensitizes us to the act of murder not by showing it—as so many horror films, and especially 1980s "slasher" films, have—but by composing its occurrence strictly through the plasticity of image, sound, and cut.

With this highly cinematic elision the viewer sees the first development of a kind of parallel movement within the style of the entire film itself. At certain points in the film, style draws us not into the purely physical act of murder but rather into the mental state possessed by the serial killer Dolarhyde, in much the same way that Will Graham will attempt to understand the killer's mind in the film's narrative. The hand-held shot up the steps is an example of this sort because it ambiguously suggests that the style we are seeing has a diegetic source—a character who manipulates the visual information seen on the screen—which in this case is Dolarhyde. But that is not what is suggested at the end of this final shot; style here helps the viewer dis-identify from the murderer, the viewer's particular experience of cinematic plasticity being a unique one that the character cannot have, for it is the work of Mann and his collaborators and *not* the work of the media-savvy Dolarhyde. This tension in the visual, sonic, plastic, and sculptural qualities of Mann's cinema—which the director himself refers to as a film's "genetic coding"—imbricates us in the tyranny of the murderer's gaze but at the same time clearly delineates our experience of watching a particular blend of cinematic effects from the much more graphic visual experiences depicted in the film's story world.[15] This intriguing parallel style keeps the viewer on edge, and as the film continues it becomes increasingly difficult to separate the dangerous gaze the viewer shares with both Graham and Dolarhyde and the expressive style of the film as an experience separate from the diegetic visual experience of the characters in the story. As I hope to show, this double meaning of style will develop important implications as the film progresses.

Sound also plays an important role throughout *Manhunter*, while also distinguishing it from other horror films. As the sinister music from the opening sequence fades out over the main titles, the sound of an ocean is mixed in: this sound establishes the beach setting in Florida where former FBI investigator Will Graham lives. This sonic connection—from the menacing score in the prologue to the ocean waves in the first scene—links Dolarhyde to Graham and finally to the viewers, the listeners of these sounds. The ephemeral quality of both the music and the ocean sounds suggests a hint of mysteriousness and intangibility in the connection between their psyches and perhaps ours as well. In this way sound complicates our experience of the film in a manner similar to the parallel tracks in the film's visual style. At what points does a subjective style of sound serve to implicate us in, or excite us about, the murderous or ethically questionable acts on screen? At what points does it serve to stylistically distance us from what is seen and heard on-screen? And at what other points does it serve the more prosaic and conventional purpose of capturing (an admittedly heavily stylized) reality? This to-and-fro movement, like the visual style of the film, is designed to keep the audience, at different junctures in the film, both involved and distanced from the events depicted on screen, and it adds an intriguing element to Mann's deployment of horror-movie tropes. *Manhunter* is not just a film about a killer's gaze (and its psychoanalytic underpinnings) and that gaze's relationship to our own emotional relationship with the film. In other words, music is not used explicitly to scare or shock us in *Manhunter*; there are no screeching violins cued on the soundtrack during on-screen or implied deaths, and even creepier parts of the score (such as the music which cues the first shots of the film) soon become dispersive after quickly reaching a crescendo. The sound rarely serves to intensify our fear, because what we hear in *Manhunter* is like everything we see: the sound and music serve to only intermittently suture us into the diegetic world of the film while at many other crucial moments placing the viewer at some degree of aesthetic distance from the narrative.

In the aforementioned scene Graham speaks to Jack Crawford about returning to the FBI to investigate the murders. As Simpson has pointed out, the FBI serves as a surrogate family for Graham, one which indeed draws him away from Molly and his son, but it is a painfully inadequate replacement, one which threatens his psychic well-being.[16] In a more oblique fashion than in some of his other films, this is yet another inquiry into an American institution in Mann's work—in this case, the family—thus making the film of a piece with other politically motivated films in the director's oeuvre such as *Thief*, *The Insider*, and *Ali*. Crawford, persuading Graham to join the investigation, hands him two photographs, saying: "If you can't look anymore, I understand." Graham looks, and what he sees are pictures of the two murdered families. In the very next shot his own wife and child walk into the frame, and thus the viewer sees the dead families and Graham's living one drawn together in a quick edit. Mann also uses the same-frame heuristic and frames within frames to separate Graham and his family from the institution of the FBI (the character of Crawford is here and throughout the film the surrogate for this larger entity). As Crawford and Molly sit in a dining room in the beach house, he tells her that he will keep Graham "as far away from it as I can"—it meaning the killer and the situations the killer creates—while the image already suggests that this promise holds little meaning for her. In the composition she is separated from Crawford by lines in the home's architecture, even though the two of them are sitting in the same room. As in *Thief*'s handling of Frank, the viewer is encouraged to identify with Graham and his family, and not with the figure of higher corporate authority, although the security of the family itself is called into question by the film.

Color-coding—a key ingredient in expressive mise-en-scène—is carefully modulated to suggest thematic motifs throughout the first act of the film. Blue is associated with Molly, sex, and the Graham family home, framed by Mann in interior shots that make it appear as if the house were somehow hovering above the ocean rather than standing upon solid ground. Blue is also associated with the Leeds family (the first of the murders, in Atlanta); when Graham enters the home for the first time blue appears before he turns on the lights. Green has a number of meanings: it is associated with searching and discovery (as in the background color in the first shot of the film, the color of the shirt Graham wears during his investigation, and the color of the blinds Graham stands in front of at the Atlanta police station). It is also linked to the family unit (the family being at stake in the search): In carefully composed shots green vegetation surrounds the Leeds family home. Later in the film, after Will Graham flees from a psychiatry ward after his first meeting with Hannibal Lecktor, Graham looks at green grass and is able to regain his composure, suggesting that family—the institution he seeks to protect—offers him a way out of his dark explorations of his own psyche.

It is the mental connection that Graham must draw between himself and the killer that concerns much of *Manhunter*. As we will see, parallels between Graham and Dolarhyde become clearer as the film's structure is retrospectively revealed in the third act of the film, but a number of scenes in the first half of *Manhunter* suggest the darker realms of Graham's mind and its correspondence to the mind of the serial killer. During his initial investigation of the Leeds home, subjective shots of Graham walking up the steps correspond exactly to the shots of the killer walking up the same steps during the very first shots of the film; in fact, the earlier shots appear, in retrospect, as only slightly modulated (through effects of slow-motion and lighting) versions of these shots associated with Graham's investigation. Indeed, such a moment distances us from Graham's experience, in that we are called on to remember an earlier moment in the construction of the film. Before too long, however, the film returns us to a consideration of Graham's mental state. After Graham investigates the home (bringing with him a tape recorder and a camera) he seems unable to continue; he walks into the bedroom's bathroom and splashes water on his face, perhaps cleansing a sense of intangible guilt. The phone then rings, and the audience hears Mrs. Leeds's voice on the answering machine. There is no one on the other end; we hear only the ghostly voice of Mrs. Leeds—"we're not home right now"—which in these moments becomes sexually and maternally associated with Graham and the water on his skin (and thus, by extension, with Graham and his own wife, both of whom are portrayed in the ocean-blue bedroom earlier in the film).

Graham is able to deduce Dolarhyde's motivations, and the mediated sensual experiences that drive his desires, by himself employing technology which aids and extends the human capabilities of vision. In a first-act scene in a hotel room, Graham carefully watches the Leedses' home movies in an attempt to theorize what the killer might have been thinking. He seems to hit a brick wall in his analysis, unable to probe further. He calls Molly but then quickly ends the conversation after exchanging only a few sentences. Ominous music fades in on the soundtrack; it seems he has needed this sensual contact, through a telephone conversation with his own wife, to tap into the darker regions of his own mind. A shot of Molly asleep and vulnerable—inserted into the sequence after the conversation between the two of them has ended—suggests that she is potentially threatened by the mindset that Graham has now found. After he returns to the chair in front of the television (the television now comprises the greater part of the shot's volume, filling the better part of left and center frame, leaving Graham narrowly boxed in compositionally) he begins directing questions to the killer (and also himself) as he gazes at the image of Mrs. Leeds on the video: "What are you dreaming? It's something you can't afford for me to know about, isn't it? God, she's lovely, isn't she? It was maddening to have to touch her with rubber gloves on, wasn't it? . . . The talcum powder came off of your rubber glove as you took it off to touch her." Graham must thus tap into his own unconscious—and by extension the potential vulnerability of his wife and child, the vulnerability of the family—in order to replicate Dolarhyde's mindset.

The parallel of killer's mind to the investigator's search is an idea also reflected in a later scene at the end of the first act. Graham, aboard a flight back to Washington from his investigation in Atlanta, places in front of him a file containing photos of the two families, and promptly falls asleep. His ensuing dream, intercut with two images of the airplane's wing and Graham sleeping, lasts for eight images and roughly twenty seconds; he dreams of Molly, his hobby of repairing boat engines, and the intense gaze he and his wife exchange with one another. The cool color of blue is associated with the sea and the boat engine, signifying the repair work Graham kept busy with before being drawn back into the FBI by Crawford, while green and white are linked to Molly. In the sequence's most striking shot, Molly, out of focus and in the foreground, approaches the camera, with green palm trees sharply in focus behind her, the wind blowing them back and forth. Graham and Molly then exchange gazes, suggesting that the look itself is rooted in the unconscious desire of this dream. These images comprise a very stylized representation of a dream; the audience is invited to share in Graham's desires but is just as much encouraged to view these slightly strange shots as cinematic constructions, an idea which once again puts in tension our identification with the protagonist and which again prompts our recognition of the way in which the film's style occasionally places us at one remove from his experiences. A sudden jump cut associates Molly with three-by-five images of the dead women from the slain families, and we realize the dream has been violently interrupted by pictures of a gruesome reality. The link between dreams and gruesome, murderous acts is quickly made, and viewers are invited to indulge in the rich composition of music and sound in this sequence before being startled by the much starker and more stylistically modest images of death.

The second act of *Manhunter*, opening with Graham's meeting with Lecktor and ending just before the appearance of Dolarhyde, turns the film into a crisp police procedural, as it details the minutia behind the investigation. But Mann, Hoenig, and Spinotti continue developing careful stylistic parallels between character experience and viewer experience, especially in one scene toward the end of the second act in which Graham and Molly rendezvous in an Atlanta hotel and in another scene in an airport café which appears in the third act. The filmmakers' approach with these two scenes is in many ways the extension of the Dziga Vertov influence evinced in the super-human shots of the camera exploring the inner workings of the technology Frank uses in *Thief*, aspects of seeing to which the characters in the film do not have access. In one evocative shot, Graham stares at the reflection of his torso in the hotel window; it is a vulnerable and damaged body, as suggested by a scar covering his stomach (the visable remnant of an injury acquired in his previous investigation of the Lecktor case). In the subsequent scene in the third act, Graham stares at the reflection of his own face in an airport café window as he becomes more determined to find Dolarhyde. What is of primary interest in each of these shots is not the significance of the scar or the reflection of his face but the style through which Graham sees these parts of himself and, in contrast, the film style through which we see him seeing. As earlier moments of the film have suggested, Graham is enabled by various media technologies to peer into the darker corners of his own mind: videotape, television, and tape recorder all assist him in his investigation of the murders. In contrast, in each of these later shots Graham finds style—a way, or a mediation, of seeing—in the glossy, reflective, abstract contours of architecture in modern society itself. While it is true that through this style Graham sees himself, as viewers of cinema we see him through a parallel but still distinctly separate confluence of sight, sound, and editing. In the hotel scene with Graham and Molly, the two of them speak of the inability to relive any moment (a thematic motif given sharper dimensions in relation to Molly in the novel, which emphasizes the death of her previous husband). It is a sentimental moment between them, a temporary triumph over their vulnerability, and an embracing of life. But Mann and Hoenig cut to a long shot of the couple during this affirmation and freeze-frame the shot of the two of them, once again sensitizing us to the ability to vicariously reexperience moments in time through frozen images and thus refiguring both Graham and Molly as highly vulnerable to media manipulation (and thus vulnerable to Dolarhyde), despite the tone of perseverance and strength in the diegesis during the scene itself.

A similar effect is produced in the airport café scene in the third act, which is comprised of two shots. In the first, a medium shot of Graham facing away from us and toward the reflection of his own face in a window, the character is placed on the left side of his frame and the reflection in the center, with rain pouring down in the background outside and other patrons vaguely reflected on the right side of the frame. Graham is intently focused on his own reflection, while a voice-over cues us into what is bouncing around in his mind: it is the Leeds answering machine message, heard earlier during his initial investigation. The voice of Mrs. Leeds—ironically and hauntingly emphasizing her family's now permanent absence with "I'm sorry, we can't come to the phone right now"—prompts Graham to raise his palm to the window and touch his own reflection, as if trying to forge some sensual connection to the dead (and perhaps to his now-exhausted self) through a distinctively different sensual experience with the glossy surface of the window. Graham's daydream is interrupted by the waitress serving him (an interruption prefigured to the audience in the reflections of other people in the window frame). This shot figures us closely with Graham: the viewer is brought into his experience through the striking composition of the reflection in the shot and the voice-over of Mrs. Leeds's voice. But the audience is also drawn outside of the character's own experience, as the window also reflects more than what Graham himself is presently focused on.

In the second shot, the filmmakers take this disconnect further, as Mann and Spinotti place the camera outside the window; Graham continues to speak to his own reflection but the rain, seen from an angle unavailable to the character, provides expressive commentary on his inner anguish. A careful parallel between styles—the character's experience through his own style of seeing and the filmmakers' composition of a style totally separate from the diegetic experiences of the characters—ensures that we are never wholly implicated in the diegetic acts of seeing. As viewers of the film we are, rather, sensitized to aspects of the world that are not a direct part of the character's experience (one might say that Graham doesn't see in widescreen as the viewer does while watching the film).

This approach is not unique to *Manhunter*; any film which provides a glimpse of subjectivity through style in addition to a crafting of a larger, outer world functions in this manner. Mann simply emphasizes his specific use of such tropes through a singular, overtly compositional widescreen style and through the themes of seeing and vision. Such themes are expanded in the third act of the film, which spends a great deal of time detailing the experience of Dolarhyde and in doing so folds back upon scenes from the first hour of the film by paralleling Graham's experience with the killer's. Dolarhyde is often portrayed wearing rectangular shades, implying a link between the killer's vision and *Manhunter*'s widescreen framings, and indicating that he sees more than the narrowly focused Graham. (In drawing a link between a character's voyeurism and the properties of cinema itself, the film here recalls Michael Powell's 1960 film *Peeping Tom*). This meaning is ultimately ironic, as I will show, for Dolarhyde's vision, like Graham's, is profoundly circumscribed; he can only see what he desires to see. These glasses, and both the interior and exterior of the lab in which Dolarhyde works, are often associated with the color blue, evoking a sensual relationship between Dolarhyde and the images he manipulates and the cool blues associated with the Grahams' bedroom early in the film. The color green appears in the background of Dolarhyde's house, suggesting a sinister inversion of the color's association with the family in the first act. And after making love, Dolarhyde and Reba (who is, importantly, blind) stand on a dock with a boat framed in the background, echoing the setting of the Graham home. Graham's own vicarious sensory experiences, mediated by television and tape recorders, parallel the similar relationship Dolarhyde holds with the photographs and home movies he keeps of the families he murders.

A number of other parallels are struck within the third act. A close shot of Graham touching evidence—including what appears to be female clothing—is matched with a subsequent cut of the Red Dragon painting inside Dolarhyde's home. Broad associations between the potential menace lying within Graham and the murderous nature of Dolarhyde are drawn in two scenes juxtaposed to one another. In the first, Graham returns to the Leeds home and imagines Mrs. Leeds lying in bed, alive, with mirrors replacing her own eyes through a startling special effect. "I see me desired by you, accepted, and loved in the silver mirrors of your eyes," Graham says, ostensibly exploring the psyche of Dolarhyde through his own particular fantasy. In the scene that immediately follows, Dolarhyde murders one of Reba's male friends out of jealousy. This scene is scored to a pop song by The Reds and the tune reaches a crescendo of clashing guitars as Dolarhyde believes he sees Reba kissing another man (in truth this man is only removing something from her eye). In neither sequence do we see these characters arrive at an understanding of what is happening before their eyes; they are too imbued with their own experiences to reach a state of wider awareness. Graham's dreamlike disorientation is suggested to us in a close-up, as a zoomlens combined with a tracking shot creates a distorted sense of space, and a similar disconnect is suggested through the song playing over Dolarhyde's jealous act of murder, its lyrics expressing an artistic understanding of a confusion that Dolarhyde only resolves through violence. Style once again provides a distanced commentary while at the same time drawing the viewer closer into the experiences of both investigator and killer.

Graham is finally able to put together the pieces of the investigation while again watching one of the Leeds family's home movies, ascertaining that the killer must have known precisely what tools he would have needed to break into the home by watching the films. Noting the processing plant where the movies were developed, Graham and Crawford are finally able to track down Dolarhyde. What follows is a climactic ending to the film set to the long version of Iron Butterfly's "In-A-Gadda-Da-Vida." Graham approaches the house alone, armed with a gun, and enters the house by crashing into a large window, thus destroying the reflective surface through which he explored the psychotic regions of his own mind throughout the film but also eradicating any artificial mediation that had previously existed between him and the killer. Dolarhyde knocks Graham out cold and proceeds to blast away posters, lights, and windows with a shotgun, thus destroying the very types of reflective surfaces which allow him to vicariously live and relive experiences. Graham and Dolarhyde are thus finally, directly paralleled in this climactic shootout as each of them attempts to destroy something around them in order to escape from their own psyches.

The violence in this sequence—repressed throughout the film through style, and now overtly on display—further inflects, in a disturbing fashion, the cathartic release Graham and Dolarhyde both experience in their final duel with each other. This release also finally imbricates the audience in the experience of the characters. Throughout *Manhunter* distinctions are drawn between the film's style and the styles employed by the main characters, who use shiny surfaces and technology as a means of experiencing. These parallel tracks are finally crossed in this climatic sequence, as Mann and Hoenig fragment and modify images by using jump cuts, slow motion, and image repetition to distort any classical sense of spatial or temporal continuity, signifying the destructive impulses of the characters and their mental states through the very materiality of the film. And for the first time the audience, through viewing these violent jump cuts (and the sudden release of diegetic violence in this sequence), experiences a mode of rather violent style similar to the characters' own.

"In-A-Gadda-Da-Vida" bridges all of these shots sonically, the guitars suggesting both a musical progression and a drug-induced improvisation that threatens to veer into disintegration. Thus a sonic parallel to the violent and fragmented visual style is developed, through music that seems to promise a similar loss of coherent structure. But the bass line and the drums—continuing the musical motif of the "heartbeat" also seen at the beginning and end of the film—provide the extended jam in the middle of this long song with a backbone it would otherwise lose. Finally, though, the powerful crescendo of "In-A-Gadda-Da-Vida" becomes associated with Graham as the song's climax scores a shot in which Graham slowly wakes up from Dolarhyde's attack. This may be a form of sonic suture: We are invited to look upon Graham slowly regaining his composure at the same moment that the soundtrack calls for us to indulge in the song's most thrilling moment, and it is perhaps at this point that any visual pleasure in the violence on display in this sequence is muted in favor of identification with Graham, the enforcer of the law. In any event, as the song descends from this apex Graham shoots the killer dead. The parallel between the detective's investigation and the killer's murders, developed so carefully across the running time of the film, is abruptly ended with the sound of a gunshot.

But has the death of Dolarhyde resolved Graham's own mind (and cleared the audience of their perhaps complicit indulgence of violent style in the final shootout sequence)? The film remains unsettled in its inexact resolution of Graham's own mental anguish and its residual effect on the protagonist's family. As Kendall R. Phillips has observed in an essay on the film, the director's cut of *Manhunter*—currently available only in an inferior workprint transfer featured as part of a two-disc DVD edition of the film—includes a brief scene excised from the film's theatrical release, in which Graham visits the family Dolarhyde had targeted for his next round of murders. "I just wanted to see you," Graham says, standing in the doorway of the family's house. Philips writes:

> The scene is shot with a great deal of ambiguity and even after we know that the figure at the door is Graham, it is unclear why he has come. His confessed

reason only heightens this ambiguity. Is Graham coming to see the family as their protector, to see the people he has fought so hard to save? Or, is Graham still struggling with the empathic mindset of Dolarhyde, his desire to see the family of an altogether different motive?[17]

One might argue that this ambiguity is actually present in both versions. Graham's family seems to be fully reaffirmed as a final shot of Graham, Molly, and Kevin facing the ocean is cued to the song "Heartbeat." However, the film ends with a freeze-frame of this shot, suggesting two separate readings. On the one hand, the shot could be the triumphant inverse of the earlier freeze frames in the film (including photographs of the murdered families and the freeze-frame of Graham and Molly in bed, discussed earlier in this chapter) in that it affirms the lives of this family rather than highlighting its vulnerability. Alternately, the shot could be read as another in a series of frozen frames in the film, suggesting that the family, while presently reunited, remains vulnerable despite the death of Dolarhyde, a reading which is, admittedly, most strongly supported in the director's cut.[18] In this interpretation of the ending the song "Heartbeat" functions with some degree of irony.

It is this latter interpretation which seems to find the most resonance within the whole of Mann's oeuvre. While a thematic focus on the institution of the family is to some degree enabled in *Manhunter* by Mann's choice of the horror genre as his canvas, the family is also a recurring theme in the director's other films. As Richard Combs has suggested, Michael Mann's concern with the American family is—perhaps unexpectedly—just as focused as in the work of a far more heralded American filmmaker, Steven Spielberg. While Combs writes that "Mann is as sentimental about families as Spielberg," families do not always find comfortable reaffirmation in Mann's work.[19] Frank destroys his vision of a perfect future, which includes a family, at the end of *Thief*; in *The Last of the Mohicans* Daniel Day-Lewis's Nathaniel Poe becomes Hawkeye as he is adopted by a new Mohican family, suggesting the malleability and ultimate impermanence of the family as a cultural institution; the future of Vincent Hanna's relationship with both his wife and stepchild is never resolved in *Heat*; Jeffrey Wigand's family is broken apart at the end of the *The Insider*; Muhammad Ali endures tense relationships with his father and a series of wives in *Ali*; and Tom Cruise's Vincent in *Collateral* briefly alludes to a troublesome past with his own family, which perhaps fuels his psychopathic tendencies. It is true that Mann views these disintegrations with some melancholy, but his portrayal of American families is not nearly as monolithically sentimental as Combs suggests. *Manhunter*, ultimately, seems a part of the intertextual thematic fabric that comprises Mann's cinema, celebrating the reunion of a family while at the same time pointing to its inevitable vulnerability.

NOTES

1. Margy Rochlin, "'Vice' is Nice . . .," *American Film* 11, no. 10 (September 1986): 56.
2. Paul Taylor, "Castles in Romania," *Monthly Film Bulletin* 52, no. 615 (April 1985): 130.
3. Mann claims he was heavily involved in the postproduction of every *Vice* episode for the first year and half up until *Manhunter*. See Gavin Smith, "Michael Mann: Wars and Peace," *Sight and Sound* 2, no. 7 (November 1992): 10.
4. Rochlin, "'Vice' is Nice," 25.
5. See a letter to the editor from Anthony Yerkovich to the *Los Angeles Times*, June 8, 1986, 107.
6. Gavin Smith, "Wars and Peace," 14.
7. Tony Williams, *Hearths of Darkness: The Family in the American Horror Film* (London: Associated University Presses, 1996), 255.
8. One critic referred to the film as overkill in terms of its style. See Walter Goodman, "Screen: *Manhunter*," *New York Times*, August 15, 1986, C6.
9. Douglas Bankston, "A Familiar Fiend," *American Cinematographer* 83, no. 10 (October 2002), 48.
10. Williams, *Hearths of Darkness*, 257.
11. Philip L. Simpson, *Psycho Paths: Tracking the Serial Killer Through Contemporary American Film and Fiction* (Carbondale: Southern Illinois University Press, 2000), 98.
12. Simpson, *Psycho Paths*, 98–99.
13. Williams, *Hearths of Darkness*, 258.
14. Simpson, *Psycho Paths*, 104.
15. Michael Sragow, "Mann Among Men," *Salon.com*, http://www.salon.com/bc/1999/02/02bc.html (accessed February 13, 2005).
16. Simpson, *Psycho Paths*, 99.
17. Kendall R. Phillips, "Redeeming the Visual: Aesthetic Questions in Michael Mann's *Manhunter*," *Literature/Film Quarterly* 31, no. 1 (2003): 14.
18. Williams also infers that the vulnerability of the family may be present in the final frame of the film. Williams, *Hearths of Darkness*, 259.
19. Richard Combs, "Michael Mann: Becoming," *Film Comment* 32, no. 2 (March–April 1996): 13.

Chapter Five

The Last of the Mohicans

After five years on the air, *Miami Vice* ended its television run during the 1988–1989 television season. Another crime show produced by Michael Mann, *Crime Story* (1986–1988), ended its run a year earlier, having lasted a season longer than many prognosticators expected, given its small audience during its first year.[1] Chuck Adamson, whose former career in law enforcement would later provide the basis for Al Pacino's character in *Heat*, and Gustave Reininger, a one-time writer for *Miami Vice*, created the show; shortly after Mann completed work on *Manhunter* he set up a production deal to bring *Crime Story* to NBC.

Crime Story's initial run of thirteen episodes took the form of a weekly serial. The storyline followed a police lieutenant, Mike Torello (Dennis Farina), whose passion and energy are directed into a tireless pursuit of a ruthless mobster named Ray Luca (Anthony Denison). Over the course of the series, Luca's cross-country crimes move the setting from the streets of Chicago in the 1960s to the glamorous backdrop of Las Vegas in the 1970s. One of the additional features of these early episodes was the intermittent use of an omniscient narrator, a style recalling the voice-overs from "March of Time" newsreels, linking this television series to a number of films noir from the cinema's past, including Stanley Kubrick's *The Killing* (1956), which used a similar style of narration.[2]

Some contemporary reviews considered *Crime Story* to be little more than a retread of *Miami Vice*. As the television critic John J. O'Connor wrote, "the surfaces of cars and rain-slicked streets are as glossy as possible. One safe-cracking scene features a cascade of acetylene-torch sparks in closeup, calculated to mesmerize any spaced-out heads in the audience . . . the show looks suspiciously as if it would be more than willing to settle for the mindless glitz of *Miami Vice*."³ But critics were only partially responsible for the show's eventual demise. Despite NBC's attempts to give the series a high profile by debuting *Crime Story*'s pilot in movie theaters, the network ultimately did a disfavor to the series by scheduling it opposite the highly popular Bruce Willis–Cybil Shepherd drama *Moonlighting*. NBC did experience a spike in the show's ratings after moving the series to a new time slot, on Fridays after *Miami Vice*, but the original serial format was at that point largely abandoned because of fears that first-time viewers tuning into the new time slot would be confused if new installments included narrative information from prior episodes.⁴

The series was renewed, surprisingly, for a second season, clearly a decision that Mann and his coproducers had not envisioned, since the final episode of the first year ended with the death of the mobster Ray Luca via the dropping of an atomic bomb. The show's writers were subsequently forced to craft a series of bizarre plot twists in which Luca (somehow) recovers from the attack. When Torello and Luca both go down in a fiery plan crash at the end of season two, NBC failed to provide the safety net for the doomed characters as they had the year before: In 1988, *Crime Story* was cancelled.⁵ Despite this setback, Mann continued his work on television during the late 1980s and early 1990s, directing the made-for-TV movie *L.A. Takedown* in 1989 (I will examine this film in greater length before my analysis of *Heat* in the next chapter) and executive-producing a three-part miniseries for NBC titled *Drug Wars: The Camerena Story* (1990), but after this work Mann would return to feature filmmaking with *The Last of the Mohicans,* an entry unlike any other in his filmography.

Throughout this study I have paid attention to the stylistic events at play throughout Mann's films—moments of impressive cinematic form which seem motivated only by the director's vision and not by requirements of narrative or genre. In a sense, *The Last of the Mohicans* is another kind of singular event within Mann's oeuvre: it is a film that, while possessing both an expressive mise-en-scène approach and an exploration of some familiar themes from the Mann's previous films, is plainly unlike anything else he had hitherto directed. *Mohicans* is the one Mann film which ruptures, if only slightly, the sense of his work as the product of a fully consistent auteur because it is the only one of his films in which his singular visual and sonic style—while certainly present at given moments—does not seem to transcend the strictures of both its genre and its debt to its source, James Fenimore Cooper's novel.

Mann nonetheless claims a personal connection to the *Mohicans* story, claiming that the 1936 production of Cooper's story was perhaps the first film he ever saw.⁶ But Mann's ability to secure studio financing for his version was anticipated, and perhaps primarily determined, by a conterminous cycle of western films that revived the dormant genre. In the early 1990s, as genre scholar Steve Neale has pointed out, Hollywood produced a string of over three dozen westerns, some of the more notable titles including *Dances With Wolves* (Kevin Costner, 1990), *Young Guns II* (Geoff Murphy, 1990), *Far and Away* (Ron Howard, 1992), *Unforgiven* (Clint Eastwood, 1992), *Geronimo: An American Legend* (Walter Hill, 1993), *Bad Girls* (Jonathan Kaplan, 1993), *Maverick* (Richard Donner, 1994), *Wyatt Earp* (Lawrence Kasdan, 1994), *Dead Man* (Jim Jarmusch, 1995), *The Quick and the Dead* (Sam Raimi, 1995) as well as a 1995 rerelease of *The Wild Bunch* (Sam Peckinpah, 1969).[7] Genre critic Tina Balio, furthermore, categorizes *Mohicans* as a "costume film," alongside contemporaneous releases such as *Robin Hood: Prince of Thieves* (Costner, 1991), *Braveheart* (Mel Gibson, 1995), and *Rob Roy* (Michael Caton-Jones, 1995). In addition to being part of a full-fledged western revival, Mann's film contributed to an even more specific genre: adaptations of the Cooper novel. As Martin Barker has pointed out, James Fenimore Cooper's source novel *The Last of the Mohicans* has spawned ten films, three plays, two television series, nine comic books, one opera, two animated cartoons, and two British radio serials.[8] Mann's film is only the most recent addition to this lineage, and the fact that it is also partially an adaptation of a prior version of the story, the 1936 adaptation starring Randolph Scott, only makes this heritage stand out in even sharper relief.

Of course, all of Mann's films are part of a genre history, but very few of them before *Mohicans* seem as inextricably linked with such a prevalent trend in contemporary genre production; the fact that the western was dormant for so many years prior to Mann's film only foregrounds the extent to which *Mohicans* was part of an overdetermined cycle. Because of this, the film is more immediately identifiable as part of the context of both the novel's and the western's own history than as a part of the history of Michael Mann. *Mohicans*'s status as a Hollywood western, a Hollywood costume epic, and a reworking of the now familiar tropes of Cooper's original novel—along with its generous display of the iconography which accompanies those genres—sometimes overwhelms one's ability to reconcile it as part of a larger piece of work alongside such stylistically distinguished films such as *Thief*, *The Keep*, and *Manhunter*. And as Mann's career has progressed into the twenty-first century, films such as *Heat*, *The Insider*, *Ali*, and *Miami Vice* seem even farther away from the American frontier.

On the related level of style, too, *The Last of the Mohicans* exists on a plane separate from Mann's other works. While it exhibits a subtle form of expressive mise-en-scène throughout much of its running time, and while it features the attention to minute realistic detail expected of a Mann film, it is clear that the film's natural setting determined much of the scope of Mann's and cinematographer Dante Spinotti's vision. The ephemera of nature—not to mention the rugged wilderness itself—offered a challenge that the urban landscapes present in Mann's other films did not pose: "I was getting inspired by things that were so transient I couldn't follow them," the director remarked in an interview.[9] In films such as *Thief*, *Manhunter*, *Heat*, and *Miami Vice*, meanwhile, the viewer gazes upon a world of concrete foundations, of brick, mortar, glass, and steel, a relatively more consistent and stable architectural world which opens up a play of light that the director can more easily control and manipulate into exact framings, colors, and angles.

In the introduction to this study, I suggested that mise-en-scène criticism implicitly initiates an analysis about more than only the director's signature: all of the collaborators who are either in front of the camera or who design the objects, settings, and compositions in the frame are "coauthors" of the style. Mise-en-scène is then never wholly reducible to direction, for it bears the mark of a confluence of creativity at work both in front of and behind the camera. The director's control of these contributions may run the gamut from tightly controlled to loosely delegated, but the coauthorial trace of collaborators is present at all times. Without the compositional style and urban settings that have characterized so many of Mann's films, *Mohicans* displays these coauthorial traces in greater abundance than any other Mann film, traces which include the work of actors, cinematographers, and editors.

At the time of the film's release, actor Daniel Day-Lewis received a good deal of media attention for his typical method-acting approach to inhabiting the character of Nathanial Poe (Natty Bumpo in Cooper's novel), an approach which complemented Mann's typical, immersive devotion to realistic visual detail during preproduction.[10] Like James Caan's preparation for the manners of his character in *Thief*, Day-Lewis spent time with American Indians in the woodlands of North Carolina, and "learned to track and skin animals, build canoes, fight with tomahawks, fire and reload a 12-pound flintlock on the run."[11] Such careful attention to detail during the planning stages allowed Day-Lewis and Mann to craft a performative visual rhetoric that was largely free of unrealistic action-movie tropes, apart from one sequence in which Day-Lewis fires two muzzle-loader shotguns simultaneously—an improbable feat that, as critic John Harkness has pointed out, would have resulted in something far less impressive than the perfect aim the character achieves in the scene.[12] *Mohicans* thus possesses a detail in both character mannerism and period setting that is also echoed in contemporaneous films such as *Braveheart* and *Rob Roy*.

Of course, some detail cannot be planned, but merely exists, and this is another factor which separates the film from Mann's other work: The wooded environment of *Mohicans*, determined to a certain extent by both its genre and its source novel, leaves behind the carefully chosen pastels and cool blues and grays with which the producer of *Miami Vice* the television series may forever be associated. This is not to say that visual beauty is neglected: The most salient aesthetic element of *Mohicans* may be its lush cinematography, comprised of greens, browns, and other autumnal colors that significantly depart from the artificial color filters used to achieve deep greens and blues in a film such as *Manhunter*. That the same cinematographer, Dante Spinotti, worked on both films attests to his versatility. Such a shift in color, of course, was to be expected, given that the film's footage was captured on location in natural exteriors found in North Carolina, including the Blue Ridge Mountains, Chimney Rock Park, and the Pisgah National Forest. Synthesizing this rough and unwieldy terrain into a coherent cinematic vision led Mann to give Spinotti free reign in his approach to filming the settings; in the final analysis *The Last of the Mohicans* may be as much a Dante Spinotti film as a Michael Mann film. "We decided to use as little lighting as we could to let the true beauty of nature stand out," Spinotti recalls. "I felt the movie needed broad strokes of light, like the techniques used by Italian Renaissance painters, rather than elaborate lights coming from specific corners." Due to torrential downpours in the mountains and woodlands during the shoot, Spinotti complemented the natural lighting with powerful Xenon lights: "These lights have a very powerful beam which can go a great distance, and it's the only light that could penetrate the depths of the forest after the natural light was gone."[13] Other problems the cinematographer faced included dampness in the viewfinder, which forced him to compose frames and calibrate lighting by eye, rather than through the precision of the film equipment; shooting footage on canoes; and manipulating the flow of a waterfall with sandbags in order to achieve the thicker downpour of water that Mann had requested.[14]

So it is not that Mann and Spinotti do not filter color and do not manipulate environment in *Mohicans*, but rather that for the first time the two of them were working in an environment which could not be wholly manipulated by cinematographic equipment; because of this, *Mohicans* loses that careful and subtle balance between a (nonetheless artificially constructed) realism and an overt, expressive artistic inflection, a combination which characterizes Mann's other films. The film instead possesses only a lightly manipulated visual reality that, while constructed primarily through the director's typical expressive mise-en-scène approach, ultimately owes more to the shape and scope of romantic Hollywood adventures—a coauthorial imprint that even a highly individualistic genre auteur like Mann cannot escape. In this aspect *Mohicans* resembles other exemplars of Hollywood genre craftsmanship executed by American directors who are otherwise acknowledged as "auteurs," a body of films including recent large-scale and somewhat impersonal Martin Scorsese productions such as *Cape Fear* (1990), *Gangs of New York* (2002), *The Aviator* (2004), and *The Departed* (2006), and an increasing body of Francis Ford Coppola films including *Bram Stoker's Dracula* (1992) and *The Rainmaker* (1997). Outside of America, too, the professionalism—and, as I will argue in the following close analysis, even some of the problematic nationalism—exhibited in *The Last of the Mohicans* is also analogous to the recent conservative turn in Zhang Yimou's career, including *Hero* (2002) and *House of Flying Daggers* (2004), both of which constitute a remarkable break from Yimou's preceding filmography.

Despite my overall reservations about *The Last of the Mohicans*, the film nonetheless weaves a number of themes that resonate within the intertextuality of Mann's oeuvre, even though much of this resonance is the product of the comparative difference between the world depicted in *Mohicans* and the urban vistas in Mann's other films. In the following close analysis I will follow these themes while at the same time indicating how *Mohicans* does occasionally rise above its commitment to genre conventions in moments of brilliantly realized and singularly beautiful cinematic form.

For the first time in Mann, opening titles are employed to set the stage of the story. But here the film is actually setting *two* stages, for the presentation of this information has a form of its own. The first words on the screen tell us that what is about to be seen portrays the third year of the French-Indian War between France and England for the possession of American colonies; then, in a separate title, it is told that "three men, the last of a vanishing people, are on the frontier west of the Hudson River." These sparse titles—a distinctive trait given that this is an adaptation of a rather turgidly written novel—are striking for what they leave out. In the juxtaposition of the evoked image generated by each title, the language used displays no cause which might connect the dispute between the French and the English, on the one hand, and the lives of the three men—some of the last of the Mohicans—on the other. The foreboding tone of the musical score does, however, rhythmically drive and thus connect these separate opening credits, prefiguring the eventual conflict between these separate worlds.

In the opening stanza of each Michael Mann film, the relationship between character and environment is established in ways that are crucial to the story. *The Last of the Mohicans* is no different, but as we will see, it introduces the space of its story and the connection of human beings (both characters and audience) to that space in a way that is markedly different from the rest of Mann's output. The camera begins on a long shot of the mountains (representing the outskirts of the Hudson River but actually shot in North Carolina). This panoramic shot is followed by a vertical downward tilt that guides us into the interior of the forest. These two images recall the first moments in *The Keep* in which Mann introduces the setting in a similar manner, giving the spectator an all-encompassing view of a vast landscape that, in *Mohicans*, no character will possess until the end of the film. But unlike *The Keep*, which attempts disorientation through such shots, in *Mohicans* the sky and the outlined detail of the mountains and the forest are presented to us in a relatively objective and unified manner. This grand unity on display in these frames is important, for even though the opening titles have already suggested that there is fragmentation between human beings on this land, the landscape itself still possesses an autonomy and a natural completeness that is totally unlike the fractured, man-made urban spaces which characterize the balance of Mann's work (and, in addition, totally unlike the subjective, dreamlike imagery which comprises *The Keep*).

This point is worth dwelling on. Mann has stated that his immersion in the natural landscape of *The Last of the Mohicans*'s setting fundamentally changed the film he was able to make. As previously mentioned, Mann has commented that during the shooting of the film he was constantly inspired by the beautiful but ephemeral imagery of the natural world, but that the burdensome process of large-scale filmmaking rendered the capturing of such instantaneous moments impossible. Such an environment not only poses a challenge for the inspired filmmaker, but it also posits a new relationship between the characters in the film and the space surrounding them, and according to Mann it is this psychological relationship between humanity and space that is different in *Mohicans* in comparison to the rest of his work:

> I didn't approach this movie the way I approached *Thief*, where I was so excited by the world Frank lives in and the way he sees his world that I made the physical world of the film appear as though it is perceived through Frank's brain. I didn't want the audience to say, "Oh I get it. I'm seeing the world the way Frank sees the world," but I did want them to feel about things the way Frank does. *Thief* was metallic, I wanted metallic colors, cyan, yellow, magentas, not reds or greens. I wanted a lot of reflection and I wanted you to feel it like a three-dimensional machine, with Frank like a rat who sees the tunnels, sees how to move efficiently through the machine of the city, to get where he wants. With *The Last of the Mohicans*, I didn't want to change the perception of the wilderness forest from how we perceive it; I just wanted it to be the way it was, because the way it was is different from what we think.[15]

If "the way it was" is different from the way we as modern viewers *now* think, Mann's frontier characters—Hawkeye, Uncas (Eric Schweig), and Chingachgook (Russell Means)—possess a relationship to natural space that is fundamentally unified. Concerning the connection between Hawkeye and the landscape, Mann has said that "it's not alien to him, he doesn't have to survive in it . . . he is it."[16]

The theme of connectedness with the land and by extension the world is captured through the form of the film. Mann's careful use of in-depth staging, for example, is evident in the first shots of the opening sequence. Hawkeye, Uncas, and Chingachgook are in pursuit of a deer when the audience first sees them. That the viewer can't exactly see what the three men are in pursuit of until the end of the sequence seems to further comment on the way in which these three men are able to apprehend their environment in a way that is now totally foreign to a contemporary audience. What one can apprehend, though, is the way in which each character, portrayed in a series of separate shots, is able to negotiate the geography of the forest physically: Even in shots where the depth of focus is somewhat flattened (the use of the anamorphic lens and the 2.35:1 frame tends to generate a relatively shallow depth of focus) the movement of characters from the foreground to the background or from the background to the foreground emphasizes the terrain covered by each of them. These characters clearly have a plan, indeed a dynamically executed one: In a single especially riveting long shot, Hawkeye's jump is timed to meet the emergence of Uncas from the left side of the frame. Of all the opening credit sequences in Mann's work, *Mohicans* is the only one to portray its characters as masterful movers within and commanders of the environment around them. Only *Thief*, in its depiction of the safecracker Frank's ability to master the techniques of his job, approaches *Mohicans* in this quality, but in that film James Caan—who is subject to the imposing space of the city at night, as depicted through Mann's careful framings—hardly moves with the breathless, assured speed of the Mohicans; Frank seems less an active agent and more of an individual whose movements and possibilities are wholly defined by the space around him.

Unity for the Mohicans also comes in the form of family. As mentioned in the previous chapter, Richard Combs has pointed out that Mann's films share a surprising trait with those of Steven Spielberg—a concern for the family and its fragmentation in modern society. But in Mann's films this theme is usually accompanied by a tense ambivalence—especially in the portrayals of the male protagonists in *Thief*, *Manhunter*, *Heat*, and *The Insider*—regarding the ability of men to successfully maintain socially productive familial relationships. If, as Christopher Sharrett has written, *The Last of the Mohicans* represents a "lost dream" of American unity implicit in the decaying postmodern landscapes of the director's other films, it is, in *Mohicans*, the theme of the loss of the family as a productive social unit which most directly foreshadows the stories of Mann films set in America's future.[17] *Mohicans* emphasizes the spiritual, emotional, and multiethnic unity of an American family that, as the film proceeds, is destroyed. Family in *Mohicans* encompasses not only human relations but also bonds with nature: After the killing of the deer, Chingachgook says a prayer over the fallen animal, bringing together the Mohicans with the land and also qualifying the killing of the animal as an act required for survival, and not for an imperialistic colonization which prompts the violence committed by the English and French in the film. The home, in the face of imperial conquest, is defined as that which the frontiersman must protect; Hawkeye's union with Cora (Madeleine Stowe) and his eventual protection and rescue of her may be read as a continuation of this theme, for he is protecting a potential future family. By way of contrast, it is also the home which the imperialist project of British (and presumably also French) colonialism is destroying: This idea is evoked in the relationship between Cora and her father, Colonel Munro (Maurice Roëves), which becomes progressively more tense as Munro's imperialistic dogma becomes more apparent, as well as in the unsuccessful attempt of the British male to propagate its authority through reproduction (Heyward fails in his attempt to romance Cora). Such aggressive and destructive behavior stands out in stark relief against the productive relationships fostered and defended by Hawkeye and the Mohicans.

The contrast between the British and the Mohicans is also implicit in Mann's expressive mise-en-scène, which generates thematic depth as the film progresses. As previously mentioned, *Mohicans* depicts the adventures of Hawkeye, Chingachgook, and Uncas through strong depth of staging; they move fluidly from background to foreground and then back again. The British, meanwhile, seem stilted against the majestic backdrop of the forest. Occasionally they are depicted as existing entirely apart from the land: a British lieutenant, attempting to recruit frontiersmen for the imperial army near the beginning of the film, is framed in a medium shot which not only prevents us from seeing him standing on stable ground but also generates a shallow depth of space between his figure and the background. By contrast, the frontiersmen, in the same scene, are positioned at varying points of depth in a number of frames, emphasizing both the sense of community they share and the connection between that community and the surrounding exterior environment. The English, meanwhile, are repeatedly associated with interior spaces: when the British major Duncan Heyward first appears, he is riding inside a carriage headed toward Albany, and the amount of unlit space in the frame, which separates him from a lone window that opens out onto nature, is striking. Later in the film, Colonel Munro and his next-in-commands, as well as the British officers at Albany, will hardly ever be depicted outdoors, and when they do venture outside they present themselves in highly ritualized military formations. Personal relationships are subject to the same arid organization, as during the first conversation between Heyward and Cora, who take their tea outdoors; this is an odd and highly mannered activity which places them in nature while obviously keeping them at a far distance from its threats. Mann, despite his commitment to realistic detail and historical accuracy in a number of areas, has little to no respect for the ability of the British to make war: a counterpoint persists throughout *Mohicans* whereby the controlled and assured movements of the army's ritualized procedures (such as their march into the forest at the beginning of the film, when Cora and Alice head toward Fort William Henry) are contrasted with the inability of that same army to defend themselves against attack without the assistance of the much less formalized fighting skill of Hawkeye and his friends.

The Mohicans' ability to dynamically traverse space renders them unique not only among Mann's other protagonists, but also differentiates them from the other Natives represented in the film; they possess an agency which seems wholly theirs, one which is unified with the natural environment they have mastered. The Huron Magua (Wes Studi), by contrast, performs a masquerade of his identity. He fools both the French and British colonizers into thinking they have successfully recruited him for their imperialist mission, when in fact he is acting only out of his desire to gain a greater deal of political economy within his own tribe. (Only Hawkeye seems aware of the game Magua is playing, when he later tells Heyward that "no Mohawk is Huron"). In the first act of the film, Magua leads a procession of British soldiers headed toward Fort William Henry—a group which includes Colonel Munro's daughters, Cora and Alice (Jodhi May), as well as Captain Heyward. Magua, of course, is really leading them into a trap: At a certain point in the forest he attacks one of the British soldiers with a machete, cueing his hitherto hidden band of Mohawks to attack the entire procession. While Magua and his group are able to attack the British fairly easily, it is clear that their strategy, to insure success, must imitate the manner of the British army to at least some extent; Magua mimics the rigid movements of the soldier in order to successfully masquerade as a loyal guide.

Indeed, Magua's role in setting this trap seems to be executed as a figurative inverse of the British army's procession. In one striking moment, Magua, proceeding straight ahead in the manner of a British soldier, suddenly turns around and begins marching in the opposite direction before attacking his victim with cold precision. The film continues to reinforce Magua's ability to masquerade, as in a later scene in which he fools a French general into believing that he is truly loyal to the French cause because he hates Colonel Munro, which, while true, is not the entire source of his motivation; his desire for political economy within his own tribe is revealed, toward the end of the film, as his ultimate goal. In both motivation and manner, Magua knows the British very well (which he himself admits during a conversation with Heyward right before the Mohawk attack): to a certain extent he must present himself as colonized in order to insure the defeat of the colonizers. By slowly unveiling his motivations, this film's Magua is an ambiguous (albeit still jingoistic) figure throughout much of the running time. In distinction from the general legacy of Native American representation in the cinema, which renders an inherent savagery as a primary motivation, Magua is broadly depicted as a smart, quick-witted character whose talents allow him to adjust the presentation of his identity according to the situation at hand. And his desire for increased political stature within his own tribe ascribes to him a motivation that, importantly, is not relative to the desires of the white imperialists but one that feeds off of those desires in order to realize itself. Mann thus gives the character of Magua a certain degree of autonomy and dignity, rare for even a revisionist western (which *Mohicans* for the most part is not). Magua is a man known not only through his violent warmaking but also through his deft ability to manipulate both meaning (through his knowledge of several languages) and appearance in order to gain respect within his own tribe.

Nonetheless, Magua's relationships with the imperialists is what prompts his demise, for Mann is careful to draw a contrast between this compromise and the motivations of Hawkeye, Chingachgook, and Uncas, all of whom avoid the world of the imperialists from which they strive to distinguish themselves. They instead connect with the spirit of the landscape around them. The visual motif of water is crucial to the film and is constantly associated with the Mohicans (and also Cora and Alice Munro later in the story). The metaphoric value of water in *Mohicans* shifts through three different symbolic meanings as the film progresses: birth, survival, and death. Initially, Mann links water to Alice Munro's first experience of the wilderness; in one shot, as she follows Hawkeye, Chingachgook, Cora, and Heyward up the stony side of a small waterfall, she stares at the water in seeming rapture. Mann foregrounds this new contact with the natural world by lowering the sound of the cascading water as Alice gazes upon it; paradoxically, reducing the sensory information of the film at this point serves to throw into relief Alice's newfound fascination with a part of the world which is very strange to her. These shots of Alice are immediately associated with a shot of Uncas looking at her, and while some critics may regard this sequence with some suspicion—one might read Uncas as associated with the mysterious world of nature here so as to render him the exotic "Other"—this moment also contains the seed of a potential biracial coupling, the birth of a new kind of relationship and the potential site of a new and potentially more progressive form of family as an institution.

If water is a site of potential birth, then it is also by extension a source for survival. As Hawkeye and the rest of the group approach Fort William Henry, they protect themselves by wading in water while Cora and Alice lay low in a canoe that the men guide toward shore. Later in the film, the theme of survival becomes even more prevalent. The protagonists escape from an unexpected Huron attack on a British procession by racing downriver in an abandoned canoe. Although the Huron are close behind, Hawkeye and the rest are able to finally escape by hiding, temporarily, in a small crevice behind a gigantic waterfall. Subsequently, in one of the film's most celebrated scenes, Hawkeye tells Cora, Alice, and Heyward that their submission to the Huron tribe is the best strategy. Hawkeye will run ahead and seek out the Huron and try to rescue the three of them at a later point. "Stay alive, no matter what occurs . . . I will find you," Hawkeye tells Cora in one of the film's most unabashedly romantic moments. What follows is an act of unequivocal heroism utterly singular in Mann's filmography: Hawkeye, in order to escape the Huron's grasp, jumps through the gigantic waterfall and lands in a stream below. Once again water has provided him with a source of survival (although in this case through a type of purely cinematic heroism which is certainly exaggerated).

Death, finally, also comes to be associated with the image of water, but it is a particular kind of death that is far different than that experienced by soldiers in the imperialist armies. The film's depicted battles between the British and the French take place on dry land, with the backdrop of the manmade Fort William Henry looming in the background of shots. These scenes brilliantly portray the way in which highly rationalized and technological approaches to war make the killing of man more efficient: as canons fire and guns are shot, we see anonymous bodies on both sides of the battle die. There is a gruesome accrual of a devastating body count here made possible through a kind of war-making which is fundamentally different from that practiced by the Mohicans and the Huron. The final act's climatic fights between Hawkeye, Chingachgook, and Uncas, on the one hand, and Magua and the Hurons on the other, possess an intimate corporeality and gravitas that Mann carefully expresses by slowing the speed of the film down as characters die and as other characters react to their deaths (a stylistic trope perhaps borrowed from the use of slow-motion in westerns directed by Sam Peckinpah), and by once again employing the visual motif of water. After Uncas is killed by Magua and subsequently thrown over the edge of the mountain, Alice reacts in horror; as Magua approaches her, she backs up to the very edge where Uncas fell. In a close-up the viewer sees drops of water gently falling in front of her face; she then makes the decision to join Uncas in death as she slowly steps off the side of the ravine. Magua, then, is subsequently murdered by Chingachgook, a witness to the murder of his son Uncas; as Chingachgook delivers a swift and final blow to Magua, the Huron falls and his death is punctuated by the slow stream of water which flows near his head. The film through its water motif has thus represented an entire life cycle, with the stream at the end of the sequence suggesting that such cycles continue regardless of the ways in which modern man attempts to manipulate and conquer the environment around him.

This mention of Cora and Alice in the preceding paragraphs also opens up a larger discussion of the representation of women in *The Last of the Mohicans*. The place of women in Mann's work is, admittedly, most often that of an addendum: they are often minor characters whose presence largely elaborates not their own intellectual and emotional lives but rather those of the men. Very rarely do the female characters function as more than the keepers of the male conscience, present to remind the men that they are failing in some regard, whether that be on the level of intimacy or on the level of family (which always seem to be the sole concerns of the women). Even when a woman seems to possess an individualistic interior life—like Kim Greist's Molly Graham in *Manhunter*, who professes a loyalty to her husband that seems to emanate only from herself and not from any particular demand by William Petersen's character, or Diane Venora's Justine in *Heat*—such qualities, in the end, serve primarily as an indication of the failure of the protagonist to conduct his behavior in a similarly coherent, conscientious way. Women in Mann's films also seem untroubled by the postmodern decay which surrounds and despairs the men at every turn; in *Manhunter* or *Heat*, they are only troubled by such landscapes implicitly, through the collective failure of their relationships with men. One might argue that this is a disturbingly umbilical relationship between women and the world in Mann, if we can imagine the umbilical cord leading straight to the patriarch; for them, contemporary experience is always mediated through the male figure.

In this respect, *The Last of the Mohicans* is at once unique in Mann's filmography (at least until the important role Gong Li is given in *Miami Vice* the film), in that it offers a larger place for its female characters in the narrative, but also troubling, in that the place on offer is not entirely progressive. Madeleine Stowe's Cora and Jodhi May's Alice come into contact with the unpredictable wilderness in a very direct way, and in this they are certainly different from other Mann women. Ultimately, of course, such contact is contained, both by the narrative itself—which demands that Hawkeye rescue Cora at the end of the film—but also by the style, which does little to express their inner emotional lives (although *Mohicans* has, in regards to all of its characters, only sketches of character interiority; even the men are more understandable through their actions than through any moments which convey their intellect or their feelings, whereas actions always seem to imply an inner existential crisis in Mann's contemporary-set films). Cora and Alice cannot, of course, defend themselves—Cora is a woman of action at certain points in the film, such as when she pulls out a gun in order to help Hawkeye with his watchman duties or when she screams at her father for his insensitivity toward the plight of the Natives—but to Mann's credit this seems largely explained by the strictures of the British society from which the women derive. In her first conversation with Heyward, Mann places Cora against the backdrop of drying laundry swaying in the breeze, as if to associate her with the world of the domestic, but such a mise-en-scène arrangement is made only because the British colonial world itself, which Mann is so careful to portray as repressive and artificial, has already placed her there. It is telling that the first time Cora appears, she is standing in a rigid pose, looking far off into the distance; the camera, meanwhile, in a contrapuntal move, is active in capturing her image as it swoops down from a high angle to meet her face down below.

The relationship between Alice and Uncas, meanwhile, is difficult for some to conceptualize as anything other than a genteel British woman encountering an exotic "Other" because Mann spends so little time developing it. Instead, most of *The Last of the Mohicans* revolves around the steadily evolving relationship between Hawkeye and Cora. For the first time in a Mann film (and for the last until *Ali* and the 2006 film adaptation of *Miami Vice*), the audience can indulge in the romantic revelry of seeing attractive stars like Daniel Day-Lewis and Madeleine Stowe unapologetically swoon over one another. Nonetheless, their bond does hold a potential for progressive expression that is absent in most Hollywood romances, and certainly in most Hollywood westerns. In an early scene between the two of them, Cora asks why frontier settlers such as John and Alexandra Cameron chose to live in such a dangerous and defenseless area of land in the first place. Hawkeye's answer is pointed: "After seven years indentured service in West Virginia, they headed out here because the frontier is the only land available for poor people. Out here they're beholden to none. Not livin' by another's leave." Hawkeye here expresses his understanding of one of the first forms of class oppression in what became modern America; much like Frank's desire to raise a family in *Thief* or Neil McCauley's ability to both hold a relationship with a woman and practice his dangerous "profession" in *Heat*, the settlers in *The Last of the Mohicans* find it difficult to survive in ways that are contingent on artificially constructed social structures that they do not fully understand.

Despite the clear way in which Hawkeye understands the troubles facing the settlers, his dazzling displays of heroism are not wholly successful, for *The Last of the Mohicans* strikes an ambivalent pitch in regards to the future possibilities open for Mann's protagonists. This tone is somewhat less evident in the original cut of the film, in which the final embrace by Daniel Day-Lewis and Madelcinc Stowe is scored to a grossly sentimental Clannad song.

In a 1999 American DVD rerelease of the film, the director excised the song and substantially lengthened the speech given by Russell Means' Chingachgook, thus rendering this final scene as less a romantic triumph and more an ambiguous gesture toward the future. Without the Clannad song in the background, the final kiss between Hawkeye and Cora seems just as much a purging of grief as it is an expression of their love; the deaths of the Mohicans and Cora's sister in this version have left a stronger and more tangible weight on the ending of the film.

If Mann's revised ending more strongly foregrounds the ambivalence surrounding individual and collective agency in modern America, another significant (and more problematic) contribution to the film was from America's cinematic past—specifically, Paul Dunne's 1936 screenplay of *The Last of the Mohicans*, which Mann tapped as a source for his own adaptation in addition to the Cooper novel. While the contents of the Cooper novel are significantly transformed in Mann's version, the 1936 screenplay provides a structural model for the 1992 film.[18] In the selection of Dunne's screenplay for adaptation, however, Mann, as he has indicated in interviews, may have found the source for his own film's mythology:

> Dunne did a very interesting thing. He was writing at a time of tremendous political struggle in the United States, a country caught in a depression and at the same time seeing events in Asia and Europe. The view here was isolationist, although some people with political agendas and attitudes saw the need to take part in international struggles against the rising tide of fascism . . . Dunne essentially gave Hawkeye the political attitudes of the isolationists . . . But then at the end of the movie, in 1936, both men—Hawkeye the proto-American individualist, and Heyward—both in love with Cora—march off to war together to face a greater common enemy.[19]

Mann's comments attest to the mythical spirit of collaboration and national unity that, in popular conceptions of history, allowed for an American victory in World War II. But these comments, unintentionally, situate the 1936 version of *The Last of the Mohicans* as something of a predecessor to films produced in America during the early 1940s, the contents of which—as regulated by the government—portrayed an illusionist unity and thus an artificial morale boost for American consumers.

John Mortin Blum discusses these avowed acts of mythologizing in his consideration of the cinema's role in propagating a certain vision of the nation to American viewers during the forties:

> Hollywood's duty was clear. It would "tell the American people about the war itself . . . how it's going and what for," it would "stimulate . . . initiative and

responsibility," but it would also demonstrate that morale, among many things, was entertainment. That did not mean that every motion picture had to be "*about* the war, or have a war background," but it did mean that every picture, romantic or dramatic or funny, would "involve a consciousness of war."[20]

While Mann assured an interviewer in 1992 that his new version of *Mohicans* contained no contemporary political messages, it is difficult not to read his adaptation, in part because of its use of the 1936 film as source material, as propagating a myth of national unity, albeit with at least the inclusion of slightly more progressive racial undertones.[21] The harmonious pairing of Hawkeye and Cora at the end of the film is a step beyond the isolationist politics of Cooper's novel, and yet this harmonious pairing itself may remind us of the united "consciousness of war"—one which glosses over all difference, racial and otherwise—Blum cites as part of 1940s American culture. Mann's *The Last of the Mohicans* is then, like a number of the aforementioned westerns made in the early 1990s, pointedly not revisionist. This film is not a despairing vision of American culture as is Sam Peckinpah's *The Wild Bunch*, for example, and it does not humanize the Native to the extent that Jarmusch's much more radical *Dead Man* does. Rather, *The Last of the Mohicans* expresses a confidence in the power of a mythical national unity, making it not unlike a John Ford work.

It may be that this vision of America is what ostensibly separates *Mohicans* from the fragmented urban settings of Mann's more typical films. But it may also be that the specter of *Mohicans* functions as a never-truly-attained dream which haunts the melancholy ambience surrounding characters in *Thief*, *Heat*, *The Insider*, *Ali*, *Collateral*, and *Miami Vice*. Christopher Sharrett has suggested as much, writing "that *Mohicans* seems in part about envisioning the lost world implicit in *Thief* and the rest of Mann's output."[22] Gavin Smith has similarly described *Mohicans* as the hopeful vision the characters in Mann's other films seek to fulfill: "If the thread running through Mann's films is the destruction that arises when worlds collide, *The Last of the Mohicans* . . . suggests the possibility that, though reconciliation of different value systems may not be achievable, understanding can be reached."[23] When the film is read in the context of the auteur's work, its romanticism, its comforting and somewhat naïve liberal-progressive worldview, its faithfulness to the conventional ideology of its genre, and its grand historical sweep become less and less interesting for their own sake and more and more captivating because such qualities correspond to an untroubled understanding of American history which, in less optimistic films such as *Thief*, *Heat*, and *The Insider*, is revealed plainly for what it is: a fantasy of unity and national purpose that is visibly absent in Mann's more characteristic visions of an overwhelmingly fragmented postmodern society. This intertext, then, tells us less about *The Last of the Mohicans* and much more about the ways in which Mann's other films, and the striking stylistic events which inflect the stories they tell, separate themselves from the fantasies of the Hollywood status quo.

NOTES

1. David Marc and Robert J. Thompson, *Prime Time, Prime Movers* (Boston: Little, Brown & Co., 1992), 238.

2. For more information on the semi-documentary/police-procedural thriller, see Frank Krutnik, *In a Lonely Street: Film Noir, Genre, Masculinity* (London and New York: Routledge, 1991), 202–8.

3. John J. O'Connor, "A Preview of NBC's 'Crime Story,'" *New York Times*, September 18, 1986, C30.

4. John J. O'Connor, "'Crime Story'—A Tale of Formula Takeover," *New York Times*, 14 December 1986, H33.

5. Marc and Thompson, *Prime Time*, 239. The show's reputation has improved in the years since its original run—so much so that David Thomson deigned the series "one of the joys of the mid-eighties" and a "true American epic." See Thomson, *The Biographical Dictionary of Film* (New York: Knopf, 2002), 551.

6. Graham Fuller, "Making Some Light: An Interview with Michael Mann," *Projections: A Forum For Filmmakers*, eds. John Boorman and Walter Donahue (Faber & Faber: London, 1992), 266.

7. Steve Neale, "Western and Gangster Films Since the 1970s," *Genre and Contemporary Hollywood* (London: British Film Institute, 2002), 33.

8. Martin Baker, "First and Last Mohicans," *Sight and Sound* 3, no. 8 (August 1993), 26.

9. Gavin Smith, "Michael Mann: Wars and Peace," *Sight and Sound* 7, no. 2 (November 1992), 10.

10. Mann has said that "I immerse myself in a film the way an actor immerses himself in a character and manipulates his immersion and accesses different parts of himself at different times." See Smith, "Wars and Peace," 10.

11. Richard B. Woodward, "The Intensely Imagined Life of Daniel Day-Lewis," *New York Times*, 5 July 1992, SM15.

12. John Harkness, "White Noise," *Sight and Sound* 2, no. 7 (November 1992), 15.

13. Brooke Comer, "Last of the Mohicans: Interpreting Cooper's Classic," *American Cinematographer* 77, no. 1 (January 1996), 30–34.

14. Comer, "Interpreting Cooper's Classic," 31–32.

15. Smith, "Wars and Peace," 10.

16. Smith, "Wars and Peace," 10.

17. Christopher Sharrett, "Michael Mann: Elegies on the Post-Industrial Landscape," *Fifty Contemporary Filmmakers*, ed. Yvonne Tasker (London: Routledge, 2002), 256.

18. Mann discusses these changes in Fuller, "Making Some Light," 267.
19. Fuller, "Making Some Light," 268.
20. John Morton Blum, *V is For Victory* (Fort Washington, PA: Harvest/HBJ Books, 1977), 25.
21. Fuller, "Making Some Light," 269.
22. Sharrett, "Michael Mann: Elegies," 256.
23. Gavin Smith, "Mann Hunters," *Film Comment* 26, no. 6 (November–December 1992): 77.

Chapter Six

Heat

Prior to helming *The Last of the Mohicans* in 1992, Mann directed a made-for-TV movie for NBC titled *L.A. Takedown* (1989). Coming after the cancellations of *Miami Vice* and *Crime Story*, and arriving before Mann's return to feature filmmaking with *The Last of the Mohicans*, *L.A. Takedown* finds the director in an awkward moment of transition: It is a film clearly influenced by the music-video montage style of *Miami Vice*, and yet it is also a story which clearly requires the larger canvas of the cinema screen.

Originally intended as the pilot for a scrapped television series titled *Hanna*, *Takedown* ended up as little more than the structural skeleton of what eventually became *Heat*: Vincent Hanna (Scott Plank), a brilliant police detective, searches for a criminal gang led by Patrick McLaren (Alex McArthur), while a number of domestic entanglements provide back stories for each character. Here any similarities with *Heat* tend to evaporate, for Hanna's and McLaren's most important decisions often seem less the product of their own internal, existential conditions and more the result of awkward plot points. Hanna's conflicts with his wife Justine (Ely Pouget) do not develop organically in the script, and are instead spurred, apparently out of nowhere, by a chance incident in a nightclub. And while McLaren searches for his antagonist Waingro (Xander Berkeley) in much the same manner as Robert De Niro's McCauley does in *Heat*, his decision, unlike the purely psychological motivation driving the same character in *Heat*, is influenced by the refusal of Eady (Laura Harrington) to fly out of the country with him; in the later big-screen version, Eady eventually agrees to leave with him while McCauley's revenge is seen to extend from his own psychological dispensation.[1]

The visual style of *Takedown* is a mix of televisual, hand-held camerawork and mannered shot compositions. The camera occasionally lingers after the end of scenes to capture fragments of street graffiti or part of a skyline, a precedent to the documentation of background textures of real settings in *Heat*, *The Insider*, *Ali*, *Collateral*, and *Miami Vice*. Several scenes, including the bank robbery and the ensuing shootout, are very well staged and provide plausible aesthetic blueprints for the visual strategies of the later film. In the end, however, *L.A. Takedown* is mostly valuable as visual evidence of how an epic screenplay can be dramatically reduced by limited filmmaking resources. As a rough draft, it is an interesting companion piece to *Heat*, but as Mark Steensland has pointed out, Mann was simply far too restricted by only ten days of preproduction and nineteen days of shooting to produce anything more in *L.A. Takedown* than merely the embryonic outline of *Heat*.[2]

Like a number of other Michael Mann films, *Heat* is an adaptation. The director himself describes the original source:

> It was a friend of mine, Chuck Adamson, who shot and killed the real Neil McCauley, in Chicago in 1963. And when Chuck told me about it, in the late 70s or early 80s, what was most striking was that he'd met McCauley; quite by accident, they'd had coffee together. And Chuck had respected the guy's professionalism—he was a really good thief, which is exciting to a detective, and he tried to keep any risks to a minimum—but at the same time he was a cold-blooded sociopath who'd kill you as soon as look at you—if *necessary* . . . Chuck was going through some crises in his life, and they wound up having one of those intimate conversations you sometimes have with strangers. There was a real rapport between them; yet both men verbally recognized one would probably kill the other. And subsequently Chuck was called to an armed robbery, saw McCauley coming out, and there was a chase: Chuck came round a corner, McCauley came up with his gun but it misfired, and Chuck shot him six times. But it was the intimacy, the mutual rapport that became the nucleus of the film.[3]

Mann first mentioned this story in a 1983 interview published shortly before the release of *The Keep*, stating that, while he was proud of *Heat* as a screenplay and wanted to produce it, he would never actually direct it himself.[4] Twelve years later Al Pacino and Robert De Niro were signed to star in the film, with Mann aboard as director. In many ways *Heat* builds upon Mann's genre work in *Thief* in its echoes of the gangster and crime film. J. A. Lindstrom has suggested that "*Heat* is a film about work and its increasing personal costs . . . the film's emphasis on the conflict between work and home—for both the criminals and the police—is a timely innovation in the gangster genre, drawing on actual trends in work during the 1990s."[5] *Heat* represents a certain kind of work that is not often displayed in Hollywood films: It portrays wealth (in the thieves' designer homes and the upscale restaurants in which they dine) and then explores with precision how that wealth is accumulated (criminal activity) and how this accumulation indeed involves the collective efforts of individuals from the entire stratum of social classes. As both Lindstrom and genre scholar Steve Neale have suggested, this emphasis on the work of the upper class is the mark of a cycle of heist pictures released in the early 1990s, including *King of New York* (Abel Ferrara, 1990) and *Sneakers* (Robert Redford, 1993). These films are in contrast to a contemporaneous cycle of independent films about lower-class gangsters such as *Reservoir Dogs* (Quentin Tarantino, 1992) and *Killing Zoe* (Roger Avary, 1994).[6] *Heat*'s criminals, in fact, can be viewed as a composite portrayal of both classes, for while De Niro and Val Kilmer's characters are well-off, others in their gang, such as the African American driver played by Dennis Haysbert, become involved in criminal activity simply to make ends meet.

Lindstrom, in citing the difficulty a number of critics have had in finding meaning in the detail of *Heat*, has in his own criticism reduced the meaning of the film's mise-en-scène to "slickness and an emphasis on style and personality," but an exploration of the film's genre by itself does not suffice to describe the specific stylistic approach Mann and his collaborators bring to the work.[7] There is something about its style that is overwhelming, however, as some critics have suggested. Richard Combs has remarked that the film "gives off a blankness, an indeterminacy, that frustrates interpretation";[8] and Nick James has remarked that the difficulty in reading the style derives from its "fulsome ambivalence."[9]

There exists no single key with which to unlock the meaning behind *Heat*'s exquisite visual style, but I suspect we can learn a great deal about the meanings and themes such style generates by considering the two directorial influences which mark its aesthetic more than any others: Stanley Kubrick and Dziga Vertov. Michael Mann has often expressed admiration for these filmmakers, naming *Dr. Strangelove, or How I Learned to Stop Worrying and Love the Atomic Bomb* (1964) as one of his ten favorite films of all time, and, as mentioned earlier, specifying Kubrick and Vertov as two of his primary influences.[10]

As suggested in the first chapter, Vertov's penchant for regarding the camera as a "superhuman" eye, able to see more than the human eye alone, was an important influence on *Thief* and its depiction of a world and a situation which its oppressed main character, Frank, could never fully see or comprehend for himself. In *Heat* the camera does not perform overtly artificial tricks such as the extreme zoom-ins and close-ups of Frank's safecracking devices in *Thief*, but its compositions and juxtapositions tend to emphasize a wealth of visual reality that its characters—inhabiting fragmented spaces in the film's depicted world—can never fully grasp. As we will see, a number of sequences visually emphasize this gap between human agency and the vast technological, industrial, and commercial landscapes evoked and captured through the technology of Mann's and cinematographer Dante Spinotti's camera. In other scenes, this gap is also directly part of the narrative itself, as in a sequence in which Vincent Hanna's crew is unknowingly photographed by the criminals. While *Thief* used this Vertovian approach to saliently point to the alienated labor of Frank in a decrepit capitalist system, the characters in *Heat* (or, at least, the ones who enjoy a privileged class position) have achieved a certain amount of independence through the accrual of wealth and visible social status. The failure of these well-off individuals to overcome their environments and find true satisfaction only intensifies Mann's melancholy regarding the possibilities of human agency in the desolate landscapes of late capitalism; an existentialist dread sets in when success in an already questionable economic system is not nearly enough for self-fulfillment.

Mann's admiration for Stanley Kubrick, meanwhile, inflects this Vertovian influence. *Heat* shares with Kubrick's work an exploration of contingency—the idea that all truth and the means of expressing what one understands as the truth are always irreducibly relative—both formally and thematically. Synthesizing Jean Mitry's eclectic film theory in his study of Kubrick, Thomas Allen Nelson writes that "Film cannot avoid the aesthetic consequences of the impersonal, concrete nature of reality—its photographic *thereness*—nor can it deny the presence of the human signifier."[11] Any frame from a Michael Mann film is similarly able to capture any portion of a sea of realities that in turn allows for a multitude of cinematographic compositional possibilities, while at the same time evoking an unwieldy, relativistic world in which the very same possibilities may be undone by the slightest unforeseen interference. Characters in *Heat* function in part as "human signifiers," and are creators of their own personal meaning, but are portrayed as inextricably a part of "the impersonal, concrete nature of reality" which threatens to upend their fulfillment at every turn. Every "true story" or adaptation is open to abstraction; in the middle of chaos, human agency can find hope or despair; and in turn a cinematic aesthetic which captures these ideas opens itself to both fluid interpretation and frustrating opacity (thus explaining the difficulty so many critics had in creating their own meaning upon viewing the film). There may be no other entry in Mann's filmography that captures this Kubrickian influence better than *Heat*.

It is worth exploring how Kubrick's influence has been traced by past critics of Mann. Richard Combs, writing on the whole of Mann's career in 1995, suggests that the director's occasionally opaque visual style might find interpretive resonance through a comparison with the director of *2001: A Space Odyssey* (1969):

Behind the sleek, self-sufficient world of *Heat*, one mainly feels the example of the maestro of this kind of cinema, the director whose signature is the sealed-up production: Stanley Kubrick. His beginnings were also in heist movies and gangster milieu, and what Mann seems to have picked up on is that confidence to stay with genre material, with stories and characters that retain the pulp feel, while turning them into perfected artworks, megaproductions operated by private rules. *Heat* is *The Killing* made by a Kubrick with the ambitions and power of *2001*. There's even a little *hommage*: a snatch of György Ligeti "space" music behind the scene where Pacino and De Niro come face to face for the first time—or rather, where the cop confronts the robber's electronically refracted image.[12]

Combs might well have mentioned *Crime Story* as part of the Kubrickian strain in Mann's work; the early episodes of the series use a narrator in "The March of Time" newsreel style in much the same manner as Kubrick's early heist picture *The Killing* (1956). While the commanding voice of the narrator in *The Killing* suggests a controlled, exacting omniscience that ironically contradicts the fragmented human activity and psychology in the film, *Heat* approaches this disparity more obliquely, winding the theme through its visual and sonic patterns rather than through the use of a narrator. Indeed, we might consider Mann and Spinotti as the "external narrators" of *Heat* in the way that the film's aesthetic density and richness offers a counterpoint to the sometimes narrow-minded determination with which its characters go about fulfilling their lives.[13]

Before exploring *Heat* in greater detail, I would like to suggest, more specifically, how this oblique external narration operates at certain points in the visual and sonic design of the film. Dante Spinotti and Mann have created a dreamlike cinematography in a number of scenes through the assistance of computerized special effects and digital compositing, achieving at times a style impossible through standard photography.[14] In one scene, characters played by Robert De Niro and Amy Brenneman converse with each other while gazing at the landscape of Los Angeles, the City of Lights. Spinotti shot these scenes against a greenscreen in order "to maintain the sharpness and brilliance of the backgrounds, and still add the night sky with its veil-shaped winter clouds,"[15] thus creating through technology a dreamscape that does not actually exist, inflecting the characters' conversation about their hopes and aspirations with an air of impossibility that prefigures the death of De Niro's character at the end of the film. This scene is not the only moment in the film in which a character will be pictured standing against a landscape of city lights and skylines, the aesthetic thus generating the consistent theme of impossible single-mindedness and determination through its visual evocation of a sea of innumerable, intangible realities. In other sequences, horizontal camera pans—perhaps the most oft-recurring type of camera movement that appears throughout the film—reveal a great density of information both along planes within the image and through latitudinal surroundings that the characters themselves do not see.

These visual effects in turn find parallels and counterpoints in the rhythms of the film's use of music and its editing. Characters are often found in spaces that do not evoke any sort of realistic sense of geography; the viewer may get a broad sense of the mood or manner of a setting, which in turn expresses character and comments on the action, but these shots do not comprise a realistic depiction of the city of Los Angeles or the locales within it. *Heat*, as suggested in the paragraph above, will often capture landscapes against which to figure its characters, but single shots in Mann's visual investigation of the particular settings within these landscapes are atomistic fragments, suggesting that each character negotiates his or her way not through a tangible, graspable sense of space but through—in Mann's cinema of desperation and solitude it could not be any other way—the inherent fragmentation of postmodern society.

This compositional strategy is thrown into relief against the film's dispersive musical sensibility. Philip Brophy has commented on the musical meanings winding through *Heat*, which uses both an original score, composed by Eliot Goldenthal and Kronos Quartet, as well as preexisting selections from artists such as Brian Eno, Moby, Passengers, Lisa Gerrard, and Michael Brook. Brophy writes:

> The ambience of *Heat*'s soundtrack is crucial to the creeping existentialism which eventually upturns the film's epic form. And just as the sound of space has become the primary erogenous zone of ambient music, *Heat*'s musical scoring is the prime means of actively spatialising the film's locations and environments—especially as a counterpoint to the highly fragmented aesthetic employed by the cinematography.[16]

Brophy is here referring to the general lack of rhythmic percussion in *Heat*'s soundtrack: an intangible, dreamlike spatialization is created through the ambience of the score, paralleling the epic spaces of cityscapes in the film's visual design and opposing, through the music's spatialized vastness, the highly fragmented and secluded spaces in which the characters live and work.

With these broad ideas in mind, specific moments in *Heat* become more approachable. *Heat* begins, as many of Mann's films do, with a man arriving at a preplanned destination by motor vehicle. *Thief* begins with Frank and Barry driving to their latest score; *The Keep* opens upon Nazis riding through the Carpathian Mountains; the serial killer Dolarhyde arrives in his van at the home of his next victims at the beginning of *Manhunter*; Lowell Bergman in *The Insider* is whisked through Tehran on a jeep while wearing a blindfold; a young Muhammad Ali encounters racism on a bus in the opening montage of *Ali*; and Vincent arrives in Los Angeles via airplane in *Collateral*. All of these scenes suggest, thematically, characters both driving and being driven, both in control of their destinations and under the control of a motor vehicle.[17] *Heat* indeed goes farther than the beginning of other Mann films in prefiguring what the ending has in store for a character (in this case, death). Neil McCauley (Robert De Niro) steps off a train onto what appears to be an unusually steep escalator.[18] This mood of risk is further heightened by the mise-en-scène of the emergency room which McCauley walks through, complete with cuts to the bloody surgeries going on around him. But in counterpoint to the unsettling sounds of oxygen pumps and defibrillators, De Niro plays McCauley as outwardly cool and collected, moving without a wasted step. Only the quick electronic beats on the music track—the opening titles by Kronos Quartet—suggests any hint of tension in McCauley. While most of the film's music will be ambient in nature, these rhythmic beats reinforce the theme of running out of time. Risk seems subtly suggested in the next scene as well, in which another member of McCauley's crew, Chris Shiherlis (Val Kilmer) buys explosives from a man who gives him a vaguely wary look.

McCauley's crew also includes Michael Cheritto (Tom Sizemore), Trejo (Danny Trejo), and, temporarily, the psychotic Waingro (Kevin Gage), all of whom are seen in the first robbery sequence, in which the gang steals bearer bonds from an armored truck. In this sequence each man is introduced to the audience separately, clearly differentiating this collective of mavericks from the unified groups of men in films by John Ford or Howard Hawks. Even McCauley and Shiherlis, who sit together in the stolen ambulance under an interstate overpass and are later depicted as close friends, are introduced in separate frames. Indeed, before the robbery itself, the only two individuals we see together are Cheritto and Waingro, a relationship that is sour from the beginning (the two, in a fit of machismo, just miss staring each other down before arriving to the score) and gets worse as the scene progresses when Waingro cavalierly murders one of the police officers in the truck.

The first scene with robbery-homicide detective Vincent Hanna (Al Pacino) appears just before this robbery, and sets a number of the character's domestic problems into motion. Hanna has no time to eat breakfast with his wife Justine (Diana Venora); and Justine's child from an earlier marriage, Lauren (Natalie Portman), frets about a missing barrette (while truly worrying about whether or not her mostly absent, disappointing biological father will show up to visit her). The home will be a battleground for Vincent throughout the film: The house (purchased by Justine's ex-husband) and its contents never really belong to Vincent and, indeed, he seems far more comfortable prowling the streets for criminals than he does with his family. This idea is clear in the scene following the armored truck robbery, in which Vincent, on the scene of the crime, delegates responsibility with an ease, authority, and panache that, while deriving from the actor's own histrionics, is ultimately the character's own. This approach to acting, emphasizing the character's invigorating rising to action, is particularly poetic in a film that thematizes the gulf between the self-control of individuals and the massive uncertainty which surrounds them. The passion Hanna puts into his own personal style attests to his desire to establish some form of human agency in the constantly threatening environment of Los Angeles.

Waingro's act of murder, which disrupts the otherwise smooth score, is no doubt a part of this threatening environment and is the first of many unexpected intrusions into carefully orchestrated plans by characters in the film. On the one hand, the action is fully explained by Waingro's particular psychology, for throughout the film the character will be figured as a renegade loner, seeking not the interest of the collective but of his own self. At the same time, his act is merely one of many psychologies intersecting with others, which thus throws the theme of contingency into relief. No one single action in the film, whether it is motivated by psychology or chance, can be illustrated as providing the domino effect which triggers the rest of the events. Shortly after Waingro is nearly shot and killed by McCauley in a diner parking lot after the first robbery, the random appearance of a police car, which temporarily distracts Waingro's new enemies, enables his escape. As McCauley, Shiherlis, and Cheritto search for him in the parking lot, the viewer sees all of the spaces in which Waingro could be hiding, none of which the criminals can exhaustively explore. At best, the film suggests that while everybody has their reasons, there may also be no profound reasons at all, a lack of meaning, a notion which is best expressed through Mann's visual design: Characters are often pictured standing on balconies, against the cityscapes of Los Angeles, a City of Lights which, in its enormity and its intangible, innumerable, infinite possibilities and limitations, can never be wholly grasped.

The first scene between De Niro and the middleman Nate (Jon Voight) emphasizes this idea: The city stands in front of them, lights twinkling in the night sky, the shot beginning with a right-to-left pan which emphasizes what to them is unseen, potentially threatening space. This idea is reinforced through the fact that the characters are discussing a plan in this scene—the selling of the bearer bonds back to their owner, the insurance company owner Roger Van Zant (William Fichtner)—which will turn out badly and interfere with the bank robbery later in the film.

If these large spaces emphasize that which the characters cannot see, the smaller spaces in which each character lives—particularly the homes of Hanna, McCauley, and Shiherlis—offer commentary on each of their lives.

Hanna's home, as noted before, is bought and paid for by Justine's ex-husband, and nothing in it is truly his besides his television set. He is appalled by its aesthetic, which he describes as "dead-tech, postmodernist bullshit," a phrase that provides, in his own mind, an equivalence between his part-time home and the decaying landscapes he surveys in his work as a detective. Even death finds its way into his domestic space: As Nick James points out, Justine is nearly always wearing black, establishing a funereal tone around the characters' relationship throughout the film.[19]

McCauley's home—seeped in blues which may remind us of the Graham family home in *Manhunter*—is utterly empty, an expression of his own desire to keep his life free of all contingencies in the event that he needs to flee from the "heat around the corner." The home has only one horizon viewable through its wide windows: the ocean. Later, McCauley will encounter the artificially rendered, dreamlike cityscape of Los Angeles on the balcony of Eady's (Amy Brenneman) apartment, the two contrasting environments suggesting the crucial presence Eady now figures in McCauley's otherwise barren life. The only member of McCauley's crew who is seen in McCauley's own apartment is Shiherlis, who sleeps there after an argument with his wife Charlene (Ashley Judd). The Shiherlis home itself is the most typical upper-class suburban home of those depicted in the film, its mise-en-scène cluttered with expensive knickknacks which put the importance of Shiherlis's family life in bold opposition to McCauley's sparse surroundings.

If some characters strive to eliminate the factor of chance by paring away the elements of their personal lives, others are more adept at negotiating a flood of information—visual or otherwise—in order to yield some sort of control over their existence. McCauley meets with Kelso (Tom Noonan), who sets up the high-risk bank score that anchors the film, a job valued in the "low-eight figures." Kelso is sitting in front of a long shot of the Los Angeles highway while a large satellite dish hangs right behind him. McCauley, initially skeptical of the job, wonders how Kelso can find such an exact estimate of the score's value.

> *McCauley*: How do you get this information?
>
> *Kelso*: It just comes to you. This stuff just flies through the air. They send this information out and it's just beamed out all over the fuckin' place . . . See, all you have to do is know how to grab it. See, I know how to grab it.

McCauley eyes Kelso with suspicion here, and for the first time he realizes that he cannot keep everything under his control; he needs the assistance of these strange machines to keep his life in order. The blocking of the scene, with Kelso sitting in front of the satellite dish, and McCauley farther away from it, is not an accident; the fact that this kind of information is "beamed out all over the place" seems vaguely threatening to McCauley. Later in the scene, when Nate informs McCauley that the deal with Van Zant is on, McCauley is figured even closer to the Los Angeles highway. "How is he?" McCauley asks of Van Zant, whom Nate has just finished speaking with via a cell phone. "He's a businessman," Nate responds matter-of-factly. Stark statements such as these, which bestow an assured confidence in the face of reasonable uncertainty, are drawn in counterpoint to the flux and flow of cars in the background.

While Mann's and Spinotti's cameras always capture more than what can be seen by the characters in the film, both the police and the criminals in *Heat* extend their range of vision and control of reality through technology in a number of different situations. For example, Hanna and his fellow detectives are able to spy on McCauley's crew with long-range cameras, while McCauley's crew pay them back in kind later in the film by using the very same technology. Unlike Frank in *Thief*, whose devices aid in the production of his ultimately exploited and alienated labor, the men in *Heat*, as evinced by their luxury apartments and designer clothes, are seeking an even greater degree of self-fulfillment within capitalism.

Technology never quite trumps chance, however, as exemplified in a scene in which the cops come very close to nabbing McCauley's crew. The gang is breaking into a metals depository, one small job before the larger bank heist. While Cheritto plugs into the building's security system with a laptop, and Shiherlis drills through a safe, Hanna and his crew watch McCauley and his counterparts through small monitors in one of the parked semitrucks. A fidgeting officer in the back of the truck makes a noise, though, and McCauley hears it and orders Shiherlis and Cheritto to abandon the job. Not even the most advanced gadgets are foolproof against peripheral intrusions; Pacino orders his officers to abort any attempt to apprehend the fleeing criminals, knowing that an arrest on charges of breaking and entering will only result in a minimum of jail time.

Tellingly, Mann is able to comment on the relationship between Hanna and McCauley in this sequence, drawing a connection between the two characters—through both the diegetic technology wielded by Hanna's crew and *Heat*'s own editing strategies—that they cannot fully make for themselves until their conversation in the café. Nick James has described this sequence well:

> That image of McCauley in negative on the monitor makes him a ghost, the counterpart to Hanna's earlier resemblance to a night creature. Surveillance brings them together, as if it's only the sensitivities of special equipment that can spot these special people. But surveillance is also the way Mann sets up a series

of teases heightening Hanna and McCauley's interest in one another, leading up to the famous coffeehouse confrontation that was both the origin of the film and its major selling point.[20]

Mann and editor Dov Hoenig juxtapose a close-up of Hanna with a close shot of the negative image on the monitor of McCauley, once again foreshadowing the thief's eventual death—through this evocation of his unsettling electronic "ghost"—and now for the first time associating Hanna directly with McCauley's eventual demise. Given that this is the first scene in which De Niro and Pacino appear together (although at this juncture never in the same frame), this is the initial and most precise articulation, in montage, of the way the two individuals parallel and echo one another in the obsessive passion which characterizes their approach to the work that they do, although the broad juxtapositions between all of their individual scenes in the first half of the film have gestured toward such an association.

This mediated confrontation precedes the one-on-one conversation Hanna and McCauley have with one another in the coffee shop. This back-and-forth dialogue is captured in a straightforward, classical shot/reaction-shot structure, which begins with three medium shots (two of Hanna as he initiates the conversation, one of McCauley as he responds) which capture the busy background in the shop. We then slide into closer shots which throw these background elements out of focus with a telephoto lens. So while Mann briefly indicates the wealth of visual information behind both actors as the shot begins—making effective use of the widescreen frame's ability to locate a close shot in a particular, detailed surrounding context—he quickly reverts to closer shots, the interest in this scene not so much in where Hanna and McCauley speak than what they say, who they are, and how they relate to each other. Not surprisingly, in this sequence the detective pursues answers more directly than the criminal: Hanna controls the direction of the conversation and asks most of the questions. Even the camera seems to share the investigator's inquisitiveness, as it is a reaction shot of McCauley—the fourth shot in the sequence—which initiates the move from medium to close shots in the depiction of the scene. The sustained and intense intimacy of this conversation—which in terms of length lasts longer than any other conversation in *Heat*—emphasizes the mirror relationship between investigator and investigated, a line of inquiry also found in the relationship between serial killer and investigator in *Manhunter*.

This relationship between investigators and criminals intersects with a discussion of *Heat*'s genre. As previously mentioned in this chapter, genre scholar Steve Neale has categorized *Heat* as a modern-day heist film concerned with upper-class gangsters, in opposition to the lower-class milieu of such films as *Reservoir Dogs*. But others working in genre have suggested that *Heat* also contains strains of the neonoir film cycle, a group which also includes *Thief* and *Manhunter*. This generic classification of Mann's work, while impressively placing the films in larger film-historical contexts, ultimately does little to describe the subtle inflections of genre *Heat* (and other Mann films) generate.

In neonoir films, the detective continues to encounter the darker realms of his psyche, always figured in the film's narrative as his encounter with the antagonist he pursues. Foster Hirsch has cited *Dirty Harry* (Don Siegel, 1971) and *Serpico* (Sidney Lumet, 1973) as early examples of neonoirs which play with the parallels between noir detectives and noir villains but ultimately retreat from the full implications of the genre through both Clint Eastwood's (in *Dirty Harry*) and Pacino's (in *Serpico*) ultimate resistance to subversive forces and identification with dominant institutions. Hirsch sees *Manhunter* and *Heat* as perpetuating this conservative hesitancy lurking through certain instances of neonoir:

> Directed by Michael Mann in a bombastic style, [*Manhunter*] emphasizes spectacle over psychology, treating its tortured protagonist more as a horror-film hero with alarming powers of self-transformation than as a noir victim or a case study of a man who knows too much. The film's glibness is apparent in [the Hollywood heroics] in the finale . . . In *Heat* . . . Mann returns to a story of an investigator obsessed with his quarry . . . The film sets up the two characters as mirror images . . . Hunter and quarry have only one face-to-face meeting, in which they confess their mutual admiration—the audience, clearly, is encouraged to read the scene in an extracurricular sense, as two crack actors . . . pay fulsome compliments to each other.[21]

For Hirsch Mann achieves only "lightly developed" themes in placing hunter and quarry in opposition, and yet this a reading achieved through a neglect of the subtleties of the film's style in relation to its genre which, as I have briefly discussed in the café scene between De Niro and Pacino, accrues more than simply extracurricular meaning. If this argument perhaps exemplifies the limitations of certain approaches to film genre in saying anything deeply resonate about the work of an accomplished stylist such as Mann, it is only because the director has given a deeper meaning to the phrase "genre stylist." Hanna and McCauley are cop and robber, hunter and quarry; in this they are archetypes before they are anything more specific. But it is in part the style of Mann's cinema, in this film and in others, which allows us to understand his characters as not simply continuing the legacy of a certain lineage of crime-film figures, but rather contributing new meaning to such a history.

Another distinguishing trait of *Heat* is its final ambivalence toward resolving this psychological parallel between its two main characters. As Hanna and

McCauley become more intertwined in one another's lives—and as the time-contingent plans of both pursuer and pursued intersect with one another, effectively thematizing the stylistic motif of chance and possibility always present in the film's long shots of Los Angeles at night—the parallel between protagonist and antagonist is never cleanly sorted out in *Heat* as it is in *Dirty Harry* and *Serpico* (and, of course, as it is not in *Manhunter*). The similarities in their behavior are not bracketed moments in the film that finally give way to a climactic sequence in which one is clearly seen as good and the other evil; although McCauley dies, Hanna's future is very much up in the air.

A closer look at the second half of the film points to ways in which parallels between the two characters are intricately developed while at the same time inflecting the exploration of the film's central theme, the clash between control and contingency. At the beginning of the bank robbery sequence—scored to the tightly wound percussive structure of Brian Eno's composition "Force Marker"—McCauley, in another prefiguring of his eventual death, slides effortlessly into the bank like a ghost, never touching the pane-glass door and very carefully and quietly stepping through the busy bank lobby. McCauley stops and surveys the scene, and an overhead shot shows us something of what he sees—the entirety of the bank—but in a manner that is clearly not approximate to McCauley's relatively limited vision, foreshadowing the impending intrusion Hanna's crew makes into an otherwise smooth job. McCauley performs his tasks with aplomb; as shot by Spinotti from a low angle, he climbs atop a series of desk and walks across them in a commanding fashion, shouting instructions to the terrified patrons. It is De Niro's most theatrical moment in *Heat*, and the only one that parallels Pacino's histrionics.

The job, of course, goes wrong, as Hanna and his fellow officers arrive on the scene. As viewers will find out later, Waingro and Van Zant have tipped off the detectives, who now know the precise location and time of the robbery. But contingency is piled atop contingency: no other scene in the film more poetically—and violently—inscribes the theme of chance in the film's style. Hanna and his crew hastily attempt to control the surrounding environment, telling the other people in the bank to calm down and barking orders for roadblocks into two-way radios. But their view isn't always clear: Trucks, confused citizens, and cars often block their way. McCauley and company, meanwhile, seem to be having a relatively easy time of it; as Cheritto, the first of the robbers to emerge from inside, makes it to the getaway car in time, he is elated. Next to leave is McCauley, walking a few steps in front of Shiherlis; they are tracked in a right-to-left camera pan which, as is generally typical of this visual strategy in *Heat*, suggests the unseen (by the characters) nooks and crannies in the spaces surrounding them—in this case, the marble granite pillars and statues of the bank's exterior plaza.

"We're going to have to take them in the car," Hanna orders his officers, "get clean shots; watch your backgrounds." But controlling environments is an impossible task for both cop and robber in *Heat*. Shiherlis is about to get inside the getaway car when he sees the police, revealed from behind a moving bus. Two or three more seconds and the robbers' fates would have been decided; the police would have taken them down in the car. As Shiherlis's expression changes from a smile to a blank stare in a single shot, he fires his machine gun in an almost mechanical reaction to the cops' presence. In the chaos that follows, what we are seeing is clearly a bravado action sequence that fits in a long line of bravado cinematic action sequences. Mann's grand bank robbery is distinct, though, in that it emphasizes, in a harrowingly realistic way, the bystanders caught in the backdrop of this showdown: Shots are often held long enough in order for the viewer to see the outline of figures sitting in cars, trying to stay low. The abstract nature of these figures (in longer shots they are nearly silhouettes, and in quicker shots their specific appearances barely register) allows viewers to quickly identify with their terrifying situation—provided that such a viewer has been scanning the depths of Mann's widescreen frame attentively. *Heat* may be a spectacle, but it is one that exists on many planes.

Genre iconography, of course, ultimately mandates that this violent confrontation happen: Why else would either cops or robbers be carrying machine guns? But through the particulars of Mann's direction and Hoenig's editing, *Heat* poeticizes this iconography and ultimately transcends it. The resulting sequence isn't scored—Eno's music is cut off the soundtrack the minute Shiherlis fires (suggesting the stopping of a heartbeat)—and the sounds of the machine guns command the sequence. The visceral impact of these sounds suggests the consequences of the violent acts these characters are committing—the gun fire on the film's soundtrack is impressively realistic. Furthermore, in shots that do not directly depict an individual firing a gun, it is impossible to sonically differentiate between the act of cop and the act of robber: Each is conflated into a situation which threatens everyone in the surrounding environment. Another more specific stylistic equivalence between cops and robbers, between Hanna and McCauley, is drawn later in the scene. Fleeing in the getaway car, McCauley makes the decision to fire into oncoming traffic, a moment portrayed in slow motion as he raises his gun (violence in Mann, as in violence in the films of Sam Peckinpah, has a gravity and seriousness to it that is reflected in this use of slow motion). A similar moment is achieved after Hanna shoots Cheritto at the end of the scene. Cheritto has picked up a young girl as a hostage, and is about to make his getaway. The importance of Hanna's decision to attempt to shoot Cheritto while he is holding the child is captured first in three jump cuts that increasingly close in on

Hanna's face. After Cheritto is downed by Hanna's fire, the camera then cuts back to Hanna walking toward the robber's body. Slow motion is used as Hanna lowers his gun and walks offscreen; the soundtrack raises his gasp of tense relief to exaggeratedly audible levels. Clearly Hanna is inscribed as the protector, the figure of the law, the vanquisher of an antagonist, and the rescuer of the young girl whose life has been threatened. But the style in which Hanna completes this action is remarkably similar to the prior use of slow motion of McCauley in the car—a poetic device not used in any other part of the sequence, thus associating the decisions of each character (and the great risk implied within them) through style, and even suggesting that these actions, in and of themselves, have a similar style to them.

The final hour of *Heat* depicts Hanna hunting for McCauley (he believes his crew has a good eight to ten hours before the robbers successfully flee Los Angeles), while McCauley makes alternative getaway plans, fearing his initial strategies have become too dangerous after the near-perilous outcome of the heist. But on the whole the final act of *Heat* is more concerned with portraying the emotional aftershocks and repercussions that the bank robbery triggers in the characters' personal lives. Hanna discovers that his wife has taken a lover, Ralph (Xander Berkeley), and he subsequently abandons the home, taking with him only a small television set, one of the few objects in the house that belongs to him. Hanna will later kick this television out of his car and onto the street, a theatrical gesture which represents both his weariness with technology, for it is technology which has so far failed in its purpose to help him arrest McCauley, as well as the exhaustion he feels regarding his domestic situation.

Hanna, later in the film, returns to his hotel room after giving up the hunt for McCauley and leaving Justine's home. The camera once again sees more than Hanna can see, for as it follows his footsteps into the room it gazes down at a soaked carpet from a leak or a flood inside the bathroom. Hanna stands outside on the balcony of his hotel room, gazing at the night sky of Los Angeles and at the intersection of highways which throughout the film have figured as unpredictable realms of possibility. He then retreats back into the hotel room, notices the flooding water, and finds that his stepdaughter Lauren has attempted suicide in the bathtub. Mann has prepared us for some sort of revelation by showing the audience the water first, a shot that also generates a great deal of suspense in that our knowledge of the impending situation is now relatively greater than Hanna's own. Tellingly, though, the viewer might expect an antagonist to emerge from the bathroom and attack Hanna; Mann is thus playing with the codes of genre and suspense here, subverting our expectations and redirecting us into the emotional world of Hanna's domestic situation.

Despite Hanna's violent disposal of his television set from his car, he will take a U-turn back into the domestic sphere with his discovery of this girl's suicide attempt. Of course, the boundaries between work and domesticity are never quite settled for Hanna; as he rushes into the hospital ER—reminding us, perhaps, of McCauley's jaunt through similar territory at the beginning of the film—he begins ordering nurses to perform certain functions, taking over the proceedings as might a surgeon and reminding us of his assured command at crime scenes. Justine appears and after she and Hanna learn that Lauren is in stable condition, the two of them discuss their future together. As Nick James has noted, the conversation is steeped in ambivalence; "All I am is what I'm going after," Hanna remarks, as Justine gives her half-hearted blessing for Hanna to leave the hospital after he receives an emergency notice on his pager.[22] As Hanna descends down the hospital staircase (and perhaps to his own death?) all diegetic sound is muted as the music of elegiac strings rises. This image is the ghostliest of Hanna in *Heat*; like McCauley drifting through the ER at the beginning of the film, or quietly stepping into the bank before the robbery, Hanna's presence is strikingly ephemeral.

Hanna is responding to an incident at the hotel Waingro is holed up in; McCauley has temporarily abandoned his escape plans and is seeking revenge. This incident has been preceded by McCauley's own domestic conflicts. He has persuaded Eady to flee with him, but not before a series of shots which depict the two of them standing against ocean landscapes in a manner which obliquely alludes to Antonioni's figuration of alienated couples in films such as *L'avventura* (1960). Dark blues dominate the color coding in this scene, reminding us of the solitary, contemplative nature of the ocean seascape outside McCauley's window and distancing us from the dense Los Angeles vista outside Eady's window; the two of them here make a decision based on nothing other than themselves.

The visual opposition between city and ocean, between dark black and blue, also decorates the mise-en-scène of later shots in which McCauley and Eady are headed for the airport in his car. McCauley calls Nate to insure that his new escape plan has been put into effect; Nate assures him that it has, and also lets him know what hotel Waingro is hiding in. "You asked so I gotta tell ya," Nate says. McCauley assures him that he doesn't care about Waingro anymore. Kronos Quartet's music, previously heard earlier during the opening titles, has by now faded in on the soundtrack; perhaps this is truly the completion of the plans McCauley set in motion at the beginning of *Heat*. Throughout this sequence McCauley's car has been driving on the highway against a backdrop of Los Angeles, with city lights starred in the distance, juxtaposed to shots of Nate on the phone in which the color of blue is displayed prominently. "So long, brother. Take it easy. You're home free," Nate says, as guitars kick in on the soundtrack (albeit at a very low level, reminding us there are no easy triumphs for characters in Mann films). "Take it easy," McCauley tells him, and hangs up the phone. Bright blues and whites flood the image as the car glides into a tunnel; the camera looks upon Eady at this point, and the hope that these colors seem to hold for her. But the colors—like the fragile strings on the soundtrack—cannot last, and as the car exits the tunnel a by-now familiar vision of Los Angeles at night intrudes. McCauley makes a quick exit from the interstate: he's set for revenge on Waingro, willfully accepting the risk.

Indeed, the only member of McCauley's gang who enjoys a complete "blue exit" is Shiherlis. Charlene, now in the custody of the police, has intentionally failed to identify her husband for the investigators; as he drives up to the apartment, she stands on the balcony and makes an intimate and very carefully modulated gesture to let him know that the situation is not safe and he should continue driving. As he exits, the hopeful color of blue refracts through his car window, although slightly unsettling music on the soundtrack reminds us he will likely never see his wife again. This close-up of Shiherlis itself seems to simply dissolve into thin air as he drives offscreen and the camera loses focus; we know that for now he is free, but as a nearly absent presence.

After murdering Waingro in the hotel, McCauley is only a few steps away from freedom, but before he gets inside his car with Eady he sees Hanna running toward him in the distance. Staring at Eady longingly, but with knowledge of the abandonment he must perform, he runs away. One of the most moving shots of *Heat* follows, in which Eady, baffled, stands motionless on the left side of the frame as Hanna, a man she has never met and never will, runs to capture his quarry on the right side of the shot. Lives quietly intersect without the individuals involved ever knowing; the camera once again paints something for us that the characters cannot see. Hanna is in motion, but he may as well be standing as still as Eady, for his motion concludes in nothing other than the death of his prey, a result which throughout *Heat* has paradoxically functioned as the means through which Hanna find fulfillment.[23]

It is this lack of fulfillment that ultimately characterizes the ambiguous coda to *Heat*. After shooting McCauley dead near an airport runway, Hanna walks up to him and holds his hand, a vaguely homoerotic image that, as Nick James has also pointed out, recalls the stone pietá seen outside the hospital at the beginning of the film.[24] On the one hand, Mann is eulogizing these men, paying tribute to their plight through the plasticity and sculptural qualities of cinema. At the same time, however, Mann gestures toward the fragility of any eulogy or artform (whether it be stone sculpture or even more fragile 35mm film): McCauley is only dead because he has lost a game of lights and shadows (it is indeed the shadow he casts against the bright lights of the airport runway which allows Hanna to locate and shoot him in this final sequence), a game with rules set not by the players involved but by unseen forces that hover above and all around them. McCauley, of course, to the very end, is determined to define all of these events as deriving from his own actions ("I told you I'm never going back," he whispers to Hanna in an allusion to the conversation in the coffee shop earlier in the film). Hanna can only emit a sympathetic "yeah" as McCauley dies. Staring out at the airport lights in the final shot of the film, figured as part of Mann's aesthetic ambivalence, he might indeed be wondering if this is any sort of triumph at all.

NOTES

1. It is worth noting that Xander Berkeley's Waingro in *L.A. Takedown* does not exude the fierce menace that Kevin Gage's performance in *Heat* achieves; Mann seems to perform his own critique of this *Takedown* miscasting in *Heat* by casting Berkeley as the meek, mousey Ralph, Justine's lover.

2. Mark Steensland, *Michael Mann* (London: Pocket Essentials, 2002), 64.

3. Geoff Andrew, "Mann to Man," *Time Out*, no. 1159 (January 17, 1996): 17.

4. Harlan Kennedy, "Castle 'Keep,'" in *Film Comment* 19, no. 6 (November/December 1983): 19.

5. J. A. Lindstrom, "*Heat*: Work and Genre," *Jump Cut*, no. 43 (July 2000): 21.

6. Lindstrom, "Work and Genre," and Steve Neale, "Westerns and Gangster Films Since the 1970s," in *Genre and Contemporary Hollywood*, ed. Steve Neale (London: British Film Institute, 2002), 37–39.

7. Lindstrom, "Work and Genre," 21.

8. Richard Combs, "Michael Mann: Becoming," *Film Comment* 32, no. 2 (March/April 1996): 10.

9. Nick James, *Heat: BFI Modern Classics* (London: British Film Institute, 2002), 14.

10. See Michael Mann, "*Sight and Sound* Top Ten," http://www.bfi.org.uk/sightandsound/topten/poll/voter.php?forename=Michael&surname=Mann (accessed February 1, 2005), and Julian Fox, "Four Minute Mile," *Films & Filming* 26, no. 4 (January 1980): 20. Mann writes of *Strangelove* in the top ten poll: "The whole picture is a third act. It codifies and presents as outrageous satire the totality of American foreign and nuclear policy and political/military culture from 1948 to 1964. And it's more effective for being wicked ridicule than any number of cautionary fables."

11. Thomas Allen Nelson, *Kubrick: Inside a Film Artist's Maze* (Bloomington: Indiana University Press, 2000), 15–16.

12. Richard Combs, "Michael Mann: Becoming," 13.

13. It is worth noting that Mann himself shies away from an exact definition of this "external narration." See Graham Fuller, "Michael Mann," *Interview* 25, no. 12 (December 1995): 34.

14. Les Paul Robley, "Hot Set," *American Cinematographer* 77, no.1 (January 1996): 47.

15. Robley, "Hot Set," 48.

16. Philip Brophy, *100 Modern Soundtracks: BFI Screen Guides* (London: British Film Institute, 2004), 128.

17. I borrow this suggestive phrase "drive and being driven" from Kent Jones who uses it to describe the effects of Tsai Ming-liang's films in a piece titled "Here and There: The Films of Tsai Ming-liang," *Movie Mutations*, eds. Jonathan Rosenbaum and Adrian Martin (London: British Film Institute, 2003), 44–51.

18. Nick James has also suggested the formal nature of this steep escalator; see James, *Heat*, 9.

19. James, *Heat*, 9.

20. James, *Heat*, 57.

21. Foster Hirsch, *Detours and Lost Highways* (New York: Limelight Editions, 1999), 160.

22. James, *Heat*, 80–81.

23. It is in this regard that *Heat* is the inverse of *Manhunter*: While William Petersen's life is drastically threatened by the work he does in hunting serial killers, Hanna's only life force seems to be the hunt for McCauley and other criminals.

24. This connection is made in James, *Heat*, 9.

Chapter Seven

The Insider

Although four years would pass before the release of Mann's follow-up to *Heat*, *The Insider* (1999), the seeds of the latter film's production were sewn decades earlier. Mann and *60 Minutes* producer Lowell Bergman had both attended the University of Wisconsin during the 1960s, but only met several years after their careers were firmly established.[1] Bergman was once a journalist for the radical *Ramparts* magazine and was mentored by the leftist political philosopher Herbert Marcuse, well known for synthesizing Marxist and Freudian theories in his political criticism.[2] In the early 1990s Bergman and Mann collaborated on a screen story about arms merchants in Marbella, but Bergman was experiencing a more personal and immediate turmoil in the very offices of the television news show he worked for.[3] The director—one of the few people Bergman felt comfortable confiding in during the experience—soon realized that his friend's conflicts at CBS would make for good drama.

Bergman's "true story" began in 1993 when he contacted Jeffrey S. Wigand, a former tobacco scientist for the Brown and Williamson tobacco company.[4] Bergman needed Wigand to translate the heavy jargon of tobacco industry literature he had unearthed while researching a story. Soon Bergman realized that Wigand knew a great deal about the possibly scandalous inner workings of the industry; the journalist suspected that a potential *60 Minutes* piece laid in the waiting. Wigand revealed to Bergman that Brown and Williamson, through the use of ammonia chemicals, were knowingly raising the nicotine levels in cigarettes in order to produce a more addictive product. But Wigand was conflicted. He had signed a confidentiality agreement with Brown and Williamson, and any public testimony about his work for the company could have left him without a severance package and facing the personal and professional consequences of a multimillion dollar lawsuit from his former employer.

Wigand eventually recorded an interview with Mike Wallace for *60 Minutes*, but soon Bergman and Wallace discovered that the CBS corporation was planning to force CBS News to bottle up the story for fear that the network would be sued by Brown and Williamson should the piece air. Don Hewitt, an executive producer for the newsmagazine, suggested that Bergman instead prepare an edited version of the story for the broadcast, one which would run without Wigand's interview and which would explain why the show could not reveal Wigand's identity or the information he had to share. The *Wall Street Journal*, meanwhile, published an article that contained a good deal of the information Wigand would have discussed had the interview aired as originally intended. Despite this public revelation of information, the truncated *60 Minutes* story aired in November 1995.

During this time Jeffrey Wigand's marriage fell apart at the seams. He took a lower-paying job teaching chemistry and Japanese to high school students. In the CBS News and corporate offices, meanwhile, conflict continued unabated. The *Wall Street Journal* revealed shortly before the airing of the modified Wigand interview that corporate influence had swayed the decision to pull the full version of the piece. The show's journalistic integrity was thus brought into question, and Bergman himself was accused by CBS of having intentionally spilled information about this corporate pressure to the *Journal* (a claim Bergman himself refutes). Only after both The *New York Daily News* and The *Wall Street Journal* revealed the complete details behind Wigand's story did CBS allow *60 Minutes* to air the unedited version of the Wigand interview.

At first glance, this subject matter does not appear especially suitable for a Michael Mann film. The choice of material becomes clearer, though, once one considers the source for Mann's screenplay, a May 1996 *Vanity Fair* article by Marie Brenner titled "The Man Who Knew Too Much."[5] Although her piece originally pivoted around the experience of Wigand, an encounter with Bergman convinced her that "the story was a double narrative" which required an equal focus on the experience of the newsmagazine producer.[6] Thus in his source material Mann had at hand two characters that could serve as both foils and parallels to one another, in broadly similar fashion to the sparring matches between doppelgangers such as Frank and his corporate bosses in *Thief* and Hanna and McCauley in *Heat*. In one sense, the characters in *The Insider* are archetypes, as are all Mann protagonists in broad form. Bergman, the idealistic journalist, struggles against capitulating to gigantic corporations, including the one he works for; Wigand, eager to contribute something meaningful to society and possessing information that could benefit the public, faces ex-employers who wield a great deal of corporate power and whose financial muscle threatens to bring down Wigand's family and his lifestyle. But these men, in their specific characteristics, prove to be rich, distinctive individuals who are often starkly opposed to one another in their motivations and their social standing (the latter of which, for Wigand, shifts as the film progresses).

Mann's film—adapted from Brenner's *Vanity Fair* piece into a screenplay by Mann and Eric Roth, whose other work includes the decidedly conservative *Forrest Gump*, a far cry from the bleaker picture of America painted in *The Insider*—uses the plasticity of cinema, as well as two sure performances by Al Pacino and Russell Crowe in the roles of, respectively, Bergman and Wigand, to suggest these similarities and differences in character. Telephone conversations and communication by fax comprise many of the scenes which include both Pacino and Crowe, moments which are depicted through an expressive montage of images in which the two protagonists, although connected intimately via technology, are nonetheless seen in completely separate locations and thus two totally different social backgrounds. Their physical, emotional, and social separation from one another, although bridged intermittently as the film progresses, is never finally reconciled through an optimistic ending; indeed, the last time the two men talk to one another in the film, it is by telephone and in a conversation that does not resolve their personal conflicts. The star personas of these two leads also contribute to our understanding of the characters and their natures: Al Pacino is experienced in playing men who brashly question and come into conflict with the power of institutions, in films such as *Serpico* (Sidney Lumet, 1973) and *Dog Day Afternoon* (Lumet, 1975), and Crowe has often played characters known for their assertive but understated individualism, traits present in characters in *The Quick and the Dead* (Sam Raimi, 1995) and *L.A. Confidential* (Curtis Hanson, 1997).

In addition to the representation of these distinctive characters, a number of broad thematic ideas circulate throughout *The Insider*. The overarching theme of the film concerns the impossibility of distinguishing between what is "inside" and what is "outside" in contemporary America; in other words, *The Insider* is about the difficulty in seeing how the world functions when one is in an environment which is constantly flooded with images and media, a situation which threatens to turn all human beings into insiders at the mercy of corporate interests. With this theme *The Insider* recalls *Thief* and the way in which James Caan's protagonist struggled against the oppression forced upon him by his corporate mob bosses. Jean-Baptiste Thoret, in a 2000 article about Michael Mann's career, suggests the presence of this theme in a scene late in *The Insider* in which Bergman learns that the CBS corporation will refuse *60 Minutes* the right to broadcast the Wigand story:

> The film brutally seesaws as the network's lawyer (Gina Gershon) calls in Lowell and his team in order to announce to them the management's decision not to

broadcast Wigand's testimony . . . In the middle of a meeting room, looking like a gigantic aquarium, the well-oiled schema of the first part [of the film] breaks down, coming to a close on this weak reply from the lawyer as she once again opens and closes a door: "We're all in this together, we're all CBS." Relegating in a single phrase the old duality inside/outside (indispensable to all strategies of counter-politics) to a mere vestige, the lawyer sounds the death knell for the political structure at work in conspiracy films of the '70s . . . the externalisation of the system is no longer possible, there is nothing left but to disappear.[7]

Thoret's assessment that this scene "brutally seesaws" the journalistic quest seen in the first half of the film may be somewhat exaggerated, for the inside/outside duality he points to is a motif inscribed in the film's very first frames and in a sense reaches only a crescendo during the sequence featuring Gershon's manipulative lawyer. Regardless, Thoret's criticism is acute, and it correctly suggests that the very structure of 1970s conspiracy and journalism films—such as *The Parallax View* (Alan J. Pakula, 1974), *All the President's Men* (Pakula, 1976), and *Network* (Sidney Lumet, 1976)—becomes in and of itself what must be recovered by the characters who struggle against monolithic reactionary forces in *The Insider*.[8] Bergman and Wigand fight for the ability to look at conspiracy from the outside; they struggle to regain the ability to say that one is an outsider, that one can speak politically, that one can say, to quote a famous line from *Network*, that one "is not going to take it anymore."[9]

As in *Manhunter* and *Heat*, the aesthetics and politics of Mann's work richly expand the genre in which he works. It is this blurring of "inside" and "outside" which constitutes *The Insider*'s major contribution to its primary genre, the journalism film. Matthew C. Ehrlich, in his book *Journalism in the Movies*, cites Hollywood film scholar Robert B. Ray's conceptions of the "official hero" and "outlaw hero" in Hollywood film, and how such archetypes function within the journalism genre:

> The outlaw hero . . . reflects "that part of the American imagination valuing self-determination and freedom from entanglements." The official hero . . . reflects "the American belief in collective action, and the objective legal process that supercede[s] private notions of right and wrong." The movies' "ideology of improvisation, individualism, and ad hoc solutions" stems form the characteristically American desire to reconcile the outlaw and official visions, or at least avoid making a permanent choice between the two.[10]

Ehrlich points out that in *The Insider* Bergman and Wigand become outlaw heroes, moving outside the boundaries of their companies in order to get Wigand's *60 Minutes* interview on the air.[11] But *The Insider* finally complicates this idea, suggesting that in contemporary society the ability to become an outlaw hero comes only at a very great cost. In Mann's film the very American ideals of individualism and self-determination (and by extension the possibilities of extending this agency into collective effort) are threatened in a corporate landscape, in which all human beings are at risk to become objectified commodities instead of agents.

Presenting the major themes and the genre framework of *The Insider* before analyzing the film itself, as I have done here, might imply that the film's aesthetic only delivers readymade a preexisting literary conception, but in actuality the film's expressive mise-en-scène generates intriguing layers which build upon the foundation provided by Bergman's and Wigand's dramatized experience. Indeed, *The Insider* functions as an exemplar of the difficulty some critics have had in digging into Mann's supposedly overwhelming aesthetic construction. Film critic and Mann appreciator Nick James, in a review of the film, writes: "In Mann's films, the *mise en scène* is so controlled, so entrancingly framed and lit, it constantly threatens to subsume or belittle the human action . . . imagine *All the President's Men* with the volume cranked up."[12] As has been my general strategy throughout this book, however, I contend that a close reading of the expressive style weaved in *The Insider* reveals a depth of meaning that, far from threatening or belittling the human action, richly comments on it and complicates it.

The film opens in Lebanon, with Bergman, in a blindfold, being driven to a secret meeting with the Imam Sheikh Fadlallah (Clifford Curtis). The purpose of Bergman's trip—to secure an interview with the sheikh for *60 Minutes*—is not directly related to the film's plot, but rather serves as a commentary on character and a contrast to the subsequent scenes introducing Wigand. The first image in *The Insider* is a subjective shot of Bergman's point of view: The entire 2.35:1 widescreen frame is shrouded in the same cloth which serves as the blindfold wrapped around his head, suggesting that both character and audience are limited in their vision, and that the ensuing events and the particular depiction of those events presented in the film will expand that vision. The shot is stunning: As a cinematic device it builds upon the failure of the Raymond Chandler adaptation *Lady in the Lake* (Robert Montgomery, 1947) in suggesting that while no film, in any exact material sense, can adequately reproduce actual human vision, it can use small amounts of such first-person technique effectively. Through the accompanying montage such images can be associated with other images to suggest what can and cannot be seen by a particular character and by the audience.

The second shot in *The Insider* identifies the driver of the vehicle in which Bergman rides, a man of apparently Middle Eastern descent. The third depicts the struggle of the camera itself to find focus on a particular object in the frame, as a back-and-forth rack focus intermittingly emphasizes both Bergman and the exteriors outside the car window, a technique which suggests that Bergman would struggle in fully grasping this unfamiliar environment through sight even if his blindfold were off. The fourth image introduces a fragment of the mechanized vehicle, an abstraction that recalls the partial views of such vehicles at the beginning of *The Keep*, *Manhunter*, and *Heat*. The next image portrays two men holding guns, inscribing this situation as a potentially threatening one to the protagonist. Subsequent profile shots of Bergman's blindfolded head continue to capture both the interior of the vehicle and the surrounding environment outside, introducing the themes of separation between what is inside and what is outside and the increasing difficulty in distinguishing between a solely insider or outsider point of view in contemporary society.

Mann and cinematographer Dante Spinotti imply in this opening sequence that their camera functions as both a Vertovian extension of human vision (which can show us things that Bergman and other characters in the film will never see) and as an equally limiting device for vision insofar as it functions as a conveyor of character point of view. Everything in this sequence, of course, captures something that Bergman himself can't see, since he is blindfolded. Certain handheld shots, which seem to be scrambling across the environment, hastily searching for something to record, suggest the struggles of vision the protagonist would experience even if his sight wasn't circumscribed. Some images frame individuals and objects from a surrounding environment that Bergman, with or without a blindfold, could not see from his position in the vehicle, such as a brief shot of a Lebanese guard smoking a cigarette. These shots fill a purely authorial, expressive function, and in this case suggest that one overarching subject of *The Insider*—the dealings of the tobacco industry—has global ramifications.

The disorientation in this opening sequence is further amplified in Bergman's meeting with Sheikh Fadlallah; the camera cuts across the 180 degree line during their conversation (in which Bergman remains blindfolded), refusing to suture the audience into a tidy shot/reaction-shot structure. Such sutures are difficult to achieve in imaginatively composed 2.35:1 widescreen frames, as is often evident in other conversations depicted in Mann films: There is always a wealth of visual detail in excess of the close-ups of characters, which complicates tidy theoretical notions regarding the exact effects of suture. As the sheikh leaves the room, the viewer sees only a shadow on the right side of the frame, suggesting his mysterious and perhaps criminal nature. One might be quick to label this caricature of a Middle Eastern man as reactionary, but as Christopher Sharrett writes, "the immediate establishing of the East as Other is transmuted [later in the film] into Brown and Williamson

CEO Thomas Sandefur (Michael Gambon)."[13] The tobacco CEOs in the film are presented as treacherous and villainously distant, suggesting that the ability to make terror exists not only in the weaponry of fundamentalist groups but also within the walls of corporate society. Indeed, when Wigand returns to Sandefur's office in a later scene, the visual depiction of the CEO's office is even more unbalanced, disorienting, and threatening than the environment depicted in Lebanon.

One of the striking aspects of this opening sequence is how Lebanon's warm weather initiates an expressive use of environment and color throughout the film. Bergman is on the trail of an important—or "hot"—story, as he seeks to secure an interview with the sheikh. But this warm, summerlike environment will not be seen again in the film. Our introduction to Jeffrey Wigand is in the relatively more mundane settings of his corporate office, and colder colors such as blue, grey, and white suggest an immediate contrast in the careers of Bergman and Wigand. These cold colors, beginning with this scene, tend to dominate the rest of the film, and suggest at various points the inner anguish the main characters experience but do not often fully express (in contrast to the confident success of Bergman's Lebanon scoop at the beginning of the film). Rain, and then snow, suggests a cycle of seasons at work as *The Insider* progresses, imagery which finally contributes to the ambivalent ending which I will discuss later in this chapter.

During this scene, which introduces Wigand to the audience, the character's reflection is captured in an office window, through which we can see his former co-workers and scientists celebrating during a lab party. Both Wigand and the other employees are visible in the same frame and yet separated by the window. As will be soon revealed, Wigand has been fired, and thus at this moment is forever separated from these people. As Wigand leaves an elevator and heads out into the Brown and Williamson lobby, foreboding music appears on the soundtrack at a very low level and only the sound of Wigand's shoes, as he walks toward the exit, breaks the silence on the film's soundtrack. As Wigand passes a company security guard, the shot begins to employ slow motion. Wigand heads toward the exit as the guard (placed in the foreground of the frame but out of focus, his presence haunting and ghostlike rather than realistic) looks at him and says something into his two-way radio. Before Wigand can reach the revolving glass exit doors—which function as a sign of the tenuous difference between inside and outside in this corporate world and which soon become one of the film's central motifs—the shot ends, and the effect achieved is something similar to a moment in Alfred Hitchcock's *Vertigo* (1958) as described by critic Robin Wood:

> There follows the accident, with Scottie (James Stewart) clinging to a collapsible gutter while a policeman, trying to save him, plunges past him to his death

hundreds of feet below . . . When we next see Scottie, he is sitting in the apartment of Midge (Barbara Bel Geddes). We do not see, and are never told, how he got down from the gutter: there seems no possible way he *could* have got down. The effect is of having him, throughout the film, metaphorically suspended over a great abyss.[14]

Mann's effect is more subtle than Hitchcock's: We can presumably infer how Wigand left the office building (he just kept on walking) because the act is not anywhere near as incredible as hanging off the edge of a building. But throughout *The Insider* the most seemingly banal moments are elevated to poetry, and as this shot of Wigand ends the viewer feels that Wigand is metaphorically ensconced within the walls of Brown and Williamson throughout the entire film. Indeed, Wigand is only able to find emotional release from this state at the very end of the film, when his complete *60 Minutes* interview airs and his children are able to see it.

Mann and cinematographer Dante Spinotti capture a number of important details about the Wigand home in the next sequence. An image of Wigand's daughter Barbara (Hallie Kate Eisenberg) sitting on a nice couch with expensive furniture around her is one of many which establishes that the family is upper-middle class. Thus we see what will be at stake personally for the characters as Wigand makes his decision to come forth with information later in the film; class will be associated with mise-en-scène very closely throughout the film's representation of Wigand, for as he loses his financial wherewithal his environs become less and less comfortable. Wigand is also associated with alcohol in this scene, as he is pictured pouring a drink while speaking to his daughter, images which foreshadow his later revelation to Bergman that he "often drinks . . . a couple times more than I should have." Editing also inflects how we pay attention to mise-en-scène: As Wigand walks outside to confer with his wife Liane (Diane Venora) about losing his job, a cut-in emphasizes his nice shoes. Clearly material comfort supports this family on the most fundamental level, and the slow removal of this comfort as *The Insider* progresses is one of the drama's central aspects.

Close-ups are of two basic varieties in *The Insider*. Mann employs standard close-ups that depict a character's face on one side of the frame in the foreground while still capturing some visual detail about the environment in which that character is placed; and extreme close-ups are also used, shots which fill nearly all of the widescreen frame with a character's visage. As previously mentioned, such close-ups do not cleanly "suture" us into the experience of the film through standard shot/reaction-shot structures; the images in Mann's films are simply too particular, too varied, too richly detailed, and too often juxtaposed with other equally unexpected images—sequences that I have signified with the phrase "stylistic events"—to operate in such a fashion. Even shot/reaction-shot structures are filmed with an overtly aesthetic tinge that complicates our emotional and intellectual involvement with the film. The extreme close-ups in *The Insider* serve to punctuate situations with intense emotion and character information and are always part of a tapestry of richly imagined compositions, each of which demands our acute critical sensitivity. For example, when Wigand's daughter Deborah (Renee Olstead) begins wheezing, Wigand brings her an asthma inhaler and holds her while she regains her breath. A frame-filling close-up of Wigand emphasizes not only his love for his daughter and his emotional investment in both caring for her ailment (which we are free to identify with), but also the scientific explanation to her of what effect the inhaler is having on her body. This moment suggests a personal contradiction in Wigand: the discrepancy between the positive social effects his knowledge of science can have and the tobacco industry job he takes to support his family. That his knowledge of science is also directly tied to his emotions and his relationships is important as well; like Bergman, he is passionate about what he does, but like Bergman and his job at *60 Minutes*, Wigand's former work environment does not properly support and sustain such integrity.

The film shifts back to Lebanon, as Bergman and Mike Wallace (Christopher Plummer) prepare to interview Sheikh Fadlallah. The scene establishes Wallace's journalistic venom (he opens the interview with a stark question: "Are you a terrorist?") and his ornery nature (he refuses to move his chair at the request of the sheikh). Bergman is clearly the mediator of the situation; his job as *60 Minutes* producer involves placating Wallace as much as it does producing stories. The two are nonetheless established as professional partners and close associates, a friendship that is tested as the film proceeds.

Bergman's family, as established in subsequent scenes and in contrast to Wigand's, is, as he himself admits, a "modern marriage." He has two older adolescent children, one his own, the other his wife's, both from previous marriages. In this his family is far different from those seen in other Mann films: If the traditional family was vulnerable in *Thief*, *Manhunter*, and *The Last of the Mohicans*, Bergman's patchwork clan signifies a messy but thriving form of familial structure to which Mann's male figures must learn to adapt. The audience is first introduced to the Bergman home when we see Pacino receive through the mail a number of important tobacco industry documents from an anonymous source for a story on smoking in bed and fire safety. The incomprehensible jargon of this literature prompts him to contact Wigand. The two of them exchange faxes but achieve no sort of fruitful communication; Wigand distrusts Bergman, suspecting that the journalist is seeking information regarding the inner workings of Brown and Williamson. During this fax session,

Wigand's tidy desk is contrasted to the busy clutter surrounding Bergman's home, perhaps prefiguring the control Wigand will relinquish over both his own life and his traditional family when he eventually decides to testify against his former employer.

After Bergman begins to suspect that Wigand may have more to share than simply knowledge of specialized industry documents, he organizes a covert meeting between the two of them at the famous Seelbach Hotel in Louisville, Kentucky, a setting which Mann and Spinotti render in a shadowy, noirlike atmosphere. In the hotel room, Bergman and Wigand are shot in separate frames; during their conversation the camera is closer on Bergman (in a telephoto shot) as he begins asking questions, while in reaction shots Wigand sits at a distance, with objects placed around and behind him in the sharper focus of a wide-angle shot. Wigand agrees to translate the documents, but refuses to share anything about his former job (information Bergman has not even requested). By disavowing his willingness to reveal anything about his ex-employers, Wigand communicates, through euphemisms and innuendo, exactly what he has to tell. It goes without saying that the journalist is intrigued by such behavior, and as Bergman gazes outside the hotel window and sees the Brown and Williamson building across the street—the same window toward which Wigand glanced as he avoided answering Bergman's questions about his employer—he becomes even more curious.

The first scenes depicting Bergman at CBS draw us into his environment very carefully. After a screening of the Sheikh Fadlallah interview—a segment which *60 Minutes* producer Don Hewitt (Philip Baker Hall) assures Wallace is "the one they'll remember you for when you're dead and buried"—Wallace invites Bergman to lunch and advises him to "bring a tie so they let us into the front door," a comment met with laughs from Bergman and others, but which implies that the former radical journalist is a not a natural fit in this upper-class corporate environment. In images which echo the revolving door Wigand heads toward in an earlier shot in the Brown and Williamson company lobby, Bergman's struggle in escaping the internal politics and procedures of CBS is prefigured in this portion of the film through three shots. In the first shot, his assistant Debi (Debi Mazar) walks in front of him and exits through the revolving door, the sun greeting her outside as she emerges, while Bergman is portrayed in shadows in the background. The next shot is closer on Bergman as he moves the doors: moving from inside a corporation to an outside position—here literally suggested in the image of the revolving doors, which spin rapidly from inside to outside in a way which metaphorically blurs the difference between the two—will become an important and difficult feat for the idealistic journalist to accomplish. An additional and not otherwise necessary shot of another CBS employee walking through the doors and into the building seems only to emphasize this idea. This theme is further developed during subsequent shots, in which Wallace walks a few strides ahead of Hewitt, Bergman, and Debi, leading this group of individuals as a corporate team even when they are outside the brick-and-mortar auspices of the company's four walls. The image of the revolving doors will appear again at the end of the film, when Bergman makes his final exit from CBS.

The expensive restaurant in which the CBS team eats lunch is juxtaposed with a shot of Wigand sitting in the Brown and Williamson lobby, waiting to meet with the company's CEO Thomas Sandefur. The lobby's revolving doors are again emphasized through images and the soundtrack: The viewer sees light and shadow cast on Wigand's face as employees enter and exit through them, and the sound of the doors, as well as the sound of a janitor's vacuum cleaner, also serve to suggest the impossibility of Wigand escaping the company's influence. After the meeting, Wigand interrupts Bergman's lunch with a phone call, telling him he has just refused to sign an even stricter confidentiality agreement with his ex-employers. Wigand believes that Bergman has ratted him out, given the further threats Brown and Williamson have now directed toward him. Mann's use of sound from the characters' environments (in this case the harsh noise of a semitruck driving past the phone booth in which Wigand stands) expresses just as effectively the brash nature of the Wigand character as does Crowe's performance. *The Insider* also continues to express feeling through weather: When Bergman appears outside Wigand's home later in the film, in order to convince the ex-tobacco scientist that he never gives up sources, a torrential downpour of rain suggests an inner anguish that the tough exteriors of these men do not reveal. And in a number of scenes—including a sequence at a driving range in which Wigand is stalked by a mysterious stranger and another during which his daughter says she sees a man walking in their backyard—Wigand's growing paranoia and the potential threats from his ex-employers are expressed not through exposition but in pools of light and shadow crafted by cinematographer Dante Spinotti.

Throughout the first half of the film, as Bergman continues in his attempts to encourage Wigand to put what he knows on legal record and do the interview with *60 Minutes*, the difference in the social backgrounds of these two men becomes clearer even as they are drawn closer together as Wigand makes the decision to put his knowledge of Brown and Williamson's company policies on record. A scene in a Japanese restaurant—like the previous scenes in Lebanon and Thomas Sandefur's office—briefly disorients us through an unexpected use of space. The sequence unfolds mostly in typical shot/reaction-shot structure but also cuts across the 180 degree line, in what is certainly a reference to Yasujiro Ozu (especially given this setting), to present three contrasting two-shots (in profile) of the men as Wigand begins to contest the ability of *60 Minutes* to really change what people think about the world. The viewer is invited to see this as both an intimate conversation and a confrontation between two men with vastly different attitudes.

Despite these intrinsic differences, it is soon apparent that Wigand's suburban existence offers him no comfort. His wife Liane reads a death threat sent through e-mail and Wigand finds a bullet in his mailbox, prompting him to contact the FBI. But the film suggests that the FBI itself may be in concert with Brown and Williamson (Mann's suspicion toward this American institution first appeared in *Manhunter* and appears again in the film version of *Miami Vice*). As Wigand runs out of his home to chase down an agent who has taken his computer, he stumbles and falls on the ground; it is a moment of hurried clumsiness that recalls Bergman's struggle through the revolving doors earlier in the film. Wigand's neighbors stand on their lawns and gaze at him curiously, and yet offer no help; for the first time Wigand's stubborn individualism, in the face of indifference from everyone around him, seems wholly justified.

At this point in the film Wigand decides to finally tape a *60 Minutes* interview with Mike Wallace. In this move, and his later decision to go on record with what he knows in a court of law, he becomes, in part, an archetype of the journalism film known as the "outlaw hero," moving outside the corporate boundaries of officialdom in his individual decision to share information about his ex-employers. The images which capture his interview—such as one shot in which television sets placed in the foreground of the compositions display Wigand's reproduced image while he sits in the background—suggest that by taping this piece with Wallace, Wigand moves both literally and figuratively outside of himself. But these visual compositions also suggest that his image is now out of his control, which foreshadows the debates within CBS News over whether or not to display his face during the broadcast of the interview. It is indeed Wigand's decision to go ahead with the interview that brings him and Bergman closer together, despite their different social backgrounds. In the interview sequence close-ups of Wigand and Bergman are juxtaposed with one another, a connection that is further enhanced in the timing of Lisa Gerrard and Pieter Bourke's score in the sequence, which matches the cuts juxtaposing the two men with lyrical piano music.

If one were to describe the structure of *The Insider* as musical, the next set of scenes, beginning with Wigand's decision to put his testimony on public record in a Biloxi, Mississippi, court, marks the end of the film's first movement. Throughout the entire film up to this point, the inside/outside dichotomy has been tightly wound; we might remember that Wigand is still metaphorically frozen inside the lobby of Brown and Williamson. As Wigand contemplates his decision to testify—with a full courtroom waiting for his appearance—he stands alone in between two trees in a long shot which emphasizes both the individual decision he has to make and his separation from Bergman. Wigand has just learned that his deposition could lead to jail time, for Brown and Williamson have filed for a gag order in the state of Kentucky. "I can't seem to find the criteria to decide," he says to Bergman after a few minutes—the word "criteria" here signifying his education and vocabulary and, at the same time, that very education's inability to help him through a confusing and debilitating situation. At this point he gazes to both his right and left: From over Wigand's shoulder, the camera pans right to the Gulf of Mexico, and then left to a cavalcade of police cars waiting to take him to the courtroom. It is an ambiguous set of images: On the one hand, the viewer might read the water as a site of possibility and freedom, and the police as restrictive; Wigand could thus be wondering how his testimony could ever possibly change these fundamental and universal meanings. But Wigand will also rely on the police and other figures of authority to protect him on the way to the courtroom and after his testimony. Wigand seems to recognize this ambiguity as he says: "What's changed . . . since whenever?" As Mann and Spinotti frame Wigand's face, alone in a single stark shot against the overcast sky as he makes the decision to testify, it becomes apparent that any symbolism derived from ocean or police is utterly relative. Wigand may search for a guiding meaning in this landscape, but ultimately the decision is his alone. This emphasis on Wigand's isolation is only furthered in the next scene; after he goes on record in the courtroom, and despite the bravura performances of his attorneys in defending what he has to say, the camera captures him alone in the frame, in front of the room.

Lisa Gerrard's operatic musical piece "Sacrifice" appears twice in this film. It is first cued in the shot in which Wigand sits alone in the courtroom, after his testimony, and it continues over a series of shots and scenes. In an exterior night scene Wigand returns to the same landscape where he first made his decision to testify, and this time both he and Bergman are figured together in the same frame; viewers are invited to read the shot as a moment of triumph in which Wigand has finally moved outside of the strictures of Brown and Williamson and also outside the boundaries of his own social background, developing a friendship with a man markedly different—and more politically progressive—than himself. These shots also foreground another striking use of weather, as the riverside breeze emphasizes the character's movement from the inside to the outside. Gerrard's piece continues briefly on the soundtrack as Bergman moves inside in the next scene, editing the Wigand piece at CBS; it is a moment of temporary triumph for the journalist, whose story is finally coming together.

At the end of this scene "Sacrifice" fades in again on the soundtrack, as the police drive Wigand back home across the Kentucky border. The wide range of emotional response welcomed by Gerrard's piece accompanies a similarly polysemic image in this sequence. When Wigand looks out the window as the driver takes the exit for Louisville, he sees an abandoned car on fire in the middle of a field; Gerrard's music reaches its peak as he gazes at this burning mass of metal, plastic, and rubber, which might seem to signify the destruction of one of *The Insider*'s signifiers of isolation (earlier in the film Bergman and Wigand secretly converse with one another inside Wigand's car, which is parked near the Ohio River in a decaying postindustrial locale as deserted as the one in which this burning car is found). Viewers might also read this automobile in flames as a product of major corporations figuratively destroyed after Wigand's searing testimony (in this implicit critique *The Insider* is at its most covertly and self-reflexively radical, for the automobile is surely one of the most celebrated products in American culture and also an object from which Mann has derived many stunning and pleasurable aesthetic effects in nearly all of his films). But the car signifies yet more potential meanings: An automobile (the Audi seen earlier in the film) is indeed an emphasized possession of Wigand's, one of many material and financial supports which keep his family afloat and one of many which are now threatened after his decision to testify. Indeed, in the signifier's perhaps most melancholic signified, Wigand himself also serves as an equivalent to the burning car: a human being abandoned in capitalism, the embodied form of so much industrial rubbish dumped aside by corporations. Triumph and despair are thus figured very closely in these shots, and it is suggested that any truly progressive political action within American systems comes at a great and irrevocable personal cost. This idea is further emphasized in the scene that immediately follows, in which Wigand discovers that Liane has left their home, taking the children with her. As Gerrard's music now fades out on the soundtrack, we realize that although Wigand has forever moved outside of old boundaries, he now also has to face new ones which draw him further and further inside his own mind as the film's final hour unfolds.

Wigand remains important to the final act of the film, but Pacino's Bergman commands most of the screen time as *The Insider* reaches its conclusion: The character becomes the journalism film's outlaw hero in the manner of Wigand, as he subverts his company's official practices and crusades to get the full version of Wigand's *60 Minutes* interview on the air. The meaning of the relationships between Bergman and his associates changes throughout the final hour of the film, associations expressed through dialogue and the placement of characters in the mise-en-scène. During Bergman's, Hewitt's, and Wallace's first encounter with CBS's lawyer Helen Caparelli, who advises them that CBS could be sued by the Brown and Williamson company if the Wigand interview is aired, Bergman is sitting close to Wallace and farther away from Hewitt, who will be the first of three to capitulate to corporate demands. The absurdity Bergman perceives in the ensuing conversation with Caparelli also highlights his outlaw status, in his (understandable) inability to comprehend the double-talk of the lawyer:

Caparelli: I've retained outside council . . . on a segment, I might add, that's already rife with problems.

Bergman: What does that mean? "Rife with problems"?

Caparelli: I'm told unusual promises were made to Wigand.

Bergman: No, only that we would hold the story until it was for him . . .

Caparelli [interrupts]: And I'm told there are questions as to our star witness's veracity . . . Our standards have to be higher than anyone else's because we are the standard for everyone else.

Bergman: As a standard, I'll hang with, is this guy telling the truth?

Caparelli: Well, with tortious interference I'm afraid the greater the truth, the greater the damage.

Bergman [pause]: Come again?

Caparelli: They own the information he's disclosing. The truer it is, the greater the damage to them. If he lied, he didn't disclose the information, then the damages are smaller.

Bergman [pregnant pause]: Is this *Alice in Wonderland*?

Bergman questions the insidious linguistic play of the lawyer, expressing outright bafflement at her words, and wonders if he hasn't fallen down Wonderland's rabbit hole. The lawyer's language—using what is in this case a menacing "we" in place of the interests of a multibillion dollar corporation—also threatens, as Jean-Baptiste Thoret has pointed out in his reading of the film, to make any distinction between "inside" and "outside" within corporate American society utterly meaningless.[15] This dialogue between Bergman and Caparelli is punctuated by a close-up of Pacino's face, the first of many close shots of the character in the final act of the film, all of which point to his growing role as a self-determined (although isolated) outlaw hero of the journalism film genre, both working within and traversing the confines of a massive corporation.

This division between Bergman and the corporate executives continues in the next scene, in which CBS vice president Eric Kluster (Stephen Tobolowsky) demands an alternative cut of Bergman's story, without Wigand's interview. An over-the-shoulder view of Bergman listening to Kluster literally beheads the executive through the framing of the shot, suggesting the facelessness of this particular businessman (a counterpoint to the intense close-ups of Pacino which pepper the rest of the film). Hewitt sides with Kluster, prompting a grand, bravura line from Pacino: "Are you a businessman, or are you a newsman?" When Wallace then makes his initial decision to toe the corporate line, Pacino and Christopher Plummer are placed at opposite ends of the widescreen frame, which makes clear the distance now between them because of Wallace's stark, scene-ending statement: "I'm with Don [Hewitt] on this one." The immediate close-shot of Bergman following this line of dialogue once again suggests his isolation within the company.

While Pacino's outlaw hero makes valiant efforts to get Wigand's interview on the air, Wigand himself is drawn further and further into the isolation of his own mind. In other words, he begins to feel the personal consequences of the journalism film's outlaw heroics in the postmodern age. His marriage having disintegrated, he spends most of his time in the same Louisville hotel in which he first met Bergman, grading papers, looking disheveled, and staring out the hotel window at the Brown and Williamson offices across the street. When the edited version of Bergman's story airs on *60 Minutes*, Wigand's isolation reaches an apex. As he listens to Mike Wallace explain on television why the piece cannot reveal the name or show the face of the tobacco insider, the camera cuts in close on Wigand. Later in this scene, a very small portion of the interview appears on the broadcast, but with Wigand's face blacked out and his voice disguised. Immediately after this moment, the film cuts to Wigand in an extreme close-up shot with a telephoto lens: all space between him and the background painting on the hotel wall has been eliminated. Later, after the segment airs, Bergman attempts to call Wigand in the hotel room, but the insider is now totally inside of himself: a subtle visual effect morphs the painting on the hotel wall into a real-life fresco of Wigand's children playing in the backyard, while the hazy, atmospheric music on the soundtrack increases in volume. This hallucination of sorts illustrates the distance between Wigand and his children, the price he has paid for placing his knowledge on a public record that has, ironically, not reached the public.

Mann emphasizes the isolation that affects both Wigand and Bergman as the film nears its conclusion. Wigand's difficult situation is emphasized when, after the interview airs, Bergman calls Wigand on the hotel phone, violently interrupting his hallucination; Mann here contrasts the narrow haunt in which Wigand has sheltered himself to Bergman's upper-class Cape Cod home. But Bergman's beautiful surroundings, as presented to us in the frame, no longer seem expansive; Bergman too seems to have lost everything.

Wigand, who is now reduced to living out of a hotel room, is apart from his family, while Bergman, standing knee-deep in the ocean after their telephone conversation, has literally lost stable ground upon which to stand. Later, while in Montana researching another story, Bergman peers out a window and sees a discarded trailer rusting under a heap of snow. This image recalls the most melancholic potential meaning of the polysemic burning car seen earlier in the film, and suggests a realization on Bergman's part that both he and Wigand have been cast aside by the corporations they worked for.

During the airing of the truncated interview the viewer also sees shots of Mike Wallace listening, watching, and reflecting upon his own image on television, reflection which apparently prompts his change in heart later in the film when he sides with Bergman's wishes to air the full story. When this full story does finally air—only after the *Wall Street Journal* and the *New York Times* publish stories about CBS having caved in to corporate demands—Lisa Gerrard's operatic "Sacrifice" reappears on the soundtrack, once again striking mixed emotional tones. The images in the ensuing montage complement this ambiguity. Wigand watches as his children are finally able to see their father share his useful information about the tobacco industry on television, clearly a fulfilling personal moment for the character. But as Bergman sits in an airport restaurant watching the story, we're invited to become skeptical as to the effects Wigand will ultimately have on the world: The people surrounding Bergman in the airport are interested in this important story to varying degrees, and some not at all.[16]

Immediately after the segment airs, Bergman gets a tip about a police raid on the Unabomber's hideout in Helena, Montana. The expressive use of weather throughout *The Insider*—weather that often takes the form of rain, which is emphasized as a metaphor for inner anguish—shifts to icy, snowy, white images in many of the shots representing Montana. The obvious and literal meaning here, that Bergman and Wigand have both been left out in the cold, also prompts the viewer to notice a slightly contrapuntal significance to the narrative content of these images: Bergman is quite successful and efficient in nabbing the Unabomber scoop out in Montana, which melancholically suggests that the only way for a journalist with integrity to accomplish good and meaningful work is to stay firmly outside of the corporate structure. Ironically, the Unabomber story also functions, for the image-consuming world, as a reason to forget Wigand's own *60 Minutes* interview. This abrupt shift to yet another transient news item reinforces the one thing Wigand feared earlier in the film: that his public testimony on television will not serve as the catalyst for a paradigmatic shift in public thinking but will rather become little more than a bit of voyeurism which evaporates once the next headline has pushed it out of view.

Bergman himself carries no illusions at this point. The ambivalence of *The Insider* is punctuated by the very end of the film, in which Bergman tells Mike Wallace he has quit his job at CBS. Bergman, a product of a messy but thriving modern marriage, perhaps recognizes from experience what Wigand has forever lost when he tells Wallace, in a statement Bergman makes to defend his choice to leave the company, that "what got broken here doesn't go back together again." We see Bergman leave the CBS office building for the final time: Sunshine greets him, but lest the viewer be too tempted to think Bergman has finally retreated from the dark effects of corporate structures, he raises his coat's hood in defense against the cold weather, a gesture in counterpoint to the sunlight flooding the frame. The image of the revolving doors, which blur the distinction between inside and outside, appears one final time as a motif, once again suggesting that although Bergman has made his exit from the brick-and-mortar corporate structure, the influence of corporate media will continue to hold sway outside the walls of the company building. The camera itself remains inside CBS, perhaps Mann's admission that, as a Hollywood filmmaker, he can never place himself wholly outside; the camera pans away from Bergman, and the screen fades to black. This is a remarkably ambivalent coda, in the tradition of all of Mann's films, and as subtly unsettling an ending as any Hollywood film is likely to offer.

The Insider is a film which cannot be read coherently without the very careful complicity of its viewers: when experiencing Mann's work one needs both visual critical capacities and sensitivities to derive meaning from the richly textured frames which comprise his films. Its poor box-office performance may suggest that media saturation itself has made it impossible for an audience to see as distinguished a film that pivots around an implicit critique and investigation into the plethora of images that surrounds us at every turn. In any event, *The Insider* remains, almost a decade after its initial release, Mann's most accomplished and searing work, and one of the most important films Hollywood produced in the 1990s.

NOTES

1. Michael Sragow, "All the Corporations' Men," *Salon.com*, http://www.salon.com/ent/col/sraq/1999/11/04/mann (accessed November 11, 2004).

2. See, in particular, Herbert Marcuse, *One-Dimensional Man: Studies in the Ideology of Advanced Society* (Boston: Beacon Press, 1964).

3. See Sragow.

4. Although the following description of the incidents surrounding Bergman's *60 Minutes* story is largely re-created in the film, I have been assisted by two sources in my description of this "true story." See David Blum, *Tick . . . Tick . . . Tick: The Long*

Life and Turbulent Times of 60 Minutes (New York: HarperCollins, 2004), 205–15, and Matthew C. Ehrlich, *Journalism in the Movies* (Urbana: University of Illinois Press, 2004), 141–143.

5. Marie Brenner, "The Man Who Knew Too Much," *Vanity Fair* (May 1996).

6. Quoted in Ehrlich, *Journalism in the Movies*, 142.

7. Jean-Baptiste Thoret, "The Aquarium Syndrome: On the Films of Michael Mann," *Senses of Cinema*, http:www.sensesofcinema.com/contents/01/19/mann.html (accessed November 15, 2004).

8. Thoret, "Aquarium Syndrome."

9. Ehrlich has suggested that all films about journalism typically pivot around "outlaw heroes" and "outlaw villains," but that in *The Insider* Bergman and Wigand "begin as official, professional types. Corporate malfeasance thrust them outside and transforms them into outlaw heroes. They successfully fight to tell the truth. . . ." See Ehrlich, *Journalism*, 142–43.

10. See Ehrlich, *Journalism*, 8; he cites Robert B. Ray, *A Certain Tendency of the American Cinema* (Princeton, N.J.: Princeton University Press, 1985), 58–63.

11. Ehrlich, *Journalism*, 142–43.

12. Nick James, "No Smoking Gun," *Sight and Sound* 10, no. 3 (March 2000): 15.

13. Christopher Sharrett, "Michael Mann: Elegies on the Post-Industrial Landscape," *Fifty Contemporary Filmmakers*, ed. Yvonne Tasker (London: Routledge, 2002), 261.

14. Robin Wood, *Hitchcock Film Revisited, rev. ed.* (New York: Columbia University Press, 2002), 110–11.

15. Thoret, "Aquarium Syndrome."

16. This point about the shot in the airport is also made in Sharrett, "Michael Mann: Elegies," 261.

Chapter Eight
Ali

As one of the most important icons in sports and popular culture in the twentieth century, Muhammad Ali is a daunting figure for any filmmaker (or, for that matter, any artist in any medium) to accurately and sensitively render. For Michael Mann, the significance of representing Ali was doubly challenging. Not only did the director have the fighter's legend to contend with, he also ventured into his first experiences with the biopic genre—as a white filmmaker, none the less, portraying the life of an African American cultural figure. Mann, as we have seen, is certainly familiar with the telling of so-called true stories, but never before had he obligated himself to telling the story of such a well-known, celebrated individual.

Although a previous Muhammad Ali biopic, *The Greatest* (Tom Gries and Monte Helleman, 1977) starred Ali himself, Mann's *Ali* is part of a later cycle of biopic films which came to prominence in the 1990s. During that decade a rising focus on North American cultural figures and "a marked increase in attention to the lives of people of colour" expanded the genre.[1] Such films included *Malcolm X* (Spike Lee, 1992, with Denzel Washington); *What's Love Got to Do With It* (Brian Gibson, 1993, with Angela Bassett as Tina Turner); *Geronimo: An American Legend* (Walter Hill, 1993, with Wes Studi); *Selena* (Gregory Nava, 1997, with Jennifer Lopez); and *Men of Honor* (George Tillman Jr., 2000, with Cuba Gooding Jr. as Carl Brashear).[2] All of these films, as is necessary in the construction of any biopic, elide various details from the depiction of each subject's life. In each instance of the genre, of course, the elisions take different forms, and for certain reviewers *Ali* simply removed too much and explained too little. *Variety*'s Todd McCarthy noted that "just about everything Mann has chosen to present is valid, substantial, and convincing, but by the end, the feeling persists that while certain essences have been grasped, only part of the story has been told."[3] A *Film Quarterly* review remarked that "the Ali [Mann] proceeds to give us is the one-dimensional version we already know from TV and magazines, and this isn't even intact. Instead of adding depth to this image, Mann's *Ali* takes an Exacto knife to it. Here is a case in which less is less."[4]

But at the beginning of the creative process behind *Ali* there was, intentionally, too much material. The writers of the original script, Stephen J. Rivele and Christopher Wilkinson (collaborators with Oliver Stone on the 1996 biopic *Nixon*, and writers of hitherto unproduced screenplays about Joe DiMaggio, Martin Luther King, Harry Houdini, and Ludwig von Beethoven) initially wrote more than was necessary for a standard feature-length film. According to Rivele, he and Wilkinson set out to craft a large script from which the film's eventual director could shape a final structure:

> We basically covered Ali's life from 1960 to the present time. Michael chose to focus on a ten-year period, from 1964 to 1974, and that's because what interested Michael was not so much Ali's spiritual journey as his sociological significance. He selected that twelve-year period and focused on the relationship between Ali's career and his religious transformation and the social context in which that occurred. That was always our intention—to create a large structure from which the ultimate director could select the vision of Ali that he wanted to portray.[5]

The events that Mann and co-screenwriter Eric Roth choose to depict in *Ali* begin with the young Cassius Clay's first fight with Sonny Liston in 1964 and end with Muhammad Ali's infamous knockout of the heavily favored George Foreman in the so-called Rumble in the Jungle fight in Zaire in 1974. Along the way the final script includes, as Rivele suggests, at least partial examinations of the monolithic social institutions—such as the Nation of Islam and the American government—which attempted to circumscribe the revolutionary aspects of Ali's cultural agency.

In a sense, then, this particular structure emphasized, at least in part, the solitary and antiheroic existential quest conducted by the protagonist against the backdrop of a sometimes overwhelming social context, a framework present in nearly every Mann film and especially prevalent in *Thief*, *Heat*, *The Insider*, *Collateral*, and *Miami Vice*. But the themes in Mann's work are derived, in their archetypal forms, from the genres through which he traverses; as we have seen, *Thief* and *Heat* dealt with their individualistic characters in ways that recalled the gangster and crime genres, and in *The Insider* both Jeffrey Wigand and Lowell Bergman are types of journalism-film characters before they are anything more specific. Likewise, with *Ali* Mann would inherit genre iconography and themes from the history of the biopic and boxing-film genres. The story of a "great individual" is indeed an expected trope of the biopic, but the boxing film also presents individuals who seek greatness. Boxing films often feature storylines that emphasize a character's movement from "chump to champ" and emphasize the boxer's struggle "against gangster pressure . . . and the need to choose between the fight game and the love of a good woman."[6] Although the young Cassius Clay is far from chump status at the beginning of *Ali* (the film begins with his championship victory over Sonny Liston), Mann's film transposes a number of other boxing-film tropes to *Ali*. The threat of the gangsters in the traditional boxing film finds its equivalent figures in *Ali* in the foreboding menace of both The Nation of Islam and the United States government. The film often situates each of Ali's three wives as concerned with both the boxer's well-being in the ring and in his business dealings outside of it, which often leads to conflicts between Ali's public and personal personas, between the "fight game and the love of a good woman." Ali never chooses between boxing and personal relationships in the film, though, because he refuses to separate the two of them. What is public for Ali is often also deeply personal, as Paul Arthur has suggested: "Ali's most intimate, self-defining human interactions occur in the ring . . . in Mann's vision, the boxing ring operates as a forum or corrida for the tentative reconciliation of Ali's public and private identities."[7]

If genre inherently determines at least part of *Ali*'s structure, it is Mann's stylistic approach to the subject matter that ultimately generates the film's meaning. In this, Paul Arthur identifies one potential conflict in Mann directing the story of a real person: The auteur's typical forms and themes may not necessarily be the best fit for telling the story of a real human being. As I have suggested, in *Ali* the boxer often emerges as another one of Mann's individualistic protagonists, attempting to affect some sort of change in the face of contingency. Would such auteurist concerns interfere with the artistic obligation to accurately relay the meaning of Ali's life? As Arthur suggestively writes:

> Slipping deftly between familiar highlights and a dense backdrop of interpersonal allegiances—handlers, wives, influential outsiders—Mann revamps a dominant theme under-girding his previous films: the opposing psychic tugs of individual autonomy and devitalizing social encumbrance. It is as if one of his patented existential loners were struggling to emerge from Ali's hyper-extroverted personality.[8]

Arthur makes clear that *Ali* walks a precarious line between grafting the expected Mann theme of the isolated individual onto a story about a "hyper-extroverted personality." In Arthur's view, Mann's treatment resulted in a dour Ali: "He seems to be having less fun and taking less pure pleasure in the spectacle of his own celebrity than in any previous account of the Ali legend."[9] Does there exist, then, beneath *Ali*'s earnest attempt to portray one period in the life of a real individual, conceptions and character constructs which emerge not from the figure's life but from Mann's previous work? In other words, what can the auteur tell us about another historical person?

To answer this question, we must look at precisely how Ali is represented in the film's aesthetic and how that aesthetic cues us to understand both him and the social context in which he lived. Auteurism—and its implicit concern with the agency of creative individuals—paves the way for a discussion of how the director inflects his use of genre iconography and tropes with a style that opens up new formally generated meanings. A theme of this critical study has been Mann's inflection, and occasional transcendence, of genre through style: Stock frameworks and tropes are often employed in his films only to then be refigured in a vast number of intricate ways through a very singular aesthetic. And while for some critics Mann's style is an intrusion into the telling of Ali's "true story," the director's formal technique—and the very subtle and inherently reflexive ways in which his technique is foregrounded *as* technique in *Ali*—ultimately generates a specificity of complicated meaning not ultimately reducible to classical auteurism's stylistic or thematic signatures (even if Ali is figured, at least in part, as an existential loner).

In crafting this aesthetic, Mann and cinematographer Emmanuel Lubezki, as well as the production designer John Myhre, were invested in articulating an accurate mise-en-scène that reflected the actual surrounding environments in which Ali lived and worked. The contribution of Ali's personal photographer, Howard Bingham (played by Jeffrey Wright in the film), was invaluable in this regard: He contributed a massive collection of photographs for Mann and Lubezki to study and was on the set to actively determine how the film would look.[10] Such attention to detail, however, does not "suture" us into a complete cinematic simulacrum of the past, but rather crafts fleeting, impressionistic images and sounds that are also overtly deliberate reconstructions. Scholar Anna Dzenis, who has also remarked upon Mann's use of a type of cinematic impressionism in *Ali*, suggests that one's prior knowledge of the boxer and his context is likely to deeply affect one's understanding of the film, despite the filmmakers' attention to realistic visual detail: "This sense of a deliberately constructed film may trouble audiences who expect a straightforward biography . . . But what is most compelling and extraordinary about this film is exactly this impressionistic re-telling of the past."[11] Dzenis goes on to note that "Mann is certainly interested in the world that Ali lived in, but he is even more interested in that world from Ali's perspective."[12]

One might also add to this observation the fact that Mann and his collaborators are interested in portraying "the world from Ali's perspective" in a way which refuses an indulgence in a reverence for the past and which generally avoids pseudo-documentary technique. "An exercise in nostalgia" is indeed that which the director deliberately wanted to avoid.[13] Instead, the film moves back and forth, in subtle rhythms, from a very carefully calculated and realistically accurate visual depiction of Ali's surroundings to an emphasis on the audience's experience of these representations as immediate impressions. This strategy does not distance the audience from the film emotionally, although Mann, in particular shots, does occasionally foreground the construction and subsequent cultural dissemination of images. But nor does the film ask for our indulgence in excessively manipulative sentiment; it instead invites our emotional and intellectual involvement in a more complex and intricate manner.

As Dzenis has suggested, Mann's later films, beginning with *Heat* but especially prevalent in *The Insider* and *Ali*, have retained a broadly expressive mise-en-scène style while at the same time inflecting that approach more overtly with moments of mannerism.[14] As suggested at earlier points in this study, expressive mise-en-scène loosely retains the idea of the image as the vehicle for narrative, but this style is no longer solely the self-effacing communicator of narrative, and instead becomes an approach which generates its meanings quite broadly, across many shots and sequences. The mannerist images in *Ali*, meanwhile, unlike the stylistically expressive moments in the film, are not vehicles for narrative at all: They are instead, as Dzenis has suggested, impressions, visual renderings of the contingent and the ephemeral moment which do not yield any particular or overt conceptual meaning. As discussed in my introduction, critics of cinematic mannerism or excessiveness are quick to label it as a self-indulgent style concerned only with itself, as a kind of self-reflexivity that ultimately goes nowhere. Such a filmic image, however, invites us to relax our interpretive reflexes and engage the image in another way; this idea is in the foreground of a film such as *Ali*, which is not exclusively mannerist. The expressive in *Ali* insures a structural backbone to the film—a thematic and aesthetic narrative consistency that allows the film to cohere as a meaningful story and which throws into relief those moments of style which are presented in a different manner—while the mannerist draws us into the film not through an organization of analyzable meaning but through the image of a contingent, fleeting moment of perception. This approach is supported, in part, through *Ali*'s handheld camera work, which often allows the camera to function as something close to an independent sense-agent. Cinematographer and camera operator Emmanuel Lubezki says that "*Ali* is about 99 percent steadi-cam and handheld work," which only increases our sense of the aesthetic's immediacy.[15]

Ali's narrative and stylistic strategy is thus very far away from classical mise-en-scène technique, and the film provides the best argument for Mann as a postclassical director. The story developed in *Ali* is crafted very broadly and is evoked, as in all of Mann's films, not so much through exposition or shot-to-shot decoupage than through overarching aesthetic designs. When government agents appear in the first act of the film, following the trail of both Ali and Malcolm X (Mario Van Peebles), their presence is never explained, and one has to infer over the course of a number of shots (inflected with foreboding music scoring the images) that they are from the FBI. One's own knowledge of history might make these connections more immediate, but on the level of the film itself Mann has developed his style of expressive and mannerist aesthetics to the level at which it challenges the way viewers perceive the meanings of the film's narrative. Later in this chapter I will examine how some of the specific and most important events in *Ali*—Ali's rejection of Malcolm X in Africa, the subsequent assassination of Malcolm X, and the utterance of Ali's famous comments on the Vietnam War and racism in America—are felt more on the overarching level of composition and editing than in the carefully modulated, shot-to-shot development of a story. If film viewers are to understand *Ali* as anything more than simply history sliced apart with "an Exacto knife," one should further analyze, in specific examples from the film, how this style functions, and how such style demands that we make associations within and across scenes. Viewers also need to intermittently relax the urge to interpret everything seen on the screen, a generally sound viewing approach to any Michael Mann film.

The opening montage of *Ali* deserves an extended analysis, for every theme present in the whole of the film is foreshadowed in its carefully constructed beginning. *Ali* begins with the sound of crowd chatter. A voice announces: "Ladies and gentlemen, right now we'd like to introduce the star of our show. The young man you've all been waiting for . . . how 'bout it for Sam Cooke!" The viewer can hear, as the main titles of the film unfold against a black screen, a drumbeat and then the loud applause of a crowd welcoming Cooke to the stage on the soundtrack. This introduction is timed in conjunction with the appearance of the name "Will Smith"—and after that, the name of the film and its subject, *Ali*—on the opening credits, implicitly suggesting that this film will be about Will Smith's development as an actor and a star and also a story about African American celebrity in general, given that Ali, Smith, and the popular singer Cooke are all obliquely figured both visually and aurally in this very brief moment. In Mann's images Cooke emerges less as a full personality (he only appears—and then very briefly—during one other moment later in the film) and more as an abstraction of the fame that will soon greet the young Cassius Clay. The fact that other black celebrities and important cultural figures appear fleetingly throughout the story to varying degrees—including Maya Angelou, Malcolm X, and Jim Brown—only serves to further emphasize the idea of cultural celebrity and its associations with the young fighter. Of course, the phrase "A Michael Mann film" precedes Will Smith's credit and thus, as Anna Dzenis has pointed out, *Ali* "reminds us this is a Michael Mann film and that his story is also being told" through the aforementioned developments, shifts, and mutations in his film style that occur throughout the film.[16]

The film doesn't open on an image of Cooke in the club, but instead begins with a brief shot (in high-definition digital video) of Ali jogging through the Chicago streets on February 24, 1964, the night before his first fight with Sonny Liston, thus establishing the immediate present from which all of the subsequent images in the opening montage derive their relationship. Subsequent shots of Cooke (David Elliott) singing in a nightclub and Ali training are all together a part of this present. Accompanying shots of Ali's childhood, Ali meeting his future assistant trainer Drew "Bundini" Brown (Jamie Foxx, in a celebrated performance), and Ali's father Cassius Clay Sr. (Giancarlo Esposito) arranging business deals, all function as sudden flashbacks, woven within this string of images to suggest that the past is always part of the present experience for Ali. These moments, taken together, broadly convey that racism in America, regardless of progress made over many decades, is a prevalent social condition—one that emerges both in single instances and across time and in memory—that the fighter must struggle against. This meaning is emphasized in the quick cuts in the montage itself, which seem to find a diegetic association in repeated shots of Ali practicing with a punching bag, as Clifford Thompson has suggested: "In the training scenes, we see a frontal close-up of the boxer as he hits a punching bag; the bag flies back and forth in front of him, making that famously pretty face appear as it would on the rapidly moving images of an old-fashioned film reel."[17]

One of the important themes introduced in this montage is Ali's encounter with images. Ali biographer Gerald Early has suggested that Ali was not an intellectual, but Mann's film suggests that Ali had an almost preternatural understanding and relationship to images from a very early age.[18] This interaction with images suggests that the film's consideration of the fighter finds the label "intellectual"—which perhaps suggests a certain degree of disembodied, unpragmatic, idealist speculation, bereft of the very embodied and passionate present of the vibrant, vital Ali—inherently limiting and invalidating too large a portion of human thought processes. At the beginning of the film, the viewer sees brief shots detailing Ali's encounter with particular images. He watches his father paint the figure of a white, blonde-haired, blue-eyed Jesus Christ. In a boardroom meeting with several white businessmen (who are never figured in the same shot as the fighter), the young Cassius Clay sits in the background behind his father, and looks up at framed photographs of champion thoroughbreds. While walking to the colored section at the back of a bus, he sees a newspaper headline screaming at him: "Nation Shocked at Lynching of Chicago Youth," with an image of the murdered and disfigured Emmett Till placed beneath. We do not hear his reaction to a particular image in a given shot; his understanding of its meaning is communicated to us in later scenes. In a conversation with Malcolm X later in the film, Ali recalls the photograph of Emmett Till he saw on the bus. When he confronts his father about changing his name from Cassius Clay to Muhammad Ali, he says he resents the financial support from white businessmen that his father has arranged: "I ain't one of their thoroughbreds." And later Ali wonders aloud what the white, blonde, and blue-eyed Jesus ever did for him during his argument with his father regarding his conversion to Islam. The way in which we have to rely on our own memories of previous shots to generate these associations across many scenes, rather than in an analysis of a single scene broken down through classical decoupage, emphasizes both the sophistication of Mann's broadly expressive mise-en-scène and the importance of memory and image analysis as themes both within the film and in Muhammad Ali's own life. Importantly, Ali does not assign a meaning to these images as he encounters them: Their contents become a crucial part of his very existence, and his thorough understanding of their greater implications arises only at moments in his own experience when such meaning becomes pertinent to his life. It is this powerful understanding of images which contributes in great part to Ali's ability to move outside of the strictures of American institutions—organizations which include his own family and his father, who is figured in all of the aforementioned shots—and critique them in his flamboyant, expressive way; in this manner Ali might remind us of the protagonists of *The Insider*.

The Insider was indeed the film in which Mann's depiction of isolated men reached a degree of hopeful collectivity after the more despairing visions of *Thief* and *Heat*, for both Bergman and Wigand must work together to get valuable information about the tobacco industry on television. Ultimately, of course, Bergman and Wigand remained separate individuals, but the gesture toward a productive social partnership, at least in the context of Mann's filmography, was significant. Although *Ali* suggests that relationships—with men or women—were often difficult for the boxer, and that he often emphasized his self-reliance in making decisions, the large cast of supporting characters throughout the film seems to implicitly figure a sort of readymade, collective support system for the boxer. Certain scenes including both Jamie Foxx's Bundini Brown and Ali's trainer Angelo Dundee (Ron Silver) accurately suggest that Ali's entourage often had a hand in crafting the verbal play he was so famous for in his interviews and television appearances.[19]

A particularly compelling moment in the opening montage suggests the particular influence Bundini had in crafting Ali's image. It is clearly a moment that Ali has internalized, for it is a flashback: We can hear the jump rope Ali is training with on the soundtrack, a sound from the diegetic present, as the flashback unravels. As Bundini approaches Ali from the left side of the frame, the boxer sits on the far right side, with a television placed in between them. Foxx makes a moving speech:

> *Bundini*: I'm called Bundini. Rhymes with Houdini. He was a Jew too. Some people call me Fastest Black, some call me Daddy Mac. Gave Sugar Ray Robinson my power for seven years, my voodoo, my magic. Now Shorty done sent me here to work for you.
>
> *Ali*: Who's Shorty?
>
> *Bundini* (looking upward): I call him Shorty. Call him Shorty because he like 'em circumcised, original people, like Moses. And I was a babe in a basket too. Born on the doorstep with a note across my chest that read, "you do the best you can for him, world." I wanna be your inspiration, your motivator, in your corner. Can I be in your corner, young man?

This is one of several virtuoso moments in Foxx's performance (perhaps the only scene that rivals it is when Bundini admits to Ali halfway through the film that he has sold the championship belt for five hundred dollars). Foxx's approach is more subtly intricate than, for example, Al Pacino's occasional scenery-chewing in *Heat*, which suggests that Foxx is the perfect type of actor for Mann's aesthetic, which places an importance on subtle inflections within an epic vision. Bundini's voodoo and magic involve helping Ali create a number of famous lines—including the most famous of all, "fly like a butterfly, sting like a bee"—which come to represent the symbolic ways in which Ali is understood in popular culture. The eloquent manner in which Foxx steals every scene he is in, even when playing opposite the star Will Smith, serves as something of a metaphor for the way in which Ali's own celebrity could never be divorced from the individuals behind-the-scenes who helped craft his public persona.

The first appearance of Ali's professional photographer in this montage, Howard Bingham, further suggests how Bingham, Bundini, and Dundee were important in crafting—sometimes literally—Ali's image, and how Mann and cinematographer Emmanuel Lubezki are also implicitly inscribed as part of this support system. In a series of four shots depicting the group sitting in a car this idea is developed. Bundini sits in the driver's seat, and looks behind him as the camera pans to the backseat with Dundee sitting on the left side. The film then cuts to a frontal close-up of Bingham taking a photograph. In the subsequent shot the viewer sees the subject of Bingham's camera: Ali. He is placed on the left side of the frame, with a flood of light coming in from the car's rear window. The frame itself resembles a photograph in its nearly static composition, but what the film itself shows us is not the corresponding point-of-view shot of what Bingham would see through his own lens. Through this change of angle, Mann and Lubezki are figured both within the film itself, with Bingham as a surrogate, and also outside of it, in that the image we see on the screen is not a diegetic creation. What is admitted very subtly in this chain of shots is that the film will both examine the dissemination of Ali's image in culture and take part in that dissemination (in a formally innovative way).

As Sam Cooke's "Bring It on Home" fades out, the montage ends; the song's conclusion is timed to Ali's arrival at a weigh-in for his first fight with Sonny Liston, suggesting that this is the moment in which Ali's celebrity attains an importance and currency similar to that of Cooke's. And if the opening salvo of *Ali* works to centrifugally draw a number of significant impressions, time periods, characters, ideas, and events together toward a single nexus—the diegetic present, in this case February 1964—then the subsequent depiction of the twenty-two year-old Cassius Clay's victory over Liston distills what would otherwise be a single grand spectacle into a montage that both analyzes the fight at a distance and revels in it emotionally (and almost physically) from the closest of possible angles.

The very first sights and sounds in this reproduction of the Clay-Liston fight clue us into the filmmakers' aesthetic strategy. On a shot-to-shot level, the fight is legible in its continuity; the boxer's most intricate moves are matched across shots. But on a broader level the sequence also juxtaposes a number of different points of view that, in a kind of back-and-forth rhythm, brings the viewer both into the fight emotionally and allows one to observe it from a distance. As Clay makes his entrance, Howard Cosell (Jon Voight) sits ringside reading an ad for a hair tonic on the radio. Throughout this first fight sequence Cosell's voice is prominent on the soundtrack when the character is himself in the shot, but it is often part of the background soundtrack at a lower level during other shots, registering as more of a sonic impression rather than as a character delivering information to the film's audience. The longest shots in this sequence foreground television cameras, and throughout the fight such shots will reappear periodically as a reminder that what is being shown is both a depiction of the construction of images themselves as well as an image construction that invites an emotional response to a character's predicament. And by the end of this fight sequence, it is clear that such legitimate pathos can quickly be co-opted: The scene is punctuated by an imposing image of Elijah Muhammad (Albert Hall), the leader of the Nation of Islam, watching the young Cassius Clay win the championship on television; throughout the film the Nation will be figured as an institution which takes advantage of Ali's celebrity.

The closest of the close-up shots in this and later fight sequences involved two particularly important techniques. One was the use of Super 35 cameras on *Ali* instead of the standard anamorphic lenses. Anamorphic film cameras are especially heavy, and Lubezki convinced Mann that shooting close-ups during the fight with such cumbersome equipment would have proven impossible; Super 35 thus allowed the director to continue to work in his preferred 2.35:1 aspect ratio with the necessary ease. In other scenes Super 35 cameras would allow for greater on-location dexterity, since most of the film was shot handheld.[20] For the extreme close-ups during the boxing scenes, which captured what it might look like to literally stand in between two fighters during a boxing match, Mann used two miniature cameras designed by Michael McAlister, who "created a rig with two tiny, surveillance-style 'lipstick cameras' that fit into the palm of [Mann's] hand."[21] Although the aspect ratio of each camera was 1.33:1, attaching two of the small cameras side-by-side allowed for the filmmakers to capture enough visual information for the widescreen frame; the footage shot by the two cameras would later be digitally "stitched" (to use McAlister's word) together by McAlister and his technicians into a single 2.35:1 composite image. "Michael made it clear that he was willing to accept slightly lesser quality in order to get the camera into places he otherwise couldn't," McAlister recalls. "He literally held a camera that was smaller than his hand. While Will Smith and the actors playing Ali's opponents were fighting, Michael was dancing around the fight, putting his hand wherever he wanted it to be."[22] Such a technique successfully conveys the impact of the boxer's punches on the body, so much so that *Ali* becomes much more than a film abstractly representing boxing matches; the audience is invited to feel the physical pain of the sport at just one remove through a very immediate and intimate stylistic technique.

The balance of the first forty-five minutes of *Ali* examines Cassius Clay joining the Nation of Islam and changing his name to Muhammad Ali. At this point in history the Nation was working to distance itself from the rhetoric of Malcolm X, and in a conversation with Ali in the film Malcolm reveals that he has been cast out of the Nation. Despite this conflict between Malcolm and the Nation, Ali joins the institution in the next scene and further distances himself from Malcolm X when the two cross paths in Africa. This abandonment of Malcolm marks the first of six moments in the film during which the audience is given an impression of Ali's own interiority through voice-over: Before Ali says to Malcolm X that he "shouldn't have quarreled with the honorable Elijah Muhammad," we hear a voice-over letting us know Ali is contemplating saying those very words aloud. Such technique allows the viewer to consider that while the Nation of Islam exerts tremendous control over Ali's business dealings and public image (a fact that is on display in other scenes), the fighter is also an independent thinker, with a mind that works beyond the grasp of those that might work to co-opt it. This technique is only an occasional strategy, but it does allow Ali's own thoughts to become part of the web of immediate detail that comprises the film. Like certain images, the meaning of these sometimes barely audible voice-overs is not always direct and cleanly apparent; the technique serves to draw viewers into the aesthetic immediacy of the film, rather than communicate a predigested message in an efficient, stylistically economical fashion.

The next hour of the film portrays Ali's refusal to fight in Vietnam, his first two marriages and his growing involvement in the Nation of Islam, and an eventual fight with Joe Frazier. It also depicts the assassination of Malcolm X, suggesting that the Nation of Islam directly ordered the murder (the three assassins were members of the institution). As Malcolm walks into a Manhattan ballroom, with a security guard on either side, the camera follows him from behind as if he were a boxer; but unlike the rhythmic music that often follows Ali into the ring, elegiac strings score Malcolm's arrival. After he is shot, the camera, in a canted angle, captures roughly what the dying Malcolm's point of view might have been at the time. With these techniques Mann both subtly foregrounds his film as an assemblage (the tone is set from the very beginning, and thus we know, assisted by our knowledge of history, that Malcolm will be shot at this moment) in a similar manner to the depiction of the first Ali-Liston fight, but nonetheless viewers are drawn into a close experience of an important event in history.

The same effect is achieved in the next scene and in many others like it throughout the film. After hearing of Malcolm's death on the radio, Ali sits in his car as Sam Cooke's "A Change Is Gonna Come" is nondiegetically cued on the soundtrack. But the version of the song we hear in the film is Al Green's live cover, recorded thirty years after the events depicted in the film, and not Cooke's original. While this musical choice was derided in at least one review which presumably thought the best musical selections would be those which would draw us directly into the time period depicted on screen, *Ali* shows us history through a contemporary construction that has no nostalgic effect or intent.[23] While many historical films use certain types of contemporary music, the deliberate employment of contemporary covers of classic pop songs is a stylistic choice that is distinctive compared to the approach of, for example, Martin Scorsese, who almost always uses only popular music that might plausibly be found in the setting and during the time depicted in his films. But *Ali* rejects this nostalgic suture effect, an effect typical of many biopics. Mann's contemporary musical selection is consistent throughout the entire film; even the opening performance of Sam Cooke's "Bringing It on Home" is a contemporary rerecording by the actor playing Cooke in the film, David Elliott. The meaning of these songs are closely tied into African American experiences of the 1960s and the concomitant fight against institutionalized racism, but by using contemporary variations the songs not only reveal feelings about the past but also indicate the relevance of those feelings to the present.

After Malcolm X's death, Ali's relationship to the Nation of Islam, the American government, and members of his own family and his entourage all become more complicated. As Paul Arthur has suggested, the boxing ring is now figured as a public site for the negotiation of the personal, as in the depiction of the second Ali-Liston fight.[24] Before the fight begins, Ali spends a great deal of time looking out into the audience where his family, his wife, and members of the Nation of Islam sit. The swift victory over Liston that follows seems like an emotional release from these entanglements and, as is true of nearly all Ali's public appearances, a statement of individual personality. Indeed, once Ali leaves the boxing ring his struggle to assert himself begins again: His first marriage is breaking up, a conflict which involves not only disputes between his wife and himself but also disagreements with his father and members of the Nation, who paternalistically assure Ali that the organization will bless the fighter's divorce. The only part of the sequence depicting Ali's experience with divorce is a shot in which Ali is figured alone in a hotel room, with melancholic blue light entering the room through the window; the film thus suggests that Ali, losing control of his personal life, will need to return to the ring and the public eye to continue to resolve these conflicts in his individualistic way.

In a further emphasis of society's encroachment upon—although not total circumscription of—Ali's own agency, the next scene shows us a woman applying makeup to Ali and thus modifying his image for an interview, while a young employee at the network tells Ali that he is to be drafted into the Vietnam War. But it is this conflict that gives the fighter a chance for one of his most important social expressions: his refusal to fight in the war. "If you accept the injunction, your life goes on," one of his lawyers tells him. But Ali refuses the draft; in a shot of Ali standing inside the government building where the injunction takes place, Mann emphasizes the volume of space above the fighter's head (including an imposing image of a strangely menacing American eagle symbol) as if to suggest the oppression weighing down on him. The social and the political here become personal for the character, and the boxing ring continues to be the site in which these conflicts are on public display; immediately after refusing the draft, Ali fights David Terrell and, upon winning, a chorus of boos greets the fighter from the crowd.

Ali's relationship with images in the aftermath of his public announcement that he will not fight in Vietnam is developed in a montage scored to a 2001 cover version of Bob Dylan's "All Along the Watchtower." After a phone conversation with the fighter, Ali's lawyer runs for cover as gunshots ring out around him. It turns out the man shot is Martin Luther King Jr. (LeVar Burton). The assassination is an incident captured in a handful of very quick shots which are just as quickly blended into an impressionistic montage featuring re-created images from around the country of late 1960s political protests and riots. Ali watches these images pass by him and in subsequent shots sees very similar events occurring in his surrounding environments; and while he works out on a roof overlooking a Chicago neighborhood, he sees buildings on fire and hears screaming in the distance. To enhance the immediacy of these moments, high-definition digital video cameras capture Ali in these widescreen 2.35:1 shots on the rooftop, giving a rough, almost documentary-like quality that serves to foreground the expressive and mannered 35mm aesthetic that defines the rest of the film. But in these shots Ali's own vision is also paralleled to the audience's experience of the stylistic events in Mann's film: no immediate reaction or analysis of meaning can come from either Ali's gaze at the burning storefronts or from our own experience of cinema at the very moment we see such things; a viewer can only strive, like Ali in his experience with images and events in the film, to see as much as possible in the immediate moment and to synthesize potential meanings and appropriate reactions at a later time.

Mann's Ali ultimately refuses passivity in light of seeing such images and events; he is inspired by these sensations. His experience in seeing and the associations he makes between images and the social reality he lives in give him a degree of cultural agency. The fighter's relationship to Howard Cosell throws this idea into relief. After visiting his now down-and-out friend Bundini in New York, Ali sits on a subway train. A cut to Elijah Muhammad announcing that Ali has just been banished from the Nation suggests that the fighter is now, like Bundini, at his lowest point. Sitting on the subway, with an electronic remix of Johnny Farmer's "Death Letter" playing on the soundtrack, Ali is being driven more than he is driving himself; in his rejection of Bundini in the previous scene, he has inscribed his own solitude. Indeed, if this were *Thief*, *Heat*, or *Collateral*, the film might have ended with this scene of the isolated Ali on the subway. But what ensues in *Ali* is one of the most optimistic passages in any Michael Mann film. As if to remedy his solitude, in the very next scene Ali approaches Howard Cosell about the possibility of an on-air interview. Cosell is wary, knowing his bosses at ABC are only interested in ratings and that Ali is facing an uphill battle with the American public after refusing the draft. Ali knows the image he will project can attract an audience: He says it will be a "momentous and historic night." The interview follows, in which Ali says that he is no longer interested in boxing because "I got a much bigger contender, a much heavier opponent, I'm fighting the entire U.S. government." But both Cosell and Ali recognize that the boxing ring is the forum in which Ali will enact resolutions of both his personal and public conflicts, and at the conclusion of the interview Ali, in a famous rhyme, makes a challenge to "Smokin'" Joe Frazier. In these scenes both Ali and Cosell seem aware that images are a construction, as their personas on camera are strikingly different from the quieter inflections in their conversations off the set. This friendship echoes the association between Bergman and Wigand in *The Insider*: Ali needs Cosell in order to make and disseminate valuable social meaning and institutional critique through the apparatus of television. Indeed, it is this potentially progressive apparatus that the characters in *The Insider* fight to recover from reactionary corporations.

Throughout the second half of *Ali* optimism about collective cultural agency reverberates. In an unexpectedly moving scene, Ali approaches Joe Frazier (James Toney) about setting up a fight. Frazier offers Ali money, knowing the ex-champion has hit hard times; the two clearly have a close friendship and an awareness of the need for such a connection in the boxing world. Later, Bundini is welcomed back into Ali's entourage, while it is Cosell who lets Ali know that the Supreme Court has overturned a judge's decision to sentence the fighter to five years in prison for refusing service in Vietnam. Despite such partnerships, Ali's social maneuverings do put his personal life into some distress, as his second wife Belinda (Nona M. Gaye) begins to criticize what she sees as his naïve associations with manipulative forces such as the Nation of Islam and, before the Rumble in the Jungle in Africa, with Don King.

Ali loses to Frazier; subsequently, Frazier loses his title to George Foreman. Although Ali wins a close decision over Frazier in a rematch, the concluding hour of *Ali* is concerned with the so-called Rumble in the Jungle fight in Zaire between Ali and Foreman. Here *Ali* covers some of the same material as the documentary *When We Were Kings* (Leon Gast and Taylor Hackford, 1996), but spends a more significant amount of time suggesting the ways in which Ali's cultural image has had a global impact. In one extended montage set to a piece of contemporary African music, Salif Keita's "Tomorrow," Ali runs with a group of children and sees a re-creation of his own image on the sides of a number of brick buildings. Ali does not comment upon or transfix a meaning to the images he sees; he merely looks as he is looked upon by the crowd around him. In one such work of graffiti, the fighter is represented knocking down mechanized instruments and vehicles of industrialized war such as airplanes, tanks, and guns; and in an image that is hard to imagine seeing in the United States, an idealistic African American, Ali, is painted as an imposing, towering figure over much smaller white soldiers. This representation of Ali is found, within the villages, in the context of a number of other cultural artifacts (which are both local and global artifacts; if we look closely we can see radios and two brief Coca-Cola advertisements hanging from buildings in the background of these shots), suggesting the figure of Ali has become part of the expressive grammar of Zaire's people. In this way, the citizens of Zaire are thus figured as what cultural studies scholars might call "textual poachers": they experience the dissemination of Ali's image on television and re-create it to serve their own local meanings.[25]

With these images and Ali's final victory over George Foreman, *Ali* concludes as the most optimistic of all Mann's films. There is a productive tension between individual accomplishment and collective spirit in the final fight. As Ali devises his now-infamous "rope-a-dope" strategy in beating the heavily favored and physically more imposing Foreman, his entourage is wholly unaware of his strategy. But this seemingly individualistic act is inspired in part through Ali's interaction with the African crowd; as he plays to the crowd they in turn chant his name. Before knocking out Foreman, Salif Keita's "Tomorrow" reappears on the soundtrack, associating the fight with Ali's earlier jog with the villagers. And while the final shots of the film proper end with Ali figured as the lone hero, a handful of shots over the end credits show people in Zaire celebrating in the rain after the fight, once again suggesting the positive charge an image in popular culture can inspire. As a producer of cultural images in the 1960s and 1970s, Ali no doubt was able to project possibilities for the future of America, African Americans, and even the world. Although this is an event in the past, a celebrated part of American history, Mann and his collaborators do not figure Ali's triumphs as part of a purely mythical utopian time we can regressively suture ourselves into. In this, the film is a major step forward from the re-creation of America's past in *The Last of the Mohicans*: *Ali*, unlike *Mohicans*, does not function as the lost dream of the existential loners in Mann's other films. It may be set in the past, but as a film, it is clearly happening *now*. If *Ali* succeeds it is because its own images, through a careful counterpoint between historical reconstruction and contemporary aesthetic immediacy, welcome and indeed demand active viewer interaction and understanding.

NOTES

1. Carolyn Anderson and John Lupo, "Hollywood Lives: The State of the Biopic at the Turn of the Century," *Genre and Contemporary Hollywood*, ed. Steve Neale (London: British Film Institute, 2002), 92–93.

2. This list is from Anderson and Lupo, "Hollywood Lives," 93.

3. Todd McCarthy, "No Sweat on Mann-Made *Ali*," *Variety*, December 17, 2001, 35.

4. Clifford Thompson, "*Ali*," *Film Quarterly* 4, no. 55 (Summer 2002): 46.

5. Don Coppola, "Brining Historical Characters to Life: An Interview with Stephen J. Rivele," *Cineaste* 27, no. 2 (Spring 2002): 16.

6. Adrian Wootton, "The Big Hurt," *Sight and Sound* 12, no. 3 (March 2002): 16–17.

7. Paul Arthur, "Lord of the Ring," *Film Comment* 38, no. 1 (January–February 2002): 33.

8. Arthur, "Lord of the Ring," 32.

9. Arthur, "Lord of the Ring," 34.

10. Jay Holben, "Ring Leader," *American Cinematographer* 82, no. 11 (November 2001): 36.

11. Anna Dzenis, "Impressionist extraordinaire: Michael Mann's *Ali*," in *Senses of Cinema*, http://www.sensesofcinema.com/contents/01/19/ali.htm (accessed October 13, 2004).

12. Dzenis, "Impressionist extraordinaire."

13. Michael Mann, Interview, *Ali* website, http:www.spe.sony.com/movies/ali/flash.html (accessed July 19, 2004).

14. Anna Dzenis, "Michael Mann's Cinema of Images," in *Screening the Past* 15, http://www.latrobe.edu.au/screeningthepast/firstrelease/fr0902/adfr14b.html (accessed January 11, 2005).

15. Holben, "Ring Leader," 36–37.

16. Dzenis, "Michael Mann's Cinema of Images."

17. Thompson, "*Ali*," 46.

18. Gerald Early, ed. *The Muhammad Ali Reader*, (New Jersey: Ecco Press, 1998), xv–xvi.

19. David Remnick, in his book on Ali, *King of the World*, quotes Ali's trainer Angelo Dundee: "We all wrote lines here and there." See Remnick, *King of the World* (New York: Random House, 1998), 148.

20. Holben, "Ring Leader," 37.

21. Holben, "Ring Leader," 37.

22. Ron Magid, "A Left-Right Camera Combo," *American Cinematographer* 82, no. 11 (November 2001): 43.

23. Thompson, "*Ali*," 46.

24. Arthur, "Lord of the Ring," 33.

25. See Henry Jenkins, *Textual Poachers: Television Fans & Participatory Culture* (London: Routledge, 1992).

Chapter Nine

Collateral

After crafting the wide cinematic canvas of *Ali*, Michael Mann returned to the small screen in 2002 as the executive producer of the police drama *Robbery Homicide Division*. The show was Mann's first television production in over a decade; its narrative followed an elite group of investigators led by Lieutenant Sam Cole (Tom Sizemore). The rest of the cast included David Cubitt and Barry Shabaka Henley, both of whom had played supporting roles in *Ali*. The show's thirteen episodes were written and directed by a variety of filmmakers, including Ami Canaan Mann, Mann's daughter.[1]

Variety blamed *Robbery Homicide Division*'s lack of success with audiences on the sense of hopelessness that the series often exuded, beginning with a premiere episode in which the main characters failed to solve a murder case.[2] A more obvious explanation for the ratings failure might have been its timeslot in the CBS schedule: It aired on Friday nights against the popular NBC drama *Law and Order: Special Victims Unit*. Ironically, *Robbery Homicide Division* was the brainchild of creator Barry Schindel, who also created the original *Law and Order*. The series eventually showed some promise when it was moved to Saturday nights in November 2002, and appeared to be finally breaking through with audiences when it won its timeslot against ABC's popular *The Agency* on December 7, 2002. Actor Tom Sizemore, however, was arrested for domestic battery on December 11, and CBS cancelled *Robbery Homicide Division* the next day.[3]

If, according to *Variety*, *Robbery Homicide Division* "was at its best with large scale-confrontation and downright hokey when it comes to one-on-one," the show's most lasting contribution to television history was in its cinematography.[4] *Robbery* was shot with high-definition digital video cameras, the same technology used during brief sequences of *Ali*. Cinematographer

Bill Roe, a veteran of other television series such as *The X-Files* and a camera operator on numerous Hollywood films, acknowledged that the technology was perfectly suited for manipulating the colors and lighting of images during on-location shooting through the use of the camera's own internal technology: "From iris pulls to color matrix menus, I've got it all at my fingertips," Roe has said. "We do 360-degree shots all the time, and I'm constantly riding the aperture to keep a good balance and maintain the look we're after. It's great to have all these options close at hand."[5]

The short-lived series would also have important consequences for Mann's film aesthetic. Although a handful of shots in *Ali* were crafted with high-definition digital cameras, nearly all of *Collateral* was shot using such equipment, which included the Thomson Grass Valley Viper FilmStream and the Sony CineAlta.[6] Mann collaborated with two cinematographers on *Collateral*: Paul Cameron, who prepped the film and shot the first three weeks of footage (his previous work includes *Gone in Sixty Seconds* [Dominic Sena, 2000], the short film *The Hire: Beat the Devil* [Tony Scott, 2001], and *Man on Fire* [Tony Scott, 2004]); and Dion Beebe, who eventually replaced Cameron because of creative differences between the cinematographer and the director.[7] (Beebe's credits include *Holy Smoke!* [Jane Campion, 1999], *Charlotte Gray* [Gillian Armstrong, 2001], *Chicago* [Rob Marshall, 2002], *In the Cut* [Jane Campion, 2003], and *Memoirs of a Geisha* [Rob Marshall, 2005]). Mann stressed that the technological choices behind *Collateral* were not made for purposes of economy: Two crews were always present on the set, one that was prepared to shoot in digital and the other that was ready to shoot certain sequences on 35mm film.[8] Digital video created images of a nighttime Los Angeles with a greater sensitivity to available source light than was possible with 35mm equipment; the twinkling, hazy lights in the background of many shots and the dark outlines of palm trees that figure against the night sky throughout *Collateral* are two of the aesthetic effects generated by the technology. For controlled lighting situations in the filming of interior sequences, the crew reverted to 35mm film; according to Beebe, digital video was a little *too* sensitive to light in such environments and as a result the color became oversaturated.[9]

The resulting film is technically a mixed-media piece in its assemblage of scenes shot on both digital video and 35mm film, and Mann, Cameron, and Beebe were able to create a tapestry of images that was wholly impossible to achieve with standard film stock alone. But while shooting exterior scenes on digital video at night—the sequences which comprise most of the film—essentially meant that the crew would only be augmenting light which was already available on location, *Collateral*'s aesthetic is not the raw, immediate, cinema-vérité style one might expect. Cinematographer Bill Roe has distinguished his "run-and-gun" work with digital video on *Robbery Homicide Division* from his meticulously composed visuals on *The X-Files*, but such a distinction does not hold true for the images in *Collateral*, which manage to render a plausible (as well as dreamlike) visual feel of Los Angeles at night while also crafting careful shot compositions that generate, across the film's duration, the broadly expressive meaning typical of most of Mann's work.[10] The director himself has described digital as a format well suited to both the realistic and the stylish:

> I like the truth-telling feeling I receive when there's very little light on the actors' faces—I think this is the first serious major motion picture done in digital video that is photoreal, rather than using it for effects. DV is also a more painterly medium: you can see what you've done as you shoot because you have the end product sitting in front of you on a Sony high-def monitor, so I could change the contrast to affect the mood, add colour, do all kinds of things you can't do with film.[11]

Mann's observation suggests the careful balance in the film's aesthetic: Digital allows for a more accurate photographic rendering of source lights, but it also enables the filmmakers to further control light not through elaborate lighting set-ups before the shooting of a scene, but during the process of shooting itself. Using these techniques, Mann, Cameron, and Beebe were able to greatly inflect the film's genre conventions through a new cinematic aesthetic. Coming after *The Insider* and *Ali*, *Collateral* marks Mann's return to the crime film and the neonoir; it is his most tightly structured genre piece since *Thief*. As critic Mark Olsen writes, "If the L.A. of *Heat* was crisp, almost photorealist in its high-gloss intensity, here the night-time cityscape is rendered with a watercolour density. *Collateral*'s after-hours timescale may be classic *noir*, but Mann's subtle night-vision . . . softens the genre's chiaroscuro tendencies."[12]

It is through the classical temporal structure of the film noir genre that Mann reintroduces his theme of the solitary individual moving through a vast landscape of sometimes overwhelming relativity and indifference. The hitman Vincent (Tom Cruise) has a limited amount of time (after sunset and before sunrise) to kill five witnesses in a major murder trial that is set to begin the next day. While characters in *Heat* also work against the clock, in that film Mann often figured the actors against the vast, widescreen cityscapes of Los Angeles, a ready-made metaphor for the contingency that greets the best-laid and most intricate plans. In the smaller-scale *Collateral*, these broad landscapes—sometimes figured in bird's eye shots of city highways looping and intersecting—are mostly represented as implicitly present in the hazy orange, blue, red, and yellow lights which the digital video captures in the distance during exterior night scenes, as well as in the background of tighter telephoto shots of the cab's interior.

Much of the film's structure derives from screenwriter Stuart Beattie's script. Although Mann rewrote certain scenes and dialogue before filming, introducing some of his favorite themes in the process, *Collateral* is the first of the director's feature films on which he receives no screenplay credit, because Beattie's structure was left largely intact.[13] The overt explanation for the film's title was eliminated in Mann's rewrite: In Beattie's script the hitman Vincent prides himself on being a clean, accurate professional killer chiefly because he has committed only two "collateral hits"—otherwise known as killings of innocent bystanders—in his entire career.[14] Despite having removed this information, Cruise's Vincent is nonetheless depicted in Mann's vision as the calculating and controlling professional that Beattie's screenplay suggests, and in his obsessive involvement with his work he recalls any number of characters from previous Mann films.

Collateral reintroduces the theme of isolated individuals in postmodern landscapes through its two main characters. Vincent recalls Frank from *Thief* and Neil McCauley from *Heat* in his elegant business attire and his composed manner. To keep a low profile as he targets his five hits, Vincent hires a cab driven by Max (Jamie Foxx). During his hectic nights, Max often gazes at a photo of a tropical island he keeps in his cab, recalling the way Frank envisioned his ideal future through his photo collage of the American Dream in *Thief*. But while Max speaks of a future in the limousine business, it is an ambition that seems more like a fantasy than a future reality given that the cabby has been driving taxis "temporarily" for twelve years.

A good portion of the film takes place inside the confines of Max's cab, initiating an intimate relationship between Max and Vincent that, in the first part of the film, at least, takes on the guise of the buddy comedy. But in the relationship between Vincent and Max, a political content is also introduced into *Collateral*. Unlike the parallels between past Mann characters such as McCauley and Hanna in *Heat* and Will Graham and Dolarhyde in *Manhunter*, Vincent and Max are not one another's doppelganger. Class sharply divides them. Max is an African American male, a member of the working class, and a timid, modest dreamer. He keeps tight control of his cab, making sure it is always clean, in a way that parallels Vincent's own composure. But the cards are stacked against Max: Vincent is white, sharply dressed (the silver fox), and looks like he could be the chief executive officer of a Fortune 500 company. Like *Heat*'s McCauley, Vincent is a criminal from a high-class milieu, and he also inherits—and adds a new wrinkle to—a particular character trait of a number of gangster-film figures. As Thomas Leitch suggests in his scholarship on the crime and gangster film genres:

Though it is ironic that films and gangs organized around breaking the rules should be so preoccupied by the rules they establish in their place, it is eminently logical for gangsters to spend their time debating rules of conduct and morality, because in opting out of the social norms that everyone else takes for granted, they are forthrightly considering the question of what rules ought to be followed and why.[15]

As a character Vincent is the messy contradiction which emerges when the gangster with a moral code—such as Paul Muni's Tony in *Scarface* (1932), Sterling Hayden's Johnny Clay in *The Killing* (1956), or McCauley in *Heat*—survives in a postmodern context. He espouses a wholly indifferent, nihilistic worldview (which I will describe in more detail later in this chapter) that tends to gloss over the importance of any moral code, even though the character nonetheless possesses an abstract code of conduct that allows him control over every situation in which he finds himself. That only he alone has to answer to such a code is another sign of his belief in a totally meaningless universe. Indeed, it is Vincent's apparent wealth—the only thing the surviving gangster-genre figure is left with—which allows him a great deal of autonomy: He can comfortably critique the American system, remarking that the United States is "a country with the fifth-largest economy in the world . . . and nobody knows each other," while at the same time offering the less privileged Max a cash offer for the all-night services of his taxi cab. Like Tony in Howard Hawks' *Scarface*, Vincent emerges (more explicitly, through dialogue, than Tony in Hawks' film) as the contradictory anticapitalist entrepreneur, the exploiter with a conscious, perhaps even subtly carrying on the old gangster tradition of "acting out viewers' . . . equivocal desire to avenge themselves on the system that has kept them down," one of the classical assumptions regarding audience response to the 1930s gangster film.[16] But whereas Tony's ascent in the capitalistic hierarchy leaves him dead at the height of his powers in *Scarface*, Vincent has already achieved the highest success imaginable before the very beginning of *Collateral*, an idea visible in the film given that we see Vincent dressed in casual corporate business attire and also apparent in his nonchalant offer to Max of six hundred dollars to drive him around for the night. Given this evidence, it appears that Vincent is not in this game for money anymore; his meaningless, destructive, and mannered style of performing his work is all that he cares about.

There exists no character in the rich films of Michael Mann that can be reduced to ideology or allegory. But character specificity and symbolic meaning are not mutually exclusive, and Vincent, as we will see, is in many ways an empty vessel of capitalistic success at the beginning of *Collateral*. He espouses a belief in action and the importance of adapting to one's environment; in this he values the superficial capitalistic ideology of "the survival of the fittest." But his posture and his beliefs are an empty illusion that produces only death and mayhem, and only his dramatic interaction with Max reveals an inner pain unperceivable in his layer upon layer of mannered cool. Max, meanwhile, is eventually driven to break out of the isolation of his cab in order to assert his agency in the same social context, implicitly rejecting Vincent's worldview. Strictly on the level of narrative, then, Vincent's deviancy is finally punished and Max's agency is finally asserted. The criminal in the crime genre, as usual, does not survive. The film's aesthetic, however, in keeping with Mann's previous films, generates a more ambivalent poetic content.

The film begins with the sound of an airplane landing. We see Tom Cruise, as Vincent, coolly making his way through a crowd in the busy airport in a medium shot. Another man (Jason Statham), unidentified, appears in a subsequent shot. The two, seemingly by accident, bump into each other and drop their identical leather briefcases; it is soon clear that they are on familiar terms. They exchange briefcases, each picking up the one that belonged to the other. Vincent and this stranger have thus staged an incident of "chance," the first sign of how we will eventually understand Vincent as a man who paradoxically believes in the ability to totally and completely control one's destiny while at the same time espousing a belief in a cosmic indifference which makes all such agency ultimately pointless. Vincent is a nihilist, but he is also remarkably efficient at what he does. What he does, of course, is stage faux improvisations that lead to murder, which only reaffirms his nihilism. His work—like all of Mann's characters, he is of course obsessed with his work—is thus a very carefully constructed form which, in these opening scenes, has absolutely no meaningful or valuable content. Vincent is thus figured early in *Collateral* as the human embodiment of a wholly destructive mannered style, and although he does possess deeper human qualities, it is only through the evolution of his relationship with Max that these are revealed. As if to emphasize this lack of meaning in Vincent's existence, throughout the film the viewer is clued into the superficial details of Vincent's process as he adapts to his environment: his manner of walking, the way he swipes an access card across an electronic reader, the way he wears a pair of sunglasses, the style with which he walks through a Korean nightclub. Until Max cracks his cool veneer later in the film, all we know of Vincent is what we see.

The next scene is a montage introducing Max and the environment in which he works. Max is finishing a crossword puzzle while waiting for his cab to return to the garage from the day shift. All around him are the sounds of drills and other devices performing maintenance on vehicles, and one can hear and see a rich mix of linguistic diversity on the soundtrack and in the images of foreign-language newspapers drivers are reading. Max gets into his cab and closes the door, and all other sound disappears; the taxi is clearly his domain, further reflected later in the film through his carefully honed ability in maneuvering the streets of Los Angeles. As Max drives out of this multicultural garage, his Caucasian boss stands on a platform above him; in a subtle top-to-bottom camera movement, Mann and his cinematographer compose an invisible vertical line which connects Max's white boss and the alcohol advertisement on top of Max's taxi, to Max himself inside of the cab, thus establishing the oblique outline of an entire power structure in one shot.[17] As Max's car exits the garage, the camera lingers on a street mural in the background which depicts a white horse corralling a black bull; the image commands a great deal of volume in the frame, and the vertical compositional relationship between it and Max's cab recalls the connection made between Max's boss, the ad on top of the cab, and Max. This connection within the composition suggests not only the racial tension in this workplace but also the idea that artistic expressions representing oppression are actually copresent (and thus possibly co-opted) in the very environments in which such oppression occurs. If Mann is drawing our attention to these expressions in his film, it is only because his camera—in his favored Vertovian way—is able to extract and compose more meaning from an environment than the naked human eye. This image, of course, is also the first suggestion of the power struggle that will be enacted between Vincent and Max.

Despite the fact that he is most comfortable in the confines of his cab, Max traffics throughout Los Angeles with a great deal of cultural know-how. He is shown speaking Spanish to employees at a gas station and he listens to a variety of music (represented on the film's soundtrack so as to blur the distinction between diegetic and nondiegetic music), thus clearly figured as a man with a skill in creatively crossing the fragmentary cultural-geographical boundaries of Los Angeles. This traversing of boundaries is also suggested through the watery, intangible imagery of his moving taxi cab's reflection against the side of paneled office building windows. His cab itself is a site of constant tension between inside and outside: Its windows open onto the world, albeit from a passive point of view.[18] Thus, despite his modesty and passivity, Max is a great deal more efficient at moving back and forth from inside (in his cab) to outside (in his dealings with gas station attendants and various fares) and then back again than the upper- and middle-class, politically minded Bergman and Wigand in *The Insider*, an idea which seems to suggest that the more one possesses the kind of social power and privilege which can engender progressive action in America, the more difficult it becomes to actually use it (a notion reinforced in the way in which the aesthetics of *Collateral*'s finale ambivalently regards Max's newfound agency).

Before he meets Vincent, Max encounters in his cab a defense attorney named Annie (Jada Pinkett-Smith). The two eventually strike up a bit of repartee; Max tells her of his plan to start his limo company. As Max drives, Groove Armada's soulful "Hands of Time" plays on the soundtrack, its lyrics suggesting both Max's subject position and desire for agency as well as the tight temporal structure of the film and city life itself, which always threatens interference in any individual's plans. The song is also clearly the type of "cool groove" (to use the character's phrase) that Max's limousine company would provide for its patrons. As the scene ends, he is able to get Annie's phone number, which not only grants him a little hope for a future relationship with this woman but also sets up the incorporation of Pinkett-Smith's character in the film's finale.

After Max drops off Annie, he picks up Vincent, and Tom Cruise's character begins espousing a melancholic worldview that reflects the fragmentary nature of the big city he dislikes; in saying such things Vincent refutes any meaningful communication between separate communities that might possibly exist within the city (and thus implicitly devalues a potential source for Max's untapped agency):

Vincent: Tell you the truth, whenever I'm [in Los Angeles] I can't wait to leave. Too sprawled out, disconnected. You know, that's me. You like it?

Max: It's my home.

Vincent: Seventeen million people. This is a country with the fifth biggest economy in the world and nobody knows each other. I read about this guy who gets on the MTA here, dies. Six hours he's riding the subway before anybody notices his corpse doing laps around LA . . . people on and off, sitting next to him. Nobody notices.

Michael J. Anderson has suggestively linked Vincent's empty, melancholic attitudes, sharply indicated in the dialogue above, with the film's rhetoric as a whole:

This focus on the city's design, though quite often exceeding the immediate exigencies of the narrative, echoes the film's moral universe . . . Indeed, both the value system expressed by Vincent in particular as well as the architecture featured so prominently throughout the film represent instantiations of postmodernism. As such, the utilisation of the nocturnal urban landscape in *Collateral* is not simply a self-justifying preoccupation of its creator, though it is this, but is also an extension of the postmodern universe that defines the film's rhetoric.[19]

This argument—which implicitly links Vincent's rhetoric with Mann's rhetoric—accurately suggests the manner in which the filmmakers' richly realized city images figure as an overarching metaphor for postmodern contingency in innumerable scenes throughout the film. However, such reasoning does not sufficiently regard the potential for both triumph and despair within postmodernism, an ambivalence that Mann's films always exude. Throughout Mann's work the codas to his films have been ambiguous; only *Thief* espouses an entirely nihilistic worldview. *Ali* in particular, through its strategy of contemporary aesthetic immediacy in the representation of an American past, suggests the prospects of both a renewed individualism and collectivism working side by side. *Collateral* depicts and articulates Vincent's worldview for the sake of the film's dramatic arc, but in the final analysis the film itself does not do so from the position of its character's amoral stance: Ultimately the film critiques Vincent's empty mannerism implicitly in its own employment of an expressive mise-en-scène and also in Max's ability to discover a greater degree of agency as the film progresses. Only the ambiguity of the ending would seem to suggest the overt despair which Vincent himself exudes.

The narrative is structured around the way in which Vincent is able to manipulate Max: He pays the cabbie six hundred dollars to hire the cab for the night, and he constantly berates him for his inability to move beyond his station in life. It is probable that Vincent believes he can get away with such manipulation since Max is a working-class man. Max, in other words, is seen by Vincent as simply too weak to rebel; he is nothing but an atom isolated in his cab. But when Vincent's first hit falls through a window and then crashes into the roof of the taxi, the hitman realizes the stakes have become higher. Max's isolation has literally been ripped apart, and the money—(which Max now realizes is dirty)—will no longer buy his loyalty.

In persuading Max to continue driving him around the city, Vincent (in addition to threatening death, of course) co-opts the rhetoric of American liberalism to get what he wants.[20] After all, like any crafty capitalist, Vincent is also a master politician. He mentions Rwanda, wondering how Max can be so concerned with the death of "one fat guy" (the man who falls on the roof of the cab) when millions are dying and starving all over the world, and later he encourages Max to talk back to his white boss. At the same time, of course, Vincent does not appear to care about what he preaches. Each of the individuals he is to kill is distinguished from the rest by a difference in gender, race, or nationality (an Hispanic man, a white man, a black man, a Korean man, and a black woman) and he pejoratively reduces the multiculturalism of Los Angeles to "disconnected sprawl," in effect also rhetorically deflating the meaning of Max's own multiculturalism, apparent in the character's bilingual skills, the music he listens to, and his ability to traverse the sprawl of the city in his cab. Mann and his cinematographer visually express the cultural gulf between Max and Vincent as they stand outside the vehicle at a gas station. In a shot perhaps reminiscent of the mural of the white horse commanding the black bull seen earlier in the film, Vincent stands to the left, away from the center of the gas station, while Max, the working-class man, stands on the right side of the frame, pumping gas, with his own bilingual skill figured in the mix of words from different languages painted on the gas station's exterior.

Vincent, the anticapitalism capitalist, thus emerges as the oppressor of Max while at the same time paternalistically governing the driver in order to get what he wants. Despite his social deviancy, Vincent functions in one sense as a figure of patriarchal law in *Collateral*, and the cops investigating his trail of murders—cops who also possess a great deal more social privilege than Max—function as his slightly more sympathetic doppelgangers. Max, by virtue of his class and job, is the one character in the film whose social position grants him the least amount of power: As we will see, he is eventually figured as stuck in the middle of the power struggles enacted by the more privileged characters represented in the film.

Indeed, although he has not seen the first two murders, Max is brought into Vincent's world when he joins him in a jazz club where the third hit is to take place. Mann's camera captures the cool intensity of the jazz players and the blue and green colors in the club in a series of close-ups. Max himself says that he "never learned how to listen to jazz," suggesting that he lacks the improvisatory skills that Vincent supposedly prizes. While listening to this music, Vincent claims to get a thrill out of Los Angeles's landscape of contingency: "Most people? Ten years from now, same job, same place, same routine, everything the same, just keeping it safe, over and over and over . . . Ten years from now? Man, you don't know where you'll be ten . . . *minutes* from now." But the filmmakers are careful to figure Vincent as decidedly apart from the improvising jazz players: While the close-ups in the montage of the various musicians' gestures and expressions emphasize the physical and emotional energy expended in playing the music, the hitman merely sits and observes. Vincent has emptied all such passion out of his external demeanor—he produces nothing in the way of art and can only eradicate.

Daniel (Barry Shabaka Henley), the trumpet player and owner of the club, is invited to sit with Vincent and Max after he is finished playing. Halfway through the conversation Vincent hints that he is there to kill Daniel, but he proposes that he will let him go should he correctly answer a question about Miles Davis. Given Vincent's staging of a chance meeting at the beginning of the film, it is reasonable to assume that this offer is pure artifice, a mock improvisation that will result—regardless of the delivered answer—in the musician's death. The fact that Vincent is not really "playing jazz" at all is evinced in the way he glances over his shoulder throughout the scene, carefully waiting to make his hit until the other employees in the bar have left, while Max, pleading for the trumpeter's life, suggests that they improvise and forget about Daniel, a comment which Vincent reacts to with a grimace. Vincent, keeping the charade going, asks Daniel where "Miles learned music," and Daniel responds that Davis, helped by his father's profitable investments in agriculture, went to the Julliard School of Music in New York in 1945. The answer is accurate, but not the complete one Vincent was looking for: Davis, Vincent says, subsequently dropped out of school to learn from Charlie Parker. Unsatisfied with Daniel's partially correct answer, Vincent shoots the jazzman dead, thus eradicating the source of the artistic improvisation he supposedly values.

After this hit, Vincent learns that Max visits his mother in the hospital every evening during his shift, and insists that the two of them pay the regularly scheduled visit so as not to arouse suspicion. In this scene we get another vision of the fragmented family in Mann's oeuvre, recalling the tatters of the venerable institution in *Thief*, *Manhunter*, *The Last of the Mohicans*, *Heat*, and *The Insider*. Much of Max's inability to act with any agency—or, at the very least, the shame engendered in being unable to do so—seems to derive at least in part from his heckling and nagging (albeit charming, to us and Vincent) mother, played by Irma P. Hall. (Hall's role is a virtual replica of her performance in the Coen Brothers' *The Ladykillers*, as Jonathan Rosenbaum has noted).[21] The fragmentation of the family is further emphasized in a conversation later in the film in which Vincent reveals to Max a possible environmental source for his sociopathic behavior: His mother died when he was young and his relationship with his father was violent and abusive. He says that he eventually killed his father, but then laughs and reveals this comment as nothing but a joke; in any event, the conversation and Vincent's laughter provide, in retrospect, a somber undertone to the slightly comedic atmosphere in earlier conversations and situations between the two characters.

Throughout the final hour of *Collateral* it is Max who will have to improvise and act in order to foil Vincent's plans. This first becomes evident in the aforementioned hospital scene. Max, it seems, has lied to his mother, telling her that he already owns a successful limousine company, as she reveals to Vincent. While Vincent chats with Max's mother, Max grabs Vincent's briefcase and runs out of the hospital room. Surely this act—Max's strongest display of agency in the film thus far—is prompted by his disgust with Vincent's crimes, but given that it occurs during this scene it also seems to derive in part from another encounter with his mother. As Max runs out of the hospital with Vincent in pursuit, both characters are figured against the backdrop of a busy city highway and its twinkling, hazy lights; this highway functions as a site of chance intersections, as in *Heat*. But at no other point in the film has the supposedly risk-taking improviser Vincent brought the two of them into such an environment. He has voiced an ideology of the survival of the fittest but has directed Max's cab to back alleys behind expensive high-rises and empty jazz clubs, avoiding, as Neil McCauley might say, "the heat around the corner" while hypocritically speaking about his desire for such heat. It is Max who prompts this encounter with the vast contingent landscape of Los Angeles, a move further emphasized when he tosses Vincent's briefcase into the oncoming traffic speeding along on the streets below.

In subsequent scenes we will see Max increase his ability to adapt to situations through his subversion of the master-slave relationship that Vincent has constructed between the two of them. Having lost his briefcase, which holds the necessary information about where and when to locate his next two hits, Vincent forces Max to retrieve backup information from his contractor, Felix (Javier Bardem). It is a win-win situation for Vincent, but a riskier proposition for Max. The cab driver must pretend to be Vincent; if he fails, Max dies and Vincent avoids Felix's wrath. If Max succeeds, Vincent gets the necessary information and is able to complete the final two hits. As Max enters Felix's nightclub, he is visibly nervous and ill at ease with the performance, but as the scene progresses he becomes more and more confident, borrowing phrases Vincent has spoken earlier in the film in order to convince Felix he can complete the job. He succeeds and leaves the nightclub with the data Vincent needs. But his successful performance is a little too successful: He is captured on the monitors of FBI agents, who are hot on the trail of the murdered witnesses and believe, like Felix, that Max is Vincent and they have their man.

Their discovery sets up the scene in the Korean nightclub, in which Max finds himself in the crossfire of Vincent, a Korean gangster's bodyguards, Felix's henchmen, and the FBI. The scene begins with an overhead shot, which establishes a rough sense of the club's interior perimeter, but subsequent shots plunge us into a sea of gyrating bodies (actual dancing seems impossible in this crammed space). The entire sequence serves as something of a frantic contrast to the intimacy in the scenes between Max and Vincent in the cab and to the free-form jazz played earlier in the nightclub; the pounding, carefully regulated beats and the lack of harmonic counterpoint in this techno music offers very little space or time for improvisation (which may then explain why the tightly wound Vincent, fond of "the jazz scene" in words but not in action, is rather successful in achieving his goals in this closed-in techno environment). Ultimately it is the paternalistic authority figures—Vincent and Detective Fanning (Mark Ruffalo)—that are able to control the situation, through violence. Vincent saves Max's life when he is threatened by one of the gang members, while Detective Fanning—before being shot dead by Vincent outside the nightclub—promises Max the protection of the law.

Despite Vincent's messy triumph in this scene—he is able to kill the fourth witness and retain Max's services in the process—the film continues to suggest that he is losing control of his ability to manipulate situations and individuals. In an earlier sequence, as Max drives Vincent to the Korean nightclub, Vincent encourages him to call the woman he met earlier in the film, telling him that life is simply too short to ignore such possibilities. There is vulnerability and sensitivity in Cruise's performance when he speaks these lines that suggests that his character's cool veneer—and by extension his empty mannerism and corrupt ideology—is beginning to crack. After this exchange, the taxi stops at a red light and a pair of coyotes crosses; at night, the coyotes' yellow eyes reflect a green and gold color, which the sensitive digital video cameras accurately capture. The camera itself seems to be reacting with surprise to the presence of these animals, which itself is rather surprising. During the production of the film the cameras were attached to the hoods of the various taxi cabs used during filming, resulting in the smooth, stable images seen throughout most of *Collateral*. But when the first coyote appears a now handheld camera zooms in on the animal in cinema-vérité style. As another coyote crosses the street, Vincent and Max simply watch in silence. These coyotes seem to represent, more saliently than any other image in the film, the unexpected sights one might encounter in an urban city; the animal itself, renowned for its unpredictability when faced with human contact, is a good metaphor for the theme of contingency in the film.

When these coyotes appear, Audioslave's "Shadow of the Sun" is cued on the soundtrack. The song will be heard again in the first scene after the melee in the Korean nightclub. Before it is cued on the soundtrack and before the coyotes appear, Max makes an open challenge to Vincent's philosophy:

Vincent: There's no good reason, no bad reason, why you live or you die.

Max: Then what are you?

Vincent: Indifferent . . . Get with it. Millions of galaxies of hundreds of millions of stars and a speck on one . . . That's us. Lost in space. The cop, you, me, who notices?

Max: What's with you?

Vincent: As in?

Max: As in, if somebody had a gun to your head and said you gotta tell me what's goin' on with this person over here or I'm gonna kill you, what was driving him, what was he thinking . . . You know, you couldn't do it, could you? They'd have to kill your ass because you don't know what anyone else is thinking. . . . The standard parts that are supposed to be there in people in you . . . aren't . . . (Max trails off).

Despite this exchange, and the potentially revelatory appearance of the coyotes which appear after it, Vincent proceeds to berate Max about his lack of success in fulfilling his dream of a limousine company. He has pushed Max toward action throughout the film, often by maliciously criticizing him for his ineffectuality and inability to accomplish his goals. Max, though, has had enough. "Shadow of the Sun" reappears on the soundtrack; as an understanding of Vincent, the song's lyrics express the internalized pain that he has carefully repressed beneath his meaningless external veneer of economic success. The ensuing lines of dialogue Jamie Foxx delivers—and Tom Cruise's reaction to them—rip Vincent's feelings out from under the surface:

> *Max*: I could have done anything I wanted to . . . But you know what? New news. It doesn't matter anyway. What does it matter anyway, if we're all insignificant out here on this big-ass nowhere . . . Says the bad-ass sociopath in my backseat . . . But you know what? That's one thing I gotta thank you for, bro, because until now I hadn't looked at it that way. What does it matter . . . What do we got to lose anyway?

As Max says this he speeds up the cab; Vincent tells him to slow down, his voice cracking and revealing once and for all an emotional vulnerability that he has hitherto carefully cloaked. This bravura moment, at least on the surface, belongs to Foxx, but the scene also, on a subtle level, features some of the most moving vocal inflections Cruise has yet to register on film. Max crashes his cab into a construction site as these emotions reach an apex, effectively eliminating the isolated vehicle, which, as a marker of his class, has defined, contained, and regulated his agency.

The subsequent scenes leading up to the finale of the film make clear both the increasing ability for social action in Max and the overwhelming landscapes of the city that in turn pose daunting challenges for such active expressions. After the car crash, Vincent escapes, but Max soon learns that Vincent's fifth and final hit will be on Annie, the lawyer he met in his cab earlier in the film. As Max tries to call Annie on her cell phone, telling her that Vincent is headed to kill her, he stands on the roof of a garage next to her building and watches her and Vincent on separate floors. This suspenseful scene recalls Jimmy Stewart's paralyzed agency as he gazes across his apartment courtyard in Alfred Hitchcock's *Rear Window* (1954), but for Max the problem is not a broken leg but the unreliable technology of his cell phone's drained battery, as well as the massive commercial and industrial structures which separate him from Annie's location.

Max and Annie are reunited after a tense sequence in which Vincent chases down Annie and is about to kill her before he is stopped short by Max. Vincent, although injured by one of Max's bullets, stays in pursuit. It is worth noting, as Manohla Dargis does in her review of the film, that on his way to help Annie escape Vincent's clutches, Max has a great deal of difficulty in figuring out how to get a gun to work, surely a unique image of an African American character in mainstream Hollywood cinema, one that also corresponds to the general shock which Max feels throughout the film after each of Vincent's murders.[22] Violence in Mann's cinema is never casual and without consequences: Often its visceral impact suggests the very real corporeality of death, and its impact on those who live through the traumatic moments in Mann's films also reflects the gravity with which death is handled throughout his work.

The ensuing finale is a mad scramble as Vincent attempts to track down Max and Annie on the Los Angeles subway system. Although expertly choreographed, filmed, and edited, this climatic sequence is in a way a standard action setpiece, and as such it may be somewhat disappointing after the originality of the scenes which preceded it; as reviewer Richard T. Kelly remarked in his *Sight & Sound* review, "the final subway chase . . . feels old, right down to the endless slamming of end-carriage doors and Vincent's uncanny indestructibility . . . They could have called this *The Terminator*."[23] Although perhaps somewhat cinematically stale in terms of narrative, the final showdown between Max and Vincent aesthetically generates the themes which have preoccupied the whole of the film. The two characters, in a confrontation on a subway car, exchange gunfire in darkness during a chance power outage. When the lights come back on, we see that it is Max who has successfully defeated Vincent; thus the narrative communicates to us Max's triumph, but also suggests that the mysteries of the big city's temporality had as much to do with his success as his own actions.

Despite its employment of well-worn genre conventions and narrative tropes, Mann's rich aesthetic approach in the depiction of the final showdown between Max and Vincent in the subway's interior is a suitable coda to the film, as it once again suggests an ambivalence only barely present in the narrative's presentation of Max's triumph over Cruise's character. This thematic content is generated through Mann's employment of digital video and computer-generated composite imagery. The interior of the subway was shot on 35mm film against a greenscreen, while the passing landscape outside the subway's windows was shot separately and later digitally composed with the film image. Such composite imagery, as theorist Lev Manovich suggests, functions as a kind of "montage within a shot" which serves not to foreground the juxtaposition of two separate spaces (as in classical Soviet montage aesthetics) but which rather creates an entirely new, imaginary space that can serve the "painterly" desires of the film director.[24] Such technology is often used to place human actors and computer-generated effects in the same spaces in such films as *Jurassic Park* (Steven Spielberg, 1993) and *Titanic*

(James Cameron, 1997).[25] In a way (albeit more subtle and less spectacular), *Collateral* is actually closer to *Titanic* in that it uses technology to render plausible imagery through composites (rather than the implausibility of human-dinosaur interaction). This marks a considerable expansion of Mann's aesthetic in the digital age. While his use of digital video on the set of the film allowed him and his collaborators to retain control over image quality during production, such technology also loses what David A. Cook calls the "privileged one-to-one relationship with reality, becoming just another set of pixels that the computer can sort and alter as it does computer-generated pixels."[26] The composition of 35mm footage and digital video within a single shot, meanwhile, is an example of a computer-generated aesthetic's "ability to generate photorealistic images directly in the computer," which "displaces live-action photography as the *only* basic material from which film is constructed."[27]

The digital technology used in the making of this scene thus crafts a dreamscape, recalling the first intimate conversation between McCauley and Eady in *Heat*, which was also shot against a greenscreen and later digitally juxtaposed, within a single shot, with a separately filmed backdrop sky of stars and lights. Ultimately, this scene in the subway, as with the mentioned scene in *Heat*, suggests an unattainable, permanently dreamy reality, which renders Max's destruction of the master-slave relationship in his murder of Vincent as an achievement somehow just beyond the possibilities our circumscribed postindustrial society will actually allow. Such ambivalence about the potential of one's ability simply *to matter* in a large, overwhelming American city is also reflected in Cruise's final line of dialogue, which recalls an earlier moment in the film: "Hey Max . . . guy gets on the MTA here, dies . . . think anybody'll notice?" This dialogue is followed first by Vincent's death and then by two juxtaposed shots of Vincent and Max, in which each is separately isolated within the vertical lines of the visual composition. This isolation is further suggested at the beginning of the film's penultimate shot of Max and Annie heading out onto the street; the two are first placed on the left side of the frame and tightly boxed-in by the side of a building which dominates the volume of the shot. Then, as they walk away from this position, the camera follows them to a crosswalk, an image that suggests the future decisions each of them will have to make during the rest of their lives in the city. The glass windows in the first image, reflecting the ghostly specter of the city's urban landscape, are as striking as images of reflective surfaces in any early Antonioni film, such as *La Notte* (1960) and *L'eclisse* (1961), in which the textures of modern society are suggestively employed as a metaphor for the ineffectuality and confusion of the main characters.

It is finally worth noting that the music which scores these last shots of *Collateral*—perhaps the most strangely beautiful of any musical selection in

Mann's work is the sonic equivalent to the computerized visual composites in the depiction of the subway, in that the sound designers have digitally remixed Antonio Pinto's orchestral "Requiem" (scored for the film, and available in its original mix on the *Collateral* soundtrack album) with the distorted guitars, percussion, and other various sonic textures of an industrial-style music (which is not named or credited on the film's soundtrack). The effect of such sonic poetry—especially for a critic not trained in musicology—is even more difficult to describe in words than the director's evocative, rich visuals. Suffice it to say that the resulting musical composite pulls, simultaneously, in two separate and distinguished stylistic directions (orchestral, "classical" music in the piece's strings and industrial-rock in its guitars and electronic beats) thus suggesting a lack of commitment to either style and as a result ambivalence in regard to each. This careful sonic design reflects the outline of a similar feeling in the film's attitude toward the possibilities of human agency in an often brutally relativistic world.

NOTES

1. See entry on Ami Canaan Mann at The Internet Movie Database, http://www.imdb.com/name/nm0542642/ (accessed February 22, 2005).
2. Phil Gallo, "*Robbery Homicide Division*," *Variety*, 7 October 2002, 33.
3. "CBS pull show, denies star was reason," *Seattle Times*, 13 December 2002, E3; and "*Robbery Homicide Division*," *TV Tome*, <http://www.tvtome.com/ tvtome/servlet/ShowMainServlet/showid-10646/Robbery_Homicide_Division/> (22 February 2005).
4. Gallo, "*Robbery Homicide Division*."
5. Jay Holben, "Shooting From the Hip," *American Cinematographer* 84, no. 2 (February 2003): 68.
6. Jay Holben, "Hell on Wheels," *American Cinematographer* 85, no. 8 (August 2004): 46.
7. Holben, "Hell on Wheels," 46.
8. Mark Olsen, "Paint it Black," *Sight and Sound* 14, no. 10 (October 2004): 16.
9. Holben, "Hell on Wheels," 48.
10. Holben, "Shooting From the Hip," 73.
11. Olsen, "Paint it Black," 16.
12. Mark Olsen, "It Happened One Night," *Sight and Sound* 14, no. 10 (October 2004): 15.
13. Olsen, "One Night,"15.
14. David Goldsmith, "*Collateral*: Stuart Beattie's Character-Driven Thriller," *Creative Screenwriting* 11, no. 4 (July–August 2004): 52.
15. Thomas Leitch, *Crime Films* (Cambridge: Cambridge University Press, 2002), 105.

16. Leitch, *Crime Films*, 111.

17. If Mann must use product placement in his work—which is not often—he will typically critique such placement obliquely (as in the Coca-Cola banners found in the African settings during the third act of *Ali*). Mann's work almost wholly evades the sticky problem of product placement, however, as a Hollywood director it seems impossible to fully avoid. The camera movement mentioned in this paragraph, and the fact that the alcohol ad is progressively destroyed as Max's taxi cab endures more physical torment throughout the film, is a different sort of product placement that nonetheless generates a formal and political meaning evident for anyone who is willing to look for it.

18. This general point about the cab's inherent inside/outside dichotomy is also made in Michael J. Anderson, "Before Sunrise, or Los Angeles Plays Itself in a Lonely Place," *Senses of Cinema*, http://www.sensesofcinema.com/contents/04/33/collateral.html (accessed February 23, 2005).

19. Anderson, "Before Sunrise."

20. In Anderson, "Before Sunrise," the author discusses this idea in his argument about *Collateral*, although does not suggest that Vincent is co-opting liberalism but that rather such liberalism is the rhetorical point of view of the film itself.

21. Jonathan Rosenbaum, "Art in Action," *Chicago Reader* (August 6, 2004).

22. Manohla Dargis, "Killer in a Cab, Doing His Job," *New York Times*, 6 August 2004, B7.

23. Richard T. Kelly, "Collateral," *Sight & Sound* 14, no. 10 (October 2004): 50.

24. Lev Manovich, *The Language of New Media* (Cambridge, MA: MIT Press, 2001), 152–53.

25. Manovich, *New Media*, 152.

26. David A. Cook, *A History of Narrative Film, 4th ed.* (New York: W. W. Norton & Company, 2004), 926; in making his observation Cook cites Lev Manovich, "What Is Digital Cinema," *BLIMP* 37 (1997): 38.

27. Cook, *Narrative Film*, 926.

Conclusion

Michael Mann and *Miami Vice* in the Shadow of New Hollywood

As I emphasized in the introduction to this book and as I have suggested in its subsequent chapters, Michael Mann's cinema does not abandon classical narrative tropes or genre frameworks, nor are his films of quite the same ilk as the self-consciously modernist interrogations of genre which characterized the filmmaking of certain Hollywood auteurs during the 1970s. The pleasures of the crime film remain intact in *Heat* and *Collateral* in a way that differs from Robert Altman's interrogation of the western, for example, in *McCabe and Mrs. Miller* (1971); the films Mann makes are, in part, enabled—if in the end not defined—by traditional genre conventions and even some of the general schemas of classical narrative. His films, rather than overhauling or explicitly critiquing genre frameworks, considerably inflect such frameworks through subtle and sometimes ineffable stylistic gestures that generate variations on conventions. These gestures do not take the form of cues which can be read in a rather straightforward manner: Instead they call for the attentive participation of the active viewer and critic to articulate the thematic meaning generated by Mann's film style. Style, for Mann, is substantive; as Christopher Sharrett has written, "Mann is an artist whose sense of the world is manifest precisely in the realization of style."[1] But like any style it is not developed in a vacuum: Mann's work always has one eye on the conventions of the past and the other on the new meanings and experiences of cinema possible in the light of inflections on genre achieved through distinctive aesthetic designs. Timothy Shary has succinctly described this idea in his review of *Miami Vice*: "It's as if genre provides Mann with an air-tight container that permits him to put style in the service of meaning."[2]

Because Mann does not turn completely away from a narrative driven by causes and effects, his characters, like those of the classical Hollywood cinema, are in part defined by the goals they seek to achieve. In Mann's crime films, there is often an instantly recognizable character motivation, be it an interest in catching a criminal or successfully robbing a bank, or in apprehending a serial killer or remaining a step ahead of the law. But soon a desire arises in Mann's characters to transcend the boundaries of a social context or institution (the mob, the FBI, corporate tobacco, the military) or an oppressive environment (cityscapes in Mann's films entrap even those characters who would initially seem to navigate their contours quite well), and such feelings lead to character motivation that is sometimes difficult to articulate in terms of clear-cut cause and effect. When Neil McCauley in *Heat* or Sonny Crockett in *Miami Vice* stand alone and stare at the ocean through a window, and a kind of existential angst seems to take over both their mood and the mood of the film, viewers may suddenly feel as if the characters' acknowledged, conscious directives are no longer enough to satisfy them. Frustrations develop when Mann's characters attempt to move beyond the patriarchal institutions and social contexts which have led them to value and desire the performance of their work; these feelings lead to the final ambivalence regarding the characters' goal fulfillment. Often, as at the end of *Heat*, *Collateral*, and *Miami Vice*, the value of the result achieved through the completion of the protagonist's task is called into question, and the ambivalent endings to Mann's films emphasize this feeling. Mann's cinema cannot be posited as an outright rejection of classical narrative structures, but the ultimate dissatisfaction in his characters in regards to the results of the kinds of goals and objectives which drive the classical Hollywood male protagonist generates an angst that is almost palpably present by the end of each Mann work.

The goal-driven narrative is not, then, wholly rejected as a framework in Mann, but classical style implicitly is, witnessed in the fact that Mann's films unfold more obliquely and in a more broadly formalized fashion than many films made strictly in the style of classical continuity. Adrian Martin's stylistic classifications of the expressive and mannerist, which I have used throughout this study, are not so much historically stable taxonomic categories of film style as they are catalysts for a criticism which seeks to articulate the specificity of films which do not traffic in the self-effacing mise-en-scène constructions of classical continuity. Films which do incorporate such classicism continue to be made, and made well: The recent work of Clint Eastwood—including films such as *Mystic River* (2002), *Million Dollar Baby* (2004), *Flags of Our Fathers* (2006), and *Letters from Iwo Jima* (2006)—are perhaps the most estimable examples in this regard. At the very same time, the terms "expressive" and "mannerist" themselves suggest that the concept of the classical looms somewhere in the background, throwing into relief the variations performed by the other two styles. This implies that the specter of the type of filmmaking which characterized the classical studio system in Hollywood remains embedded in the work of any auteur whose style either modulates content in a broad manner (as do most of Mann's films) or dispenses entirely with the communication of content through the display of a mannerist style. This seems quite natural in a Mann film given that the goals of the classical protagonist also remain even though these are ultimately questioned.

If, on this conceptual level, the classical grants the expressive and the mannerist existence, this should not suggest that any departure from stylistic economy is always in the end commensurable with the ideals of cinematic classicism itself. Mann's films remain distinct from a classical poetics even though the very concept of classical style assists viewers in recognizing the variations performed upon such a style. Classical filmmaking and the studio system have also provided the director with a veritable storehouse of genres, themes, and character types which function as a kind of palette upon which Mann's aesthetic designs go to work. These genres, themes, and character types do not determine the meaning of Mann's films, but they do, at least in part, enable the reformulations made upon them through their very use. Indeed, as Mann's body of work has grown over the course of thirty years, his own oeuvre has begun to provide him in recent films with a grab bag of narrative tropes, psychological types, snippets of dialogue, and even pieces of music which are constantly reshaped into consistently distinctive aesthetic effects and thematic meanings in each subsequent film. Shary, making a similar point in his review of Mann's film adaptation of *Miami Vice*, has suggested that this is the result of Mann's "Kubrickian perfectionism: just as *Heat* originated in the pilot for Mann's aborted *L.A. Takedown* (1989), *Miami Vice* is loosely based on the series pilot written by Anthony Yerkovich."[3] David Bordwell has suggested that all contemporary Hollywood filmmakers work "in the shadow of enduring monuments," those great films from the studio era; but at the same time he acknowledges that Mann's works seem peculiarly self-enclosed (a point Sharrett makes in his article as well).[4] The fact that Mann's are genre films suggests a history or a lineage, but the manner in which they reformulate conventions within these genre frameworks—and the manner in which they reshape the more idiosyncratic motifs and tropes of prior Mann films—leads to work that is utterly singular and, in another sense, self-perpetuating.

Mann's distinction largely rests, then, in the significance of his style. His work is not a glossy type of filmmaking in which style trumps content, but rather one in which style generates content. While it should be clear at this point that I value Mann as a major filmmaker, I have carefully avoided making a value judgment as to his exact place in the lineage of recent American auteurs. The avoidance is due partially to the nature of this study itself: I have sought to articulate the meanings behind what I see as a highly idiosyncratic and singular genre aesthetic, and in the very attempt to defend such a position I may have made the road toward categorizing Mann in a collective group of filmmakers even more difficult. Despite the fact that he works in genre, Mann's filmography as a whole simply does not fit altogether comfortably within the contours of lineages already established. His films flirt with modernism in their aesthetic attributes, most notably in the way his style subtly calls attention to itself through such means as the occasional lack of establishing shots (which lead to extreme close-ups and the exploration of the aesthetic values of the surfaces of the worlds on display in his films) and the presence of music which generates qualities of feeling and attitude that are sometimes difficult to localize within specific narrative moments. These aspects of Mann's work might suggest a relation to the directors of the New Hollywood cinema of the late 1960s and 1970s. But to attribute to Mann's style a cinematic self-reflexivity, without qualification, is problematic. The reflexivity of Mann's cinema demands an acutely active and attentive viewership, but the cues for a modernist cinema—exhaustive interrogation and deconstruction of narrative structures, genre frameworks, and a thorough questioning of film realism—are conspicuously absent. His realism hones up to its artificiality, and in fact any trace of the "real" in Mann derives from the power generated by this very quiet acknowledgement, in the films themselves, of the artificial construction that comprises any work of art. But at the same time Mann has remained thoroughly interested in presenting the more or less realistic detail of the dramatic situations he has carefully researched and he is committed to a belief in logical character psychology. The result is rather a kind of amplification of a certain sense of reality presented within and through the bounds of genre, a reality which cannot exist outside of the image itself and which is enabled by convention, but which nonetheless has its moorings in a particular understanding of the world outside of film.

Where modernist film (and the study of modernist film) delights in intertextuality and the revelation of self-expression as myth, Mann's work hardly ever refers to other films or filmmakers and his interests in self-expression seem quite earnest. If his films are highly cinematic, they are not cinematic in an overtly referential manner but rather in a way meant to be slowly discovered or sensed. This may be seen to differ from the genre work of Spike Lee, Quentin Tarantino, Brian De Palma, Steven Soderbergh, or Martin Scorsese, whose works are self-consciously cine-literature and unabashedly and aggressively cinematic from the very first frames. As viewers, critics, and scholars, I think that we should live with films by directors such as Lee, Tarantino, De Palma, Soderbergh, and Scorsese for awhile to fully understand them, rather than pronouncing judgment the minute we exit the movie theater; but with Mann this becomes less a desire and more an outright necessity. The value of his work lies in nothing less than that which, in the end, every cinephile and film scholar craves: rich rewards for attentive cinema spectatorship. The fact that Mann—or any other genre film auteur—works within genre should not be seen as reductive of this value.

If neatly categorizing Mann is difficult (and in fact it may also prove undesirable), the political tinge of his films would suggest that as a director he is sympathetic with a number of the New Hollywood films which emerged in the 1960s and 1970s. I have, throughout this study, placed a thorough discussion of the politics of Mann's work in the background, in order to discuss at length the aesthetic experience his films present and the thematic material generated by this aesthetic. There has been, of course, an implicit political aspect to the thematic material that has emerged in the previous chapters. Mann's films, as Sharrett has previously suggested, function in part as "elegies on the postindustrial landscape": the cityscapes of the classical Hollywood cinema, so often a site for the celebration of (white) male agency and goal fulfillment, have become the backdrop to ambivalence and frustration.[5] The most optimistic film in Mann's oeuvre is *Ali* (and perhaps also, in its final although overly sentimentalized vision of transcendence, *The Jericho Mile*), and the success of that film is largely attributable to the broadness of Mann's aesthetic vision, which has proven just as capable in creating a sense of the politically revolutionary personality of Muhammad Ali as it has been in suggesting the lack of agency held by Mann's other protagonists. The aesthetic immediacy of *Ali*, however, as explored in Chapter Eight, suggests a political content of relevance to our contemporary lives, resulting in a film that avoids celebratory nostalgia in favor of the implication that there is still a great deal wrong with the institutions that comprise American life (the revolutionary aspects of Ali's life, the film suggests, are still a work in progress, open for completion by the viewers of the film). In all cases Mann's protagonists are marked by the institutions in which they work, or by which they are directly or indirectly affected. Frank in *Thief* and Bergman and Wigand in *The Insider* are all held in check by the mandates of corporate capitalism, and are almost entirely unable to act outside of these strictures when they prove too restrictive. The talents of the detective Will Graham in *Manhunter* are used in a rather unethical manner by the FBI, and there is some suggestion in the director's cut of the film that this use results in a permanent vulnerability in his personal life. Vincent Hanna in *Heat* and Max in *Collateral* both achieve goal fulfillment at the end of their narratives, and each represents the triumph of the law over the transgressor, but the actual value of their fulfillment is questioned at each film's end. Meanwhile, the divided personalities of both Tubbs and Crockett in the recent film version of *Miami Vice* seem to exist wholly within the confines of monolithic corporate structures (either those operated by the government or the criminal underworld), and the only attempt to transcend these structures (Crockett's romance with Isabella) ends—at least for Crockett—in failure and frustrated desire.

The failure depicted within Mann's most remarkable films is chiefly the failure of male protagonists, and the type of failure on display is in many ways the image of a hero no longer able to act in the same manner as the protagonists of many of the films of the classical studio era (and indeed many of today's blockbusters). Mann's protagonists, to different degrees, develop attitudes, thoughts, and desires that lead ultimately to a questioning of the institutions into which they have been positioned throughout their adult lives. In *Thief*, Frank remains fairly naïve of the nature of social oppression (both that which he enacts over his own employees and that which is enacted upon him by Leo's crew). As a result the film is Mann at his most Vertovian, given that his aesthetic etches into view a world of power relations that Frank himself cannot overcome. Frank's ultimate inability to articulate the pain such oppression has generated in him—the bloody conclusion of *Thief* contains very little dialogue, and many of its most moving shots, including the final moment Frank spends in the backyard of his home, unfold nearly in silence—results in the violence he enacts during the film's final moments, as he murders his bosses and sets both his home and his workplace on fire. This violence is thrown into relief against the backdrop of the alienating world on display in the film and as a result Frank's actions are rendered inexorable. In *Heat*, in spite of the fact that Vincent Hanna finally catches McCauley, the elegiac ending to the film suggests that no lasting fulfillment has been found. In *Collateral* Max learns, first and foremost, the value and possibility of his own agency, but in the film's finale some of Vincent's own nihilism seems to have slowly leaked into Mann's aesthetic, placing Max in a highly uncertain relationship to his own future. The characters in *The Insider*, meanwhile, work within corporate institutions that wield enormous power. It is up to Bergman and Wigand to use such power to politically efficacious ends, but Mann's film calls into question the very possibility of media conglomerates, and by extension those who work within them, being at all "politically efficacious" (to any progressive end).

This begs the question of the political intent of Mann's cinema itself. Mann's cinema is Vertovian in that his images compose more, suggest more, than his characters—always deeply engaged with their own actions, obsessions, and desires—fully realize or understand. (This idea becomes complicated in films such as *Manhunter*, *The Insider*, and during some passages of *Miami Vice*, all works in which the obsessions and desires of the main characters become increasingly dependent on their ability to harness the same powers of visual mediation that Mann and his collaborators wield in realizing their own vision). Mann respects the actions of his protagonists—and the way they define themselves through the work they perform—too much to affect an attitude of superiority through this Vertovian influence, even if his films often encompass a larger view of the world than any single one of his characters can attain, and at times this respect outweighs any articulation of a clear ideological stance that may have otherwise existed in the films. Whether or not this is a flaw in his work is open to debate: The politics of his cinema may only be implicit in the way in which his films tell stories about the work his men perform with skill and passion but through which they are ultimately unable to find fulfillment. Alternately, one could point out, as Sharrett has, that this respect for the protagonists results in an overidentification with the male characters on Mann's part, resulting in a "eulogizing of the male subject [which] raises more than a few questions about his political focus," a sentiment on Mann's part which cannot fully attain the crucial critical distance required to achieve a sustained political perspective within the context of the films themselves.[6]

To some extent the work performed by the characters may then echo the very work of the director himself. In the chapter on *The Insider* I suggested that the final shot of the film—wherein Mann's camera remains inside the building of the CBS corporation while Al Pacino's Lowell Bergman is seen exiting to the bright exteriors—expresses poetically the predicament of Mann's own creativity. How to say something politically progressive in Hollywood, an institution which depends on the exchange of massive amounts of capital within a system that Mann's films question, or at the very least, depict ambivalently? Can Mann ever possibly reach an audience sensitive to his aesthetics—and through his style, his themes and politics—by way of the Hollywood machine? It is debatable the extent to which even the most politically articulate works of the New Hollywood era actually effected changes in consciousness in the audiences which watched the films. What finally guarantees the ambiguity of Mann's politics—although they seem generally leftist in nature—is the deep ambivalence present in nearly all of his films, especially in their endings. Each Mann film drives inexorably to an ending that questions fundamentally the ultimate value of the goals the obsessive and calculating protagonists have achieved (or failed to achieve). There is a kind of existential angst and affect to much of Mann's work and it would probably be difficult to articulate this emotional timbre within a political program, given that in Mann such emotion is often the result of a kind of dispersive, slightly abstract atmosphere which exists across the body of all of his work. In other words, it may be that the very quality of Mann's broadly but subtly expressive style does not easily lend itself to the inclusion of a didactic political message.

The most useful way to place Mann in a lineage of auteurs, given the political leanings implicit (if not fully, consciously developed) within his aesthetic, may then be to suggest that he stands in the shadow of New Hollywood cinema. His films aspire to greatness and significance and in this they suggest, counter to the claims of the many nostalgic film critics who cut their professional teeth on films released in the decades of the 1960s and 1970s, that the end of the period we now know historically as New Hollywood did not spell the ending of meaningful filmmaking in the industry. But given the nature of Mann's work and the trajectory of his career—his rise to the status of a powerful figure within the film industry is the inverse of the gradual fall from grace which affected directors such as Arthur Penn, Robert Altman, and Sam Peckinpah—this categorization introduces possible objections; Mann's own gradual success occurred in the same industrial context that essentially banished the likes of Altman and Peckinpah from the industry. In this respect it is appropriate that the final chapter of this book discuss in some detail Michael Mann's recent film version of *Miami Vice*, not only in order to explore Mann's latest work for its own aesthetic and thematic significance but also to conclude this study by suggesting what place Mann holds within the lineage of contemporary Hollywood cinema in the light of a recent film that for some critics, on the face of it, might be prime evidence for Mann's irrelevance.

Miami Vice is a directorial choice which may initially disappoint many of Mann's most devoted followers, given that a remake of a 1980s television series does not exactly rest comfortably besides relatively prestigious, stylistically accomplished, and socially aware pictures such as *The Insider* and *Ali*. Some supporters of the director, at the very least, seemed nervous: in an issue of *Sight and Sound* released shortly after the film's release in Britain, Mark Wrathall suggested that in the light of *Miami Vice* a good many Mann fans, including himself, were "suffering our most profound crisis of faith."[7] Jonathan Rosenbaum (admittedly not a terribly passionate supporter of Mann in the first place) was more severe, claiming that the real vice within the film is the supposed evidence of "a gifted director letting his talent go to seed."[8] It is thus possible that Mann's position within a lineage of progressive auteurs might for some be mitigated by the fact of his remaking a glossy cultural product from the conservative decade of the 1980s. (It should be noted that distinguished critics and cinephiles such as Manohla Dargis of the *New York Times* and both Ed Gonzalez and Nick Schager of the online *Slant* magazine placed *Miami Vice* on their lists of the ten best films of 2006, alongside the more widely heralded artistic achievements of films such as *Three Times* [Hou Hsiao-Hsien], *L'Enfant* [Jean-Pierre Dardenne and Luc Dardenne], and *Inland Empire* [David Lynch]).[9]

If, for a number of critics and scholars, the merit and significance (aesthetic, thematic, and political) of contemporary American films is often thrown into relief against the influential specter of the New Hollywood directors, the achievements of the previous generation offer a basis of comparison for the merit of the new one. The question becomes: If New Hollywood is the yardstick against which recent achievements (or lack thereof) must be measured, does Mann's work suffer or hold up in such a comparison? Given that pessimism exists among film critics and scholars of a certain age regarding the quality of Hollywood/American films of the 1980s and 1990s, it should come as no surprise that the value of Mann's films, both as aesthetic objects and as at least partially formed critiques of the patriarchal contexts in which his narratives take place, is rarely trumpeted. Oftentimes the feeling that the American cinema has declined in recent decades finds expression—occasionally explicitly—as nostalgia for New Hollywood. As Alexander Horwath has written in the preface to the engaging anthology *The Last Great American Picture Show: New Hollywood Cinema in the 1970s*, "If you have come of age as a cinema-goer during the heyday of the New Hollywood cinema—sometime between *Bonnie and Clyde* and *Taxi Driver*—you've probably experienced the main brands of post-1970s American cinema by necessity as less rich, less intelligent, less political, as retrograde."[10] David Thomson has expressed a similar sentiment:

> It was not just in moments that we had to pay attention to these movies. Many of them had unfamiliar shapes, new narrative structures or strategies. They began late. They switched course. They didn't say this guy is reliably good and that one write-off bad. They didn't stick to the rules. And they did not end well, or happily, or comfortably. Sometimes they broke off in your hands or your mind.[11]

For films that do not end "well, or happily, or comfortably," I can point to the ambivalence embedded within the conclusion of films such as *Thief*, *Heat*, *The Insider*, *Collateral*, and, *Miami Vice*, which all echo the Thomson quote above. If Mann's films exude a degree of the political liberalism similar to the New Hollywood cinema's left-leaning attitudes, one may indeed wonder why Mann has rarely been included in a discussion of a type of Hollywood filmmaking that significantly continues the tradition of Scorsese, Altman, Peckinpah, and Penn.

Thomson himself might offer the beginnings of an answer. In his *Biographical Dictionary of Film*, Thomson implies that Mann's most significant achievement was his production of the television series *Crime Story*, broadcast on NBC during the 1980s. Thomson is rather unique in being both a passionate defender of the New Hollywood films and a critic interested in the contours of American television. Noel King has pointed out that critics such as Pauline Kael despised the way in which "the cinema post-New Hollywood 'televisionises' itself . . . squanders its aesthetic obligation to perform specifically cinematic work on and with the image . . ."[12] It is highly unlikely, of course, that Thomson would disagree with Kael's sentiment regarding the slow waning of a film culture in America which celebrates the specificity of cinema and its achievements. What is important is that the pleasure Thomson finds in *Crime Story* might suggest that there is a televisual specificity worth celebrating, which in turn would suggest that Mann's achievements within the realms of television—that "bad object" for a number of cinephiles and intellectuals—might be a crucial part of his importance, and indeed might contribute to an argument regarding Mann's worth in the light of the bygone New Hollywood age. (To this end both *Miami Vice* the series and *Crime Story* provide ground for further criticism and scholarship beyond this present volume). Indeed, *Vice* might even offer ground for the development of a political perspective within Mann's work; as Sharrett has pointed out, the original television series was "often about the failure and contradictions of the justice system, and the tensions within and failure of the male group."[13] In turn, this is relevant to a discussion of *Miami Vice* the film: If the 1980s series provided a legitimate palette of stories, characters, situations, and plots that might be richly reworked in a new version, in a new style, and with a thematic significance that echoes Mann's previous films, perhaps his history as a television producer—and his subsequent decision to remake *Miami Vice* as a 2006 film—might not automatically prove to be a conservative aspect of his legacy.

It is immediately apparent that while Mann has continued a tradition of meaningful filmmaking which holds its own in comparison to the best New Hollywood films, his work's potential success cannot be understood on the terms which the legacy of New Hollywood has set—terms which place importance on the deconstruction of genre as contained in the work of Peckinpah, Altman, and Penn—but rather in the terms of how Mann explores and uses genre, as an employment of convention that acts as a canvas upon which a new style and subsequently a new thematic significance is sketched. Given that *Miami Vice* looks and sounds nothing like its television predecessor, and that in terms of both its aesthetics and its themes it seems to emerge in great part from concerns in Mann's previous films, it is appropriate to begin a discussion of the film by suggesting the themes it holds in common with earlier films as well as the new stylistic direction the film takes in its presentation of those themes. As a continuation of the worldview developed in films as valuable as *Heat*, *The Insider*, and *Ali*, *Miami Vice* can then be seen less as an undesirable anomaly or a purely commercial concession in the director's career and more as another intriguing exploration of ideas that have concerned the director over the course of ten films.

Miami Vice tells another crime story, familiar to viewers of both the original series and the director's previous crime films. A short plot summary can begin to suggest some of the film's key themes. Detectives Sonny Crockett (Colin Farrell) and Ricardo Tubbs (Jamie Foxx), along with detectives Trudy Joplin (Naomie Harris) and Gina Calabrese (Elizabeth Rodriguez), are engaged in detective work in an effort to bring down the drug czar Arcángel de Jesús Montoya (Luis Tosar) through undercover negotiations with Montoya's middleman Jose Yero (John Ortiz). The film is densely populated with sequences depicting dangerous undercover operations in South America, and Mann's focus on the details of each particular setting and situation gives the viewer a good sense of the immediate risk Crockett and Tubbs face at nearly every moment. Along the way Crockett falls in love with Montoya's business associate and lover Isabella (Gong Li) in a relationship which echoes that between McCauley and Eady in *Heat*: It promises a transcendence from circumstance that in the end can never be consummated. (The sequence near the conclusion of *Vice* which depicts Crockett and Isabella heading in a car toward separate, solitary futures directly echoes a similar moment involving McCauley and Eady in the earlier film.) Near the end of the film, the personal and the professional completely lose their distinction, as they do in most Mann films, as Trudy herself is kidnapped shortly after Yero becomes suspicious of the intentions of the undercover cops. A final shootout between Crockett, Tubbs, and an army of cops on the one side, and Yero and his henchmen on the other, suggests a sense of narrative completion, but both the split between Isabella and Crockett and the fact that Montoya himself escapes arrest generates a familiar Mann ambivalence about the value of the work his male characters perform against sometimes highly melancholy landscapes of vast urban and industrial space (which echo the varieties of landscapes which Christopher Sharrett has explored in his analysis of Mann films up to *The Insider*).[14] The final images of Montoya's empty, abandoned mansion in South America directly echo the sparseness of the private spaces populated by most Mann protagonists, implying that the failure of the protagonists to successfully "complete the job" and heroically catch the criminal is directly tied into the physical and psychological isolation which often affects them. *Miami Vice*'s familiar plotline functions as a canvas for Mann's aesthetic designs and the subsequent generation of thematic material which echoes the director's previous films.

The characters of Montoya and Yero, for their part, are both variations on the classical gangster figure which has persisted throughout the history of Hollywood cinema. And Crockett and Tubbs, due in large part to the nature of the undercover work they perform, and in the usual fashion of the Mann protagonist, are the doppelgangers of the criminal figures. The development of the gangster figure within Mann's cinema is a theme explored throughout this book in the chapters dealing with Mann's crime films. Robert Warshow's conception of the classical gangster film (as discussed in Chapter Two) suggested that the gangster could never survive alone, and yet the paradox of the gangster's predicament is the individual eminence that results from success.[15] It is this achieved individuality which, ironically, spells the gangster's doom. The gangster cannot help but be an individual in the light of his material wealth and individual distinction, and it is this distinction that functions as a prelude to his eventual downfall. In *Miami Vice* the film, as in the television series, the display of the signifiers of wealth such as nice clothes and fancy cars, as well as technological know-how, is not limited only to the criminals but it also pertains to the cops, especially Sonny Crockett. Crockett's behavior—never fully contextualized within a private life and thus only on display in his professional existence—often comes so close to mirroring that of his quarry that Tubbs occasionally has to remind him of his professional duties. But the gangster figures in Mann films, and their counterparts like Crockett who to some extent emulate them, also desire a certain degree of social adjustment in order to efface the very nature of their solitary existences: Crockett's escape from his psychological conflicts is embodied in *Miami Vice* in Isabella, just as Frank seeks a house and home with Jessie in *Thief*. But for Mann's characters, once individual eminence is achieved through the performance of work—whether it is the eminence of a seasoned thief or a skillful detective—it is hard to disappear back into the quotidian world. Indeed, unlike nearly all of Mann's previous films, *Miami Vice* contains very few images of anything resembling an autonomous quotidian world: While socially acceptable normality is symbolized in the figure of Jessie in *Thief* or Eady in *Heat*, family and relationships are inextricable from the decaying professional world of both Crockett and Tubbs in *Miami Vice*, especially given that each of them love a woman who is embroiled in the same profession or situation as they are.

As also mentioned in chapter 2, the actual behavior which leads to the success of the traditional gangster figure is kept in the background, but in Mann these figures (who often blend the line between the law and the criminal) are in fact defined by the work they do and the actions they perform, all of which is on display (in meticulous, carefully researched detail) in each film's imagery. The elaborate attention to the tools used, jargon spoken, and actions performed by each character are clearly evident in all of the films and for good reason: These characters express themselves, at least in part, through the manner in which they perform their work. For both the cops and the criminals their labor is not something to hide: Their work is instead the very expression of the value and the meaning of each character's understanding of his existence. This focus on and obsession with work, as well as the intertwined natures of the cops and the criminals, is nowhere more apparent than in the characters who populate *Miami Vice*. Mann dedicates entire sequences to illustrating how Crockett and Tubbs transport drugs for Yero during their undercover operations; when they fly an airplane over restricted airspace in an attempt to make a delivery for Yero (they fly behind another jet in order to prevent their own from appearing on the monitors of air traffic controllers), it is possible to forget for a moment that they are on the side of the law and to simply immerse oneself in the exquisitely presented depiction through image and sound of a skillfully performed undercover operation that is in fact a criminal act. Jose Yero, meanwhile, when he is not organizing a drug deal with Crockett, Tubbs, or Montoya, is depicted carefully overseeing the operations of Montoya's casinos; indeed, the roulette wheels which appear on his desk monitors function as motifs reminding us of the theme of contingency in Mann's cinema, which is once again prevalent in *Vice*.

On the most obvious level, chance is of course a theme that relates to the subject matter of *Vice*: undercover work, after all, is a risky operation. But the film is most moving when it explores how its characters attempt to fulfill desires against the backdrop of indifferent and vast cityscapes and industrial environments, desires which occasionally come into conflict with the work that they are called upon to perform. As in other Mann films, protagonist and antagonist in *Miami Vice* are often defined by the similarity of their desires and/or the manner in which they seek to fulfill their desires in the face of sometimes overwhelming contingency. The figures in *Miami Vice* attempt to overcome the circumstances which threaten to derail their carefully designed plans through the harnessing of technologies and sophisticated systems of intelligence that grant them a wider scope of vision, control, and surveillance. They do not seek to use such technology for socially or politically meaningful ends, as do the characters in *The Insider* and *Ali*. Their behavior is almost antisocial in the way that it attempts to circumscribe the contingencies of society through surveillance for the fulfillment of purely personal interests (the work characters perform in *Miami Vice* is never moralized; Crockett and Tubbs seem less interested in the war on drugs than they are in the lives such a war allows them to lead). The fact that these characters eventually seek to transcend the very situations and institutions that lead them to develop such behavior suggests a nascent social awareness, although for them it can only be articulated through a personal language of desire. In this they are similar to characters in both *Thief* and *Heat*, but the wide array of technologies the characters in *Vice* wield exceeds the previous films to a great degree; the narrative moments in *Vice* in which Crockett and Tubbs must leave behind these technologies in order to perform improvisatory undercover work only throws into relief those other sequences in the film where they are dependent on such instruments in order to perform their jobs.

Mann develops other themes in *Vice* which are also familiar to viewers of his previous films. The theme of the heteronormative family and its vulnerability—an important strand in nearly every Mann work, but especially pervasive in *Thief*, *Manhunter*, and *The Insider*—reappears in *Miami Vice* as well. Families in *Vice* are as fragmented and patchwork, relative to the norm, as any previously seen in a Mann film. The characters of Tubbs and Trudy have an intimate relationship, and it is implied that the bond between Tubbs and the FBI informant Alonzo (John Hawkes) constitutes a family; shortly after introducing Alonzo at the beginning of the film, Mann pans across a series of photos in Alonzo's apartment which capture Tubbs and Alonzo's family sitting together. However, the fact that all of these bonds are formed within the context of alienating institutions—and the fact that both Trudy and Alonzo either die or come close to dying as direct consequences of their obligations to such institutions—suggests that the health of the family as a unit, no matter what the particular nature of its makeup, is as tattered as ever in *Vice*.

These tatters are evident at several points in the narrative. Early in the film Crockett and Tubbs apprehend Alonzo on a Miami interstate (the scene recalls the passage in *Heat* in which Hanna tracks down McCauley on the Los Angeles highway); Alonzo is a FBI informant who fears for his family's lives upon giving up sensitive information about undercover agents to members of Yero's operation. After Tubbs informs Alonzo of the murder of his family by the criminals to whom he gave up the information, Alonzo gazes past Tubbs, Crockett, and the highway at a dark and indifferent Miami horizon that is oceans away from the brightly lit daytime pastels of the original television series (Alonzo's gaze is represented through one of those signature Mann shots in which visual information in the foreground of the frame is thrown out of focus in favor of a deep focus on the contours of background planes in the image). Alonzo then suddenly kills himself by walking into oncoming traffic; the slow decay of the notes in the musical score after his death implies the loss of a human spirit within the inhuman nocturnal environment of Miami represented on the film's visual track (echoing the death of Vincent at the end of *Collateral*). The fact that his death takes place against what is for Mann a familiar cityscape of alienation poetically emphasizes the link between landscape and affect present in many of the director's films, and here such affect is directly linked to the dissolution of the heteronormative family unit. Other moments in the film also inform Mann's thematic focus on the family. The last image of Tubbs and Trudy in the film is an image of their hands clasped together as they hold one another, with Trudy near death in the hospital (Trudy is severely injured in an explosion triggered by Yero in the final act of the film). While it is suggested that Trudy ultimately survives, Mann captures their hands in a (so quick to be almost imperceptible) freeze-frame, a method which echoes both the use of the same technique in *Manhunter*, in which it implied the vulnerability of familial bonds, and the earlier still photographs of Tubbs sitting with Alonzo's ill-fated family. The only reference to Crockett's childhood family life, meanwhile, comes during a discussion between him and Isabella in Cuba; Crockett implies that his father was unlucky, and this echoes the final conversation and ensuing separation between Crockett and Isabella at the end of the film ("Time is luck; luck ran out").

In addition to this focus on the characters' use of technology and the vulnerability of the family, *Miami Vice* continues Mann's interest in the exploration of the gravity of the violence his characters cause, as some of the film's first critics have pointed out (such as Stephanie Zacharek in her *Salon.com* review).[16] The consequences of violence tend to be represented stylistically through different methods across Mann's body of work. In *The Last of the Mohicans* the death of Magua, the film's villain, is given a palpable weight through the employment of slow motion as the character is slain. In the climatic shoot-out between the groups of cops and robbers in *Heat*, the innocent bystanders caught in the crossfire are a deeply felt presence, and Mann once again uses slow motion in that film to depict the wielding of violent weapons by both the cop Hanna and the robber McCauley. Only in *Collateral* is violence occasionally treated lightly and associated with a sense of humor, and such moments seem out of place in this director's oeuvre, although they may be explained as the product of Vincent's dark, nihilistic worldview (which, arguably, seeps into the film's own aesthetic at times and certainly by the film's end). In *Miami Vice* Mann employs slow motion during a failed drug bust at the beginning of the film; from the inside of an undercover police vehicle we see the bodies of FBI agents being ripped apart in gruesome detail by bullets. Mann focuses on this sequence not for the sake of gratuitousness and not only to establish the risk Crockett and Tubbs will themselves face but also to register the moment with gravitas through its representation in the film's dense, high-definition, almost photorealistic imagery. Likewise, near the end of the film in the trailer-park sequence, Tubbs kills one of Trudy's kidnappers with such suddenness that the very immediacy of the moment is startling; the moment has not been predigested into a form of crowd-pleasing narrative spectacle. The deaths within the film—even those which are not represented with slow-motion technique—are, in general, handled in a manner that recalls Peckinpah's focus on the corporeal aspect of dying, and the viewer receives from the rendering of such moments a sense of real life being extinguished from real bodies, and not simply the cynical accrual of an immense body count in another slick Hollywood action picture.

So even though some viewers have perhaps been unable to progress beyond the very title *Miami Vice* in order to discuss intelligibly the aesthetic object which the film actually is, I hope to have suggested that the value of the film is largely perceptible in the persistence of those themes in the film which have recurred throughout Mann's work. Such themes include, to summarize, the wielding of technology in order to control and potentially overcome the contingencies of society; the blurring of the line between the actions of the protagonist and the actions of the antagonist; the ambivalence regarding goals achieved or not achieved as well as a gradually increasing desire to transcend the patriarchal institutions which generate a desire for those goals in the first place; a depiction of the gravity and the consequences of violence; and the vulnerability of the family (whether that family be the potential one envisioned by Sonny and Isabella or the makeshift one formed not only by Tubbs and Trudy, but also by Tubbs and the FBI informant Alonzo, which is implied briefly at the beginning of the film). By citing particular themes from the film in this manner I want to suggest that *Miami Vice*, while by its very nature a more commercial choice than some of Mann's earlier and more "prestigious" pictures, nonetheless continues to weave variations upon ideas which the director has developed with great seriousness throughout his entire career. Commercial considerations, such as the use of a familiar genre, are not incommensurate with the making of successful motion picture art; as with *Thief*, *Heat*, and *Collateral*, the value of *Miami Vice* largely rests in the aesthetic and thematic significance Mann and his collaborators are able to achieve within genre frameworks.

Miami Vice, then, is not only interesting for its themes, but for the manner in which its style suggests and inflects its themes and ultimately creates a substantial worldview. The aesthetics of Mann's films and the power (or lack of power) that the characters themselves attain through vision and technological instruments of sight have been an intriguing counterpoint in a number of the director's films. As suggested earlier, in *Miami Vice* the characters for the first time wield instruments of surveillance and detection that go above and beyond those used by characters in the director's previous crime films. The vision enabled through the use of these devices nonetheless never quite equals Mann's own. Mann describes the interaction between his protagonist and his aesthetic in the earlier *Thief* by mentioning that "I wanted a lot of reflection and I wanted you to feel it like a three-dimensional machine, with Frank like a rat who sees the tunnels, sees how to move efficiently through the machine of the city, to get where he wants."[17] The mental image of a small animal skillfully navigating a terrain which nonetheless dwarfs it is a telling description of the relationship between figure and city in many of Mann's films, but in *Miami Vice* the relationship "collapses into one frame," to borrow a line of dialogue spoken by Jamie Foxx in the film. *Miami Vice*, unlike *Thief*, does not always give us a thoroughly contextualized visual sense of the worlds Crockett and Tubbs inhabit: Most sequences in *Miami Vice* lack a clear establishing shot, and the geography of space is often developed within scenes in a rather oblique manner. In *Miami Vice* Mann is more likely to begin a scene not by introducing us to a full setting but by exploring the metallic shine of the side of a car, the purplish tinge of the almost palpably humid Miami sky, or abstracted portions of architecture. This visual strategy, although familiar from other Mann films such as *Heat*, *The Insider*, and *Collateral*, has nonetheless been registered as a flaw by some critics: Jonathan Rosenbaum has written that Mann "tends to neglect [the characters'] visual contexts," implying (somewhat untenably, or at least confusingly) that *Miami Vice* as an aesthetic object is not itself a "visual context."[18]

Perhaps, though, *Miami Vice* has almost too much visual context in terms of the cinematic depiction of its world. As a counterpoint to its visual sense of abstraction and fragmentation, Mann and cinematographer Dion Beebe, through their use of high-definition digital video cameras, also capture an immense depth of field in certain shots that renders the world in which Crockett and Tubbs live as simply overwhelming, too much to experience visually in a single viewing of the film. At certain points while watching the film during its initial theatrical release I myself felt an acute desire to hold onto individual film frames for longer than Mann was willing to let them linger on the screen (this feeling has continued to sustain itself over several theatrical viewings as well as pause-button-resistant viewings on DVD). In *Miami Vice* the individual film frame—existing outside the parameters of the unobtrusive classical continuity system—becomes almost like a photograph hanging on a wall (a quality that, as pointed out in the chapter on *Thief*, is often regarded as anticinematic by some critics who are harsh on Mann), and yet a photograph which is nonetheless carefully knitted into the temporality of a broadly expressive style, meaning that as a film image it is not as self-consciously reflexive as what is often included in modernist, Brechtian films, but that it nonetheless also possesses a visual sense that is not fully commensurable with the idea of film images as self-effacing vehicles for narrative information.

As a result of this approach it is sometimes as if the viewer can see only an abstract portion of the film's environment. But as I have suggested, there is also a counterpoint to this aspect of the film's visual aesthetic, since just as often viewers are likely to feel that there is simply *too much* image to apprehend in a single viewing of a given shot. Manohla Dargis has nicely described this feeling:

> *Miami Vice* is a gorgeous, shimmering object, and it made me think more about how technologies are irrevocably changing our sense of what movies look like

than any film I've seen this year. Partly shot using a Viper FilmStream camera, the film shows us a world that seems to stretch on forever, without the standard sense of geographical perspective. When Crockett and Tubbs stand on a Miami roof, it's as if the world were visible in its entirety, as if all our familiar time-and-space coordinates had dropped away, because they have.[19]

Mann's highly formalized visuals in *Miami Vice* compose his characters within isolated environments they know completely and intimately (sometimes as a result of the technologies of mediation and surveillance which they wield) but, contrapuntally, both the depth of the visuals and their juxtapositions stitch such environments within larger worlds that extend far beyond the immediate milieu characters inhabit and also beyond the immediate visual grasp of the viewer. The fact that Mann repeatedly pairs extreme close-ups and other types of visual abstractions with shots possessing an immense depth of field suggests a bifurcated intent to immerse us into the psychological world of the detective work performed in the film (from this psychology there emerges a feeling of confidence within characters and perhaps also viewers in the way worlds and settings are controlled and surveyed) while at the same time constantly reaffirming a Vertovian depiction of an immense, contingent, and, in the end, ungraspable world. As Crockett in particular slowly realizes a desire to transcend the circumstances of his world, Mann's very aesthetic design—a design which suggests both a free agency within a familiar social milieu and a sense of entrapment within the borders of Mann's carefully composed film frame—becomes a source of much of *Miami Vice*'s drama. Far from being a retreat into the Hollywood netherworld of misconceived, emptily ironic television remakes, then, *Miami Vice* contains the complex relationship between innovative visual style and thematic meaning characteristic of his entire body of work.

Because a rich relationship between aesthetic design and thematic material is a crucial aspect of any Mann film, the particular means Mann and his collaborators employ to achieve their aesthetic designs is always of interest. The painterly images in *Miami Vice* might at first recall Mann's and cinematographer Dion Beebe's previous experiments with the capabilities of high-definition video to manipulate color in *Collateral*. While this sort of manipulation does in part define the aesthetic of *Miami Vice*, at the same time the style of *Vice* differs from Mann's previous films, *Collateral* included. While *Miami Vice* continues Mann's predilection for expressive mise-en-scène—the manner in which Mann establishes both the world of *Vice* and the characters within that world is developed through the same dispersive, broad quality of mise-en-scène construction as in Mann's other films—it is important to note that the images themselves, in many respects, look like nothing else in the director's filmography. As mentioned earlier, while *Vice* continues to employ the Thomson Grass Valley Viper FilmStream and Sony CineAlta high-definition digital video cameras (previously used in capturing the night sequences in *Collateral*), the camera has been used for different aesthetic purposes in this new film. Whereas interior sequences in *Collateral* were mostly shot on film, nearly all of *Miami Vice*'s sequences—including exterior and daylight sequences—were shot in high-definition. Beebe, who shot most of *Collateral*, has said:

> We went back down the digital path, but we weren't looking to reproduce the look of *Collateral*. We used the experience we gained shooting nights on *Collateral* to develop the night look on *Miami Vice*, but . . . We went for more contrast with hard light, as opposed to the soft, wraparound look we did on *Collateral*. We also had to deal with daylight, which was a new challenge for me in HD.[20]

Instead of substituting film cameras for high-definition cameras on certain entire sequences as was the case in *Collateral*, Mann and Beebe used 35mm film cameras only for those particular shots which were impossible to capture in high-definition, such as extreme close-ups and high-speed shots.[21] The result of this approach is that the high-definition video cameras paint the entire world of *Miami Vice* with a depth of field so immense and varied that virtually every single experience of the film is guaranteed, at least on the level of attention to composition and background details, to be a fundamentally different one.

The images which comprise *Miami Vice* are thus intriguing counterpoints between careful visual compositions which generate abstract views of the surrounding urban and industrial environments in which the characters work, and a rigorous depth of field granted through the use of high-definition video (almost every object in every frame seems visible and almost tangible, whereas many shots in *Collateral*, a more intimate drama, register background detail with a more opaque luminosity). The film's formalism also incorporates a kind of on-the-fly, handheld-camera aesthetic which grants the images a sense of immediacy, especially effective during those moments in the narrative when the cops need to leave behind their systems of surveillance and communication in order to perform more improvisatory and risky undercover work. This particular approach, while distinctive from Mann's previous films, nonetheless contains a recurring interest in presenting realistic and carefully researched dramatic situations while at the same time amplifying those situations through a highly controlled and carefully modulated formalism.

The interest in *Miami Vice* largely rests, then, not only on the presence of familiar thematic material which Mann has explored throughout his career, but also on the broad interplay between the director's aesthetic and the vision and desires possessed by the characters themselves. These ideas are apparent from the opening montage of the film, which drops viewers into the middle of things: Sonny Crockett and Ricardo Tubbs are staking out a band of sex traffickers in a Miami nightclub. They are assisted by intelligence analyst Trudy, an associate of Crockett and Tubbs and the girlfriend of the latter, and Gina, also an undercover cop. While Crockett, Tubbs, Trudy, and Gina stand back and observe (waiting for the right time to leap into action), fellow detective Larry Zito (Justin Theroux) sets up an elaborate surveillance system on the roof of the nightclub; meanwhile, detective Stan Switek (Domenick Lombardozzi) poses undercover as a client and stands talking with one of the traffickers, a pimp named Neptune (Isaach De Bankolé), attempting to lure him into the trap which the detectives as a team have set up. Mann's purpose with this kinetic opening montage is twofold: It seeks to establish the rhythms and feeling of this Miami nightclub (the manner in which the music on the soundtrack shifts gracefully from diegetic to nondiegetic suggests the extent to which Mann uses music to establish both the feeling of a particular setting and the feeling of the film itself, almost as if in lieu of an establishing shot), and at the same time the montage puts into play the existential crisis facing Mann's male characters, a crisis which involves a conflict between desire and the work that they are compelled to do.

As mentioned earlier, such a conflict is initially illustrated in *Vice* through Mann's recurring interest in drawing both professional and psychological parallels between his protagonists and antagonists. When we first encounter Switek, it is unclear whether he is a criminal observed by Tubbs and Crockett or the undercover agent he actually is; only when he appears on the roof with the rest of the detectives is his true identity completely inferable. (An additional opening scene preceding the scene now under discussion in an extended cut of *Miami Vice* released on DVD clarifies Switek's relationship to Crockett and Tubbs at an earlier point in the narrative, but to the detriment of the power of the nightclub sequence in the theatrical cut). Additionally, while the sex trafficking sting is put into place, Crockett is depicted flirting with a bartender and giving her a rather generous tip. This moment might be read as a socially acceptable form of behavior on Crockett's part that will nonetheless echo the actions of the sex traffickers, in that he is exchanging money for the promise of future sexual favors. At the very least it suggests a broad, potential psychological similarity between Crockett and the criminals, which echoes the relationship between the detective and the serial killer in *Manhunter* or between Vincent Hanna and Neil McCauley in *Heat*. But Mann complicates this idea by inserting a discontinuous shot of Trudy into the middle of the conversation between Crockett and the bartender, implying—perhaps because for the first time in a Mann film the primary female characters share the same profession as the male ones—that Sonny is at least partially aware of the gravity of the violence (emotional, psychological, and physical) done to women in society (his job is, supposedly, to protect against such violence) and thus his behavior is never quite a direct parallel to that of his quarry (even if it dangerously flirts with it). Any predilection Crockett has for the criminal mindset (to recall a word used by the characters in *Manhunter*) is tempered by his understanding of the violence done by those he pits himself against. One of Crockett's desires, as the film unfolds, is to break free of this conflict by pursuing a relationship with Isabella that promises a kind of utopian transcendence from the worlds they both inhabit.

Rarely in Mann's work has the thin line between protagonist and antagonist been sketched so deftly and subtly as in this opening sequence, but this idea does not determine the nature of every character in the film. For example, Foxx's Tubbs is the one character who, while not breaking his bond with or loyalty to his more cavalier partner, occasionally reminds Crockett of the dangers of identifying too closely in undercover work with the criminals they are attempting to corner. Despite his fairly conventional heroic guise, Tubbs nonetheless echoes previous figures of the law in Mann films—such as William Petersen's detective in *Manhunter* and Al Pacino's Vincent in *Heat*—in the occasional ambivalence the film holds in relation to the character's own stature as an effectual protagonist. This idea is initially suggested in the opening sequence. Tubbs is depicted carefully watching the behavior of Neptune, and reacts violently when he sees the criminal's rough physical handling of a prostitute; he proceeds to fight a number of Neptune's security guards. The fact that Tubbs fails to reach Neptune in this scene foreshadows the ineffectuality that results when Tubbs attempts to protect women in the manner of a valiant classical hero throughout the film. Indeed, the only truly "heroic" moment for Tubbs—the kind of heroism the viewer expects from a protagonist in an American action film—comes later in the film when he kills the drug boss Yero, suggesting that he can only enact his heroism when the very figures he desires to protect—women—are missing from the immediate surroundings.

The fact that Mann has placed two prominent female characters in the middle of the dramatic situation in the film's opening scene, however, points to an interesting question which the beginning of *Miami Vice* poses: What will be the role of women in relation to the male protagonists in this film? While significant female characters such as Jessie in *Thief*, Alice and Cora Munro in *The Last of the Mohicans*, Eady and Justine in *Heat*, Liane Wigand in *The Insider*, and Annie in *Collateral* seem to exist outside of the world populated by the male figures, or have a connection to that world only through the men, in *Miami Vice* Mann's men and women share the same profession and are often thrown into the same dangerous situations. The female characters in *Vice* are some of the strongest in Mann's career by virtue of this very fact, although even their strength is still a marginal concern in Mann's vision because of his insistence on depicting the predicaments and situations of his male characters. Mann's greatest limitation as a director and a writer—his inability to depict women except through the concerns and crises of men—is thus expanded to only a small degree in *Vice*, but the strong impression both Trudy and Gina register as characters is in large part due to the striking performances and presences of Naomie Harris and Elizabeth Rodriguez in these roles. Many of the film's most bravura sequences—Trudy telling off the smooth-talking informant Nicholas (Eddie Marsan) and Gina saving Trudy's life in the final act of the film—suggest behavior which, far from being defined by a relationship to the men in the film, is autonomous.

If the women exude confidence, the men in *Miami Vice* face the same kind of existential crisis familiar to previous Mann characters. They struggle when the goals they seek to achieve within the institutions for which they work come into conflict with their own desires. But if the film were concerned only with character psychology in the absence of relating that psychology to larger aesthetic emotions and ideas, it would be of only cursory interest. Another theme, which encompasses Mann's typical interest in contrasting protagonist to antagonist, is achieved through Mann's stylistic innovation. Innovation of style and form was an important aspect to a number of New Hollywood films, but form achieved its value only insofar as such innovation reflected thematic meaning that was not suitable to the construction of the types of goal-oriented classical Hollywood cinema that the New Hollywood films criticized and threw into relief. Like those films, *Miami Vice* as an aesthetic object shapes itself to reflect its director's central recurring themes, suggested earlier in this chapter: the sometimes overwhelming contingency and conscription of agency felt by his characters and at work throughout the often alienating world his films sketch. The presence of this theme throughout Mann's work has often been linked to the presence of his characters within a social world characterized by its industrial backdrops and vast cityscapes, a world that operates according to forces and interests which the characters themselves do not fully understand. I have used the word "Vertovian" to describe this aspect of Mann's style, following Mann's own claim, discussed earlier in the book, that he has been influenced by a certain strand in Dziga Vertov's work, the idea that the camera is "superhuman," that it can function as an eye which sees more than any single human being can envision. That all of Mann's characters desire an autonomy and an individual agency is clear: that they desire this against the landscape of a social world they can never quite wholly comprehend (despite their best efforts to wield instruments of technology to help them reign in that vast world) is the source of much of the dramatic and aesthetic conflict within his work.

Thus in *Miami Vice* the viewer sees the social fact of a world which extends beyond either the viewer's or the characters' understanding even though the struggle to control and reign in this world through technology—and, in the wake of understanding that the world can never quite be fully reigned in, to finally transcend that world—is dramatized. The desire for transcendence, in the end, trumps the desire to control one's existence within the very social milieu that prompts the want for transcendence in the first place. In *Miami Vice* Crockett's relationship with Isabella throws light onto this theme. The two quickly develop a relationship (instigated by a series of glances exchanged during meetings between Crockett and Tubbs's and Isabella's employers). Finally the two of them consummate their relationship outside the purview of either Montoya's operations or Crockett's undercover work by traveling to Cuba. The expanse of the ocean surrounding the two characters, as they travel in Crockett's speedboat to Cuba while Patti LaBelle's variation on Moby's "One of These Mornings" plays on the film's soundtrack, suggests that the two have succeeded in moving outside of the institutions which have positioned them as subjects. Later in the film, a conscious recognition that they are from very different social milieu ends their relationship; the film's coda, which pictures Crockett bidding goodbye to Isabella, implies the ultimate failure of the former to progress beyond the environment in which he lives and works.

The environment within which Mann's characters perform their work is not one predesigned by the filmmakers for the successful completion of goals, as are the fully presented worlds depicted within the illusionist continuity system of classical Hollywood. In other words, Mann does not assemble his images and sounds in order to lay the ground for the heroic navigation of an environment by strong, damsel-in-distress–saving protagonists, a formula that has been intact in the cinema at least since the days of D. W. Griffith and which persists today. Toward the end of the film, in perhaps the most elegiacally beautiful sequence in Mann's entire filmography, Crockett and Tubbs speed in their boats against the nocturnal backdrop of an industrial locale in Miami in an attempt to rescue Trudy, who has been kidnapped by Yero's henchmen and is being held in an urban trailer park near the Miami airport. Mann depicts Crockett and Tubbs together in profile, on the right side of the frame, as they exchange information with their associates and drive their vehicles against the impressionistic sky rendered through Mann's and Beebe's painterly use of high definition video. A typically somber piece of music—Moby's shimmering "Anthem (Cinematic Version)"—plays on the soundtrack. As Crockett, Tubbs, and their associates jump out of their boats and into a pair of police vehicles, fragments of architecture (including the brightly lit blue color of a bridge) hover in the background, drenching each shot in a cold, melancholy blue color. This is one of those Mann images that seems utterly without precedent in cinema, as if it was pulled out of a book of modernist photography; its effect is similar to the "heavy blue or amber casts [which] convey an icy or autumnal effect" that Christopher Sharrett has noted in other Mann films.[22] The urban cityscape and postmodern world that Mann has captured and to some extent created is utterly indifferent, in these kinds of sequences, to the lives of its inhabitants. And there is no sense from these sights and sounds that what is about to transpire is a heroic act. It is instead an act that the characters must perform due to the nature of their desire for their work (and their attempt to overcome its consequences), but without any guarantee of success. The cinematic world weaved around Crockett and Tubbs gives no indication that their endeavor to rescue Trudy will be successful (indeed, her life hangs in the balance by the end of the film). There is in fact no indication that their actions mean anything at all. Indeed, after Trudy is rescued by the cops (she is ultimately saved not by one of the men but by Gina, who shoots the Yero thug who holds a gun to Trudy's head) the moment is not represented as triumphant or as a vindication of law enforcement; an anguished variation of "Anthem (Cinematic Version)" appears on the soundtrack in rhyme to the earlier moment in the sequence, as Yero, from his position of surveillance in South America, dials a number on his cell phone which triggers the explosion in the trailer park that results in Trudy's serious injury.

I do not mean to imply through this enthusiasm for the film that *Miami Vice* does not contain limitations. Its attitudes toward the patriarchal world it portrays are occasionally mitigated by certain weaknesses. One of these, its general characterization of women, has already been mentioned (although within the context of Mann's other films *Vice* feels like an advance in this regard). And as discussed earlier, Mann's identification with his male characters largely prevents *Miami Vice* from developing a full critical distance toward the world it depicts, even if that world is nonetheless represented with almost palpable melancholy. Then there is the simple fact of Mann being a Hollywood director. The ending of *The Insider* suggested that, in the end, Mann was perhaps complicit with the very institutional practices (the corporate control and dissemination of images) he was critiquing. Nonetheless, *The Insider*—which I still believe is the touchstone of Mann's career to date—developed a highly sensitive poetic sense which in the end elevated itself above and beyond any mitigating commercial concerns. *Miami Vice*, by its very nature as a television remake, would seem to suggest a retreat from socially engaged cinematic poetics. In this concluding chapter I hope to have suggested the film's greater, and likely more enduring, value, which is clearly on display in the film and available to any spectator willing to look for it.

In its final moments, in fact, *Vice* suggests that, far from being a director out of ideas, Mann has been rejuvenated with a new sense of purpose through his return to the crime genre. *Miami Vice* ends with a stirring parallel montage that depicts Trudy slowly emerging from a coma with Tubbs by her side while Crockett and Isabella part ways on the shores of Florida. The last shots depicting the final moments between Crockett and Isabella, he on the shore and she in a boat sailing away, are drenched in blue, and recall not only earlier, more hopeful points in their relationship (the boat ride to Cuba in the middle of the ocean and the erotic scene between the two of them in the shower) but may also remind viewers of the final moments McCauley and Eady share in *Heat*, as McCauley drives against the blue-tinged backdrop of a Los Angeles highway tunnel, or the blue rendering of lovemaking between Will Graham and his wife in their beachside home in *Manhunter*. Tubbs and Trudy, meanwhile, share an embrace as the latter emerges from her coma, contact which is captured by Mann in a close-up of their hands tightly bound together; as mentioned earlier, he quickly freezes the frame to suggest a preservation of this moment in time (which implies that Trudy, after all, may not make it). The second to last shot of the film focuses on Isabella alone, as she faces a future without Crockett, and the moment is without precedent in Mann's films since it suggests — in contradistinction to the failure of the men — the possibility of a successful, happy, and autonomous future for one of the director's female characters. (The fact that Isabella is heading to Cuba — decidedly separate from the alienating American contexts Mann typically depicts in his films — suggests that she finds what is for a Mann character an unprecedented redemption).

In the final shot of the film, Crockett is depicted walking, in the distance, back into the hospital to rejoin Tubbs. Although this building is, on a literal level, a hospital, it also functions metonymically as the institution and social context to which Crockett belongs and which he, in the wake of his failed stab at transcendence with Isabella, ultimately cannot progress beyond. Mann's camera, in the inverse of its position during the final shot of *The Insider*, stays outside, watching Crockett head back inside in a long shot that recalls any number of final images in Mann films which depict a protagonist either walking away from the viewer or standing alone in the frame. So while the director has once again sketched the failed attempt of characters (excepting Isabella) to overcome the circumstances of their lives, the very position of Mann's camera in this final shot suggests that his own cinema may indeed continue a valiant struggle to find a place outside of circumstance and compromise. It is an optimistic ending, in terms of Mann's career, even if the events in the diegetic world do not end well. This shot, and indeed this entire riveting final sequence, like much of Mann's work, suggests signs of life within an industry that has largely been proclaimed dead in the demise of

New Hollywood, or at the very least aesthetically, politically, and socially decadent (if not dangerous). Even if *Miami Vice* does not quite scale the heights of *The Insider* or *Ali* (it is nonetheless arguably his best crime film), it contains more than its share of moments which should remind viewers of Mann's importance as a filmmaker, and it continues to find new stylistic possibilities and fresh significance in thematic material which has preoccupied him for close to three decades. Filmgoers can only hope for more such films from Mann in the future.

NOTES

1. Christopher Sharrett, "Michael Mann: Elegies on the Post-Industrial Landscape," *Fifty Contemporary Filmmakers*, ed. Yvonne Tasker (London: Routledge, 2002), 254.

2. Timothy Shary, "Which Way is Up," *Sight and Sound* 16, no. 9 (September 2006): 17.

3. Shary, 15. In a later issue of *Sight and Sound*, a reader took issue with the claim that the film was based only on Yerkovich's pilot, arguing instead that in fact the film as an adaptation synthesizes moments from other episodes of the television series and other moments in Mann's films. Nonetheless, Shary's general point is still relevant. See John Debney, "Letter of the Month," *Sight and Sound* 17, no. 1 (January 2007): 96.

4. David Bordwell, *The Way Hollywood Tells It: Story and Style in Modern Movies* (Berkeley: University of California Press, 2006), 24, 26; and Sharrett, "Michael Mann: Elegies," 254.

5. Sharrett, "Michael Mann: Elegies," 253–63.

6. Sharrett, "Michael Mann: Elegies," 262.

7. Mark Wrathall, "*Michael Mann*," *Sight & Sound* 16, no. 12 (December 2006): 95.

8. Jonathan Rosenbaum, "*Miami Vice*," *Chicago Reader*, http://onfilm.chicagoreader.com/movies/capsules/30056_MIAMI_VICE (accessed August 22, 2006).

9. See, respectively, Manohla Dargis, "Not for the Faint of Heart or Lazy of Thought," *New York Times*, 24 December 2006, AR7, AR22; and Ed Gonzalez and Nick Schager, "2006 Year in Film," *Slant*, http://www.slantmagazine.com/film/features/2006yearinfilm.asp (accessed January 11, 2007).

10. Alexander Horwath, "The Impure Cinema: New Hollywood 1967–1976," in *The Last Great American Picture Show: New Hollywood Cinema in the 1970s*, eds. Thomas Elsaesser, Alexander Horwath, and Noel King (Amsterdam: Amsterdam University Press, 2004), 9.

11. David Thomson, "The Decade When Moves Mattered," in *The Last Great American Picture Show: New Hollywood Cinema in the 1970s*, 74.

12. Noel King, "The Last Good Time We Ever Had," in *The Last Great American Picture Show: New Hollywood Cinema in the 1970s,* 30.

13. Sharrett, "Michael Mann: Elegies," 254.

14. Sharrett, "Michael Mann: Elegies," 253–63.

15. Robert Warshow, *The Immediate Experience: Movies, Comics, Theatre, and Other Aspects of Popular Culture* (Cambridge, MA: Harvard University Press, 2001), 102–3.

16. Stephanie Zacharek, "*Miami Vice*," *Salon.com*. http://www.salon.com/ent/movies/review/2006/07/28/miami_vice/index_np.html (accessed November 1, 2006).

17. Gavin Smith, "Michael Mann: Wars and Peace," *Sight and Sound* 7, no. 2 (November 1992): 10.

18. Rosenbaum, "*Miami Vice*."

19. Dargis, "Not for the Faint of Heart or Lazy of Thought," AR22.

20. Jay Holben, "Partners in Crime," *American Cinematographer* 87, no. 8 (August 2006): 53.

21. Holben, "Partners in Crime," 56, 58.

22. Sharrett, "Michael Mann: Elegies," 255.

Michael Mann Filmography

The Jericho Mile (1979). Production: ABC Circle Films [U.S.]. Distribution: American Broadcasting Company [U.S.]. Director: Michael Mann. Producer: Tim Zinnemann. Screenplay: Patrick J. Nolan and Michael Mann. Cinematographer: Rexford L. Metz. Editor: Arthur Schmidt. Aspect ratio: 1.33:1.
Cast: Peter Strauss (Rain Murphy), Richard Lawson (R. C. Stiles), Roger E. Mosley (Cotton Crown), Brian Dennehy (Dr. D), Geoffrey Lewis (Dr. Bill Janowski).

Thief (1981). Production: Mann/Caan Productions. Distribution: United Artists. Director: Michael Mann. Producers: Richard Brams, Jerry Bruckheimer, Ronnie Caan, Michael Mann. Screenplay: Michael Mann, based on *The Home Invaders*, by Frank Hohimer. Cinematography: Donald E. Thorin. Editor: Dov Hoenig. Aspect ratio: 1.85:1.
Cast: James Caan (Frank), Tuesday Weld (Jessie), Willie Nelson (Okla), James Belushi (Barry), Robert Prosky (Leo), Tom Signorelli (Attaglia), Dennis Farina (Carl).

The Keep (1983). Production: Associated Capital and Capital Equipment Leasing. Distribution: Paramount Pictures. Director: Michael Mann. Screenplay: Michael Mann, based on *The Keep*, by F. Paul Wilson. Cinematographer: Alex Thomson. Editors: Dov Hoenig and Chris Kelly. Aspect ratio: 2.35:1.
Cast: Scott Glenn (Glaeken Trismegestus), Alberta Watson (Eva Cuza), Jürgen Prochnow (Captain Klaus Woermann), Robert Prosky (Father Fonescu), Ian McKellen (Dr. Theodore Cuza).

Manhunter (1986). Production: De Laurentiis Entertainment Group (DEG) and Red Dragon Productions S.A. Distribution: De Laurentiis Entertainment Group (DEG). Director: Michael Mann. Screenplay: Michael Mann, based on *Red Dragon*, by Thomas Harris. Cinematographer: Dante Spinotti. Editor: Dov Hoenig. Aspect ratio: 2.35:1.

Cast: William Petersen (Will Graham), Kim Greist (Molly Graham), Joan Allen (Reba McClane), Brian Cox (Dr. Hannibal Lecktor), Dennis Farina (Jack Crawford), Tom Noonan (Francis Dolarhyde), Stephen Lang (Freddy Lounds).

L.A. Takedown (1989). Production: Ajar Inc., Movies Film Production, World International Network. Director: Michael Mann. Screenplay: Michael Mann. Cinematographer: Ronald Víctor García. Editor: Dov Hoenig. Aspect ratio: 1.33:1.

Cast: Scott Plank (Vincent Hanna), Alex McArthur (Patrick McClaren), Michael Rooker (Bosko), Ely Pouget (Lillian), Vincent Guastaferro (Cerrito), Laura Harrington (Eady).

The Last of the Mohicans (1992). Production: Morgan Creek Productions. Distribution: Twentieth Century Fox Film Corporation. Director: Michael Mann. Screenplay: John L. Balderston, Paul Perez, Daniel Moore, Michael Mann, Christopher Crowe, based on *The Last of the Mohicans*, by James Fenimore Cooper and the screenplay *The Last of the Mohicans* (1936), by Philip Dunne. Cinematographer: Dante Spinotti. Editor: Dov Hoenig. Aspect ratio: 2.35:1.

Cast: Daniel Day-Lewis (Hawkeye/Nathaniel Poe), Madeleine Stowe (Cora Munro), Russell Means (Chingachgook), Eric Schweig (Uncas), Jodhi May (Alice Munro), Steven Waddington (Major Duncan Heyward), Wes Studi (Magua).

Heat (1995). Production: Warner Bros., Regency Enterprises, Forward Pass, Monarchy Enterprises BV. Distribution: Warner Bros. Director: Michael Mann. Screenplay: Michael Mann. Cinematographer: Dante Spinotti. Editor: Dov Hoenig. Aspect ratio: 2.35:1.

Cast: Al Pacino (Vincent Hanna), Robert De Niro (Neil McCauley), Val Kilmer (Chris Shiherlis), Jon Voight (Nate), Tom Sizemore (Michael Cheritto), Diane Venora (Justine Hanna), Amy Brenneman (Eady), Ashley Judd (Charlene Shiherlis), Mykelti Williamson (Sergeant Drucker), Wes Studi (Detective Casals), Ted Levine (Bosko), Dennis Haysbert (Donald Breedan), William Fichtner (Roger Van Zant), Natalie Portman (Lauren), Tom Noonan (Kelso), Kevin Gage (Waingro), Hank Azaria (Alan Marciano), Danny Trejo (Trejo).

The Insider (1999). Production: Blue Light Productions, Forward Pass, Kaitz Productions, Mann/Roth Productions, Touchstone Pictures. Distribution: Buena Vista Pictures. Director: Michael Mann. Screenplay: Eric Roth and Michael Mann, based on the *Vanity Fair* article, "The Man Who Knew Too Much," by Marie Brenner. Cinematography: Dante Spinotti. Editors: William Goldenberg, David Rosenbloom, Paul Rubell. Aspect ratio: 2.35:1 (Super 35).

Cast: Al Pacino (Lowell Bergman), Russell Crowe (Jeffrey Wigand), Christopher Plummer (Mike Wallace), Diane Venora (Liane Wigand), Philip Baker Hall (Don Hewitt), Lindsay Crouse (Sharon Tiller), Debi Mazar (Debbie De Luca), Gina Gershon (Helen Caperelli), Stephen Tobolowsky (Eric Kluster).

Ali (2001). Production: Columbia Pictures Corporation, Forward Pass, Initial Entertainment Group (IEG), Moonlighting Films South Africa, Overbrook Entertainment, Peters Entertainment, Picture Entertainment Corporation. Distribution: Columbia Pictures. Director: Michael Mann. Screenplay: Gregory Allen Howard (story), Stephen J. Rivele, Christopher Wilkinson, Eric Roth, Michael Mann. Cinematography: Emmanuel Lubezki. Editors: William Goldenberg, Lynzee Klingman, Stephen E. Rivkin. Aspect ratio: 2.35:1 (Super 35).

Cast: Will Smith (Cassius Clay/Cassius X/Muhammad Ali), Jamie Foxx (Drew "Bundini" Brown), Jon Voight (Howard Cosell), Mario Van Peebles (Malcolm X), Ron Silver (Angelo Dundee), Jeffrey Wright (Howard Bingham), Mykelti Williamson (Don King), Jada Pinkett Smith (Sonji), Nona M. Gaye (Belinda Ali), Michael Michele (Veronica Porche), Giancarlo Esposito (Cassius Clay Sr.), Barry Shabaka Henley (Herbert Muhammad), LeVar Burton (Martin Luther King Jr.), Albert Hall (Elijah Muhammad).

Collateral (2004). Production: DreamWorks SKG, Paramount Pictures, Parkes/MacDonald Productions. Distribution: DreamWorks SKG. Director: Michael Mann. Screenplay: Stuart Beattie. Cinematographers: Dion Beebe and Paul Cameron. Editors: Jim Miller and Paul Rubell. Aspect ratio: 2.40:1.

Cast: Tom Cruise (Vincent), Jamie Foxx (Max), Jada Pinkett Smith (Annie), Mark Ruffalo (Fanning), Peter Berg (Richard Weidner), Bruce McGill (Pedrosa), Irma P. Hall (Ida), Barry Shabaka Henley (Daniel), Javier Bardem (Felix), Emilio Rivera (Paco).

Miami Vice (2006). Production: Universal Pictures, Forward Pass, Michael Mann Productions. Distribution: Universal Pictures. Director: Michael Mann. Screenplay: Michael Mann, based on the television series created by Anthony

Yerkovich. Cinematographer: Dion Beebe. Editors: William Goldberg, Paul Rubell. Aspect Ratio: 2.35:1.

Cast: Colin Farrell (Detective James "Sonny" Crockett), Jamie Foxx (Detective Ricardo Tubbs), Gong Li (Isabella), Naomie Harris (Trudy Joplin), Ciarán Hinds (Fujima), Justin Theroux (Zito), Luis Tosar (Arcángel de Jesús Montoya), Barry Shabaka Henley (Castillo), John Ortiz (José Yero), Elizabeth Rodriguez (Gina Calabrese), Domenick Lombardozzi (Switek).

Bibliography

BOOKS

Bettelheim, Bruno. *The Uses of Enchantment: The Meaning and Importance of Fairy Tales*. New York: Vintage, 1989.

Blum, David. *Tick . . . Tick . . . Tick: The Long Life and Turbulent Times of 60 Minutes*. New York: HarperCollins, 2004.

Blum, John Morton. *V is for Victory*. Fort Washington, PA: Harvest/HBJ Books, 1977.

Boorman, John and Walter Donahue. *Projections: A Forum for Filmmakers*. London: Faber & Faber, 1992.

Bordwell, David. *The Films of Carl-Theodor Dreyer*. Berkeley and Los Angeles: University of California Press, 1981.

———. *Narration in the Fiction Film*. Madison: University of Wisconsin Press, 1985.

———. *The Way Hollywood Tells It: Story and Style in Modern Movies*. Berkeley: University of California Press, 2006.

Bordwell, David, Janet Staiger, and Kristin Thompson. *The Classical Hollywood Cinema: Film Style & Mode of Production to 1960*. New York: Columbia University Press, 1985.

Brophy, Philip. *100 Modern Soundtracks: BFI Screen Guides*. London: British Film Institute, 2004.

Caldwell, John Thornton. *Televisuality: Style, Crisis, and Authority in American Television*. New Brunswick, NJ: Rutgers University Press, 1995.

Cook, David A. *A History of Narrative Film. 4th ed.* New York: W. W. Norton & Co., 2004.

———. *Lost Illusions: American Cinema in the Shadow of Watergate and Vietnam, 1970–1979*. New York: Charles Scribner's Sons, 2000.

Crowther, Bruce. *Captured on Film: The Prison Movie*. London: B.T. Batsford Ltd., 1989.

Early, Gerald. *The Muhammad Ali Reader*. Hopewell, New Jersey: Ecco Press, 1998.

Ehrlich, Matthew C. *Journalism in the Movies*. Urbana: University of Illinois Press, 2004.

Elsaesser, Thomas, Alexander Horwath, and Noel King, eds. *The Last Great American Picture Show: New Hollywood Cinema in the 1970s*. Amsterdam: Amsterdam University Press, 2004.

Elsaesser, Thomas and Warren Buckland. *Studying Contemporary American Film*. London: Arnold, 2002.

Engel, Joel. *Screenwriters on Screenwriting: The Best in the Business Discuss Their Craft*. New York: Hyperion, 1995.

Feeney, F. X. *Michael Mann*. London: Taschen, 2006.

Gernster, David A. and Janet Staiger, eds. *Authorship and Film*. London: Routledge, 2003.

Harris, Thomas. *Red Dragon*. New York: Random House, 1981.

Hirsch, Foster. *Detours and Lost Highways*. New York: Limelight Editions, 1999.

Hohimer, Frank. *The Home Invaders: Confessions of a Cat Burglar*. Chicago: Chicago Review Press, 1975.

James, Nick. *Heat: BFI Modern Classics*. London: British Film Institute, 2002.

Jenkins, Henry. *Textual Poachers: Television Fans and Participatory Culture*. London: Routledge, 1992.

Jones, Kent. *L'Argent: BFI Modern Classics*. London: British Film Institute, 1999.

Krutnik, Frank. *In a Lonely Street: Film Noir, Genre, and Masculinity*. London and New York: Routledge, 1991.

Leitch, Thomas. *Crime Films*. Cambridge: Cambridge University Press, 2002.

Manovich, Lev. *The Language of New Media*. Cambridge, MA: MIT Press, 2001.

Marc, David and Robert J. Thompson. *Prime Time, Prime Movers*. Boston: Little, Brown & Co., 1992.

Marcuse, Herbert. *One-Dimensional Man: Studies in the Ideology of Advanced Society*. Boston: Beacon Press, 1964.

Milne, Tom, ed. and trans. *Godard on Godard*. London: Secker & Warburg, 1972.

Mussman, Toby, ed. *Jean-Luc Godard*. New York: E. P. Dutton, 1968.

Naremore, James, ed. *Film Adaptation*. New Brunswick, NJ: Rutgers University Press, 2000.

———. *More Than Night: Film Noir in its Contexts*. Berkeley and Los Angeles: University of California Press, 1998.

Neale, Steve, ed. *Genre and Contemporary Hollywood*. London: British Film Institute, 2002.

Nelson, Thomas Allen. *Kubrick: Inside a Film Artist's Maze*. Bloomington: Indiana University Press, 2000.

Ray, Robert B. *A Certain Tendency of the American Cinema*. Princeton, NJ: Princeton University Press, 1985.

———. *How a Film Theory Got Lost and Other Mysteries in Cultural Studies*. Bloomington and Indianapolis: Indiana University Press. 2001.

Remnick, David. *King of the World*. New York: Random House, 1998.

Rosenbaum, Jonathan. *Essential Cinema: On the Necessity of Film Canons*. Baltimore: John Hopkins University Press, 2004.

Rosenbaum, Jonathan and Adrian Martin, eds. *Movie Mutations*. London: British Film Institute, 2003.
Self, Robert T. *Robert Altman's Subliminal Reality*. Minneapolis: University of Minnesota Press, 2002.
Simpson, Philip L. *Psycho Paths: Tracking the Serial Killer Through Contemporary American Film and Fiction*. Carbondale: Southern Illinois University Press, 2000.
Steensland, Mark. *Michael Mann*. London: Pocket Essentials, 2002.
Tasker, Yvonne, ed. *Fifty Contemporary Filmmakers*. London: Routledge, 2002.
Thompson, Kristin. *Storytelling in the New Hollywood*. Cambridge, MA: Harvard University Press, 1999.
Thomson, David. *The Biographical Dictionary of Film*. New York: Knopf, 2002.
Truffaut, François. *Hitchcock*, rev. ed. New York: Simon & Schuster, 1985.
Warshow, Robert. *The Immediate Experience: Movies, Comics, Theatre, and Other Aspects of Popular Culture*. Cambridge, MA: Harvard University Press, 2001.
Wexman, Virginia Wright, ed. *Film and Authorship*. New Brunswick, NJ: Rutgers University Press, 2003.
Wildermuth, Mark E. *Blood in the Moonlight: Michael Mann and Information Age Cinema*. Jefferson, NC: McFarland & Co., 2005.
Williams, Tony. *Hearths of Darkness: The Family in the American Horror Film*. London: Associated University Presses, 1996.
Wilson, F. Paul. *The Keep*. New York: William, Morrow & Co, 1981.
Wood, Robin. *Hitchcock's Films Revisited. Rev. ed*. New York: Columbia University Press, 2002.

JOURNAL ARTICLES

Andrew, Geoff. "Mann to Man." *Time Out*, no. 1159 (January 17, 1996): 16–17.
Arthur, Paul. "Lord of the Ring." *Film Comment* 38, no. 1 (January–February 2002): 32–34.
Auster, Al and Leonard Quart. "Thief." *Cineaste* 11, no. 3 (1981): 38.
Baker, Martin. "First and Last Mohicans." *Sight and Sound* 3, no. 8 (August 1993): 26–29.
Bankston, Douglas. "A Familiar Fiend." *American Cinematographer* 83, no. 10 (October 2002): 48–61.
Combs, Richard. "Michael Mann: Becoming." *Film Comment* 32, no. 2 (March/April 1996).
———. "Violent Streets." *Monthly Film Bulletin* 33, no. 569 (June 1981): 121–22.
Comer, Brooke. "Last of the Mohicans: Interpreting Cooper's Classic." *American Cinematographer* 77, no. 1 (January 1996): 30–34.
Coppola, Don. "Bringing Historical Characters to Life: An Interview with Stephen J. Rivele." *Cineaste* 27, no. 2 (Spring 2002): 16–19.
Debney, John. "Letter of the Month." *Sight and Sound* 17, no. 1 (January 2007): 96.
Fox, Julian. "Four Minute Mile." *Films & Filming* 26, no. 4 (January 1980): 19–25.
Fuller, Graham. "Michael Mann." *Interview* 25, no. 12 (December 1995).

Goldsmith, David. "*Collateral*: Stuart Beattie's Character-Driven Thriller." *Creative Screenwriting* 11, no. 4 (July–August 2004): 50–53.
Harkness, John. "White Noise." *Sight and Sound* 2, no. 7 (November 1992): 15.
Holben, Jay. "Hell on Wheels." *American Cinematographer* 85, no. 8 (August 2004): 40–42, 44, 46–51.
———. "Partners in Crime." *American Cinematographer* 87, no. 8 (August 2006): 52–63.
———. "Ring Leader." *American Cinematographer* 82, no. 11 (November 2001): 34–49.
———. "Shooting From the Hip." *American Cinematographer* 84, no. 2 (February 2003): 66–73.
James, Nick. "No Smoking Gun." *Sight and Sound* 10, no. 3 (March 2000): 14–17, 46–47.
Kelly, Richard T. "*Collateral*." *Sight and Sound* 14, no. 10 (October 2004): 50.
Kennedy, Harlan. "Castle 'Keep.'" *Film Comment* 19, no. 6 (November/December 1983): 16–19.
Lindstrom, J. A. "*Heat*: Work and Genre." *Jump Cut*, no. 43 (July 2000): 21–30.
Magid, Ron. "A Left-Right Camera Combo." *American Cinematographer* 82, no. 11 (November 2001): 42–43.
Manovich. Lev. "What Is Digital Cinema?" *Blimp* 37 (1997): 38.
Martin, Adrian. "Mise-en-scene is Dead, or The Expressive, The Excessive, The Technical, and The Stylish." *Continuum: The Australian Journal of Media & Culture* 5, no. 2 (1990): 87–140.
Newman, Kim. "The Keep." *Monthly Film Bulletin* 52, no. 615 (April 1985): 127–28.
Olsen, Mark. "It Happened One Night." *Sight and Sound* 14, no. 10 (October 2004): 14–15.
———. "Paint it Black." *Sight and Sound* 14, no. 10 (October 2004): 16.
Phillips, Kendall R. "Redeeming the Visual: Aesthetic Questions in Michael Mann's *Manhunter*." *Literature/Film Quarterly* 31, no. 1 (2003): 10–16.
Robley, Les Paul. "Hot Set." *American Cinematographer* 77, no. 1 (January 1996): 46–50.
Rochlin, Margy. "'Vice' is Nice . . ." *American Film* 11, no. 10 (September 1986): 20–25, 56, 58.
Routt, William D. "L'Evidence." *Continuum: The Australian Journal of Media & Culture* 5, no. 2 (1990): 40–67.
Shary, Timothy. "Which Way is Up." *Sight and Sound* 16, no. 9 (September 2006): 14–18.
Smith, Gavin. "Mann Hunters." *Film Comment* 28, no. 6 (November-December 1992): 72, 75, 77.
———. "Michael Mann: Wars and Peace." *Sight and Sound* 2, no. 7 (November 1992): 10–12.
Sterritt, David. "Short Takes," *Christian Science Monitor*, April 16, 1981.
Taylor, Paul. "Castles in Romania." *Monthly Film Bulletin* 52, no. 615 (April 1985): 129–31.
Thompson, Clifford. "Ali." *Flim Quarterly* 4, no 55 (Summer 2002): 46.
Wood, Robin. "Questions of Value." *Cineaction* 62 (2003): 1.

Wootton, Adrian. "The Big Hurt." *Sight and Sound* 12, no. 3 (March 2002): 16–18, 34–35, 52.

Wrathall, Mark. "*Michael Mann*." *Sight and Sound* 16, no. 12 (December 2006): 95.

MAGAZINES, NEWSPAPERS, AND TRADE JOURNALS

Brenner, Marie. "The Man Who Knew Too Much." *Vanity Fair* (May 1996).

Canby, Vincent. "Screen: 'Thief,' With Caan and Tuesday Weld." *New York Times*, (27 March 1981), C12.

"CBS Pulls Show, Denies Star Was Reason." *Seattle Times*, December 13, 2002.

Chase, Chris. "At the Movies." *New York Times* (3 April 1981): C6.

Dargis, Manhola. "Killer in a Cab, Doing His Job." *New York Times*, August 6, 2004, B7.

———. "Not for the Faint of Heart or Lazy of Thought." *New York Times* (24 December 2006): AR7, AR22.

Dargis, Manohla and A. O. Scott. "The Lights, The Actors, The Issues, The Camera. Discuss." *New York Times* (16 December 2004): 1, 20.

Farber, Stephen. "TV Series to Be Broadcast in Stereo." *New York Times* (9 July 1984): C18.

Gallo, Phil. "*Robbery Homicide Division*." *Variety* (7 October 2002): 33.

Goodman, Walter. "Screen: *Manhunter*," *New York Times* (15 August 1986): C6.

Honeycutt, Kirk. "Made-for-TV Films—Hollywood's Stepchild Comes of Age." *New York Times* (19 August 1979): D1.

McCarthy, Todd. "No Sweat on Mann-Made *Ali*." *Variety*, December 17, 2001, 35.

O'Connor, John J. "'Crime Story'—A Tale of Formula Takeover." *New York Times* (14 December 1986): H33, H40.

———. "'Matt Helm,' 'Bronk' in Detective Ranks." *New York Times* (20 September 1975): 59.

———. "A Preview of NBC's 'Crime Story.'" *New York Times* (18 September, 1986): C30.

———. "TV Weekend: Natalie Wood Sparks ABC's 'Cracker Factory.'" *New York Times* (16 March 1979): C30.

Rosenbaum, Jonathan. "Art in Action." *Chicago Reader* (5 August 2004).

Sloane, Leonard. "ABC On Its Way Out of the Cellar." *New York Times* (9 November 1975): F1–F2.

Woodward, Richard B. "The Intensely Imagined Life of Daniel Day-Lewis." *New York Times* (5 July, 1992): SM14–SM19, SM30.

Yerkovich, Anthony. Letter to the editor. *Los Angeles Times* (8 June 1986), 107.

ARTICLES ON WEBSITES

Anderson, Michael J. "Before Sunrise, or Los Angeles Plays Itself in a Lonely Place." *Senses of Cinema* http://www.sensesofcinema.com/contents/04/33/collateral.html (accessed February 23, 2005).

Dzenis, Anna. "Great Directors: Michael Mann." *Senses of Cinema* http://www.sensesofcinema.com/ contents/ directors/02/mann.html (accessed January 11, 2005).
———. "Impressionist extraordinaire: Michael Mann's *Ali*." *Senses of Cinema* http://www.sensesofcinema.com/contents/01/19/ali.htm (accessed January 11, 2005).
———. "Michael Mann's Cinema of Images." *Screening the Past* http://www.latrobe.edu.au/screeningthepast/firstrelease/fr0902/adfr14b.html (accessed January 11, 2005).
Gonzalez, Ed and Nick Schager. "2006 Year in Film." *Slant Magazine*, http://www.slantmagazine.com/film/features/2006yearinfilm.asp (accessed January 11, 2007).
The Internet Movie Database. http:/www.imdb.com (accessed October 12, 2004; November 13, 2004; February 15, 2005; 22 February 2005).
Mann, Michael. Interview, *Ali* website. http:www.spe.sony.com/movies/ali/flash.html (accessed July 19, 2004).
———. "*Sight and Sound* Top Ten." *Sight and Sound*. http://www.bfi.org.uk/sightandsound/topten/poll/voter.php?forename=Michael&surname=Mann (accesseed February 1, 2005).
Piter, Stéphane. *The Keep* fan website http://www.the-keep.ath.cx/default_en.htm (accessed January 29, 2005).
"*Robbery Homicide Division*." *TV Tome*. http://www.tvtome.com/tvtome/servlet/Show/MainServlet/showed-10646/Robbery_Homicide_Division/ (accessed February 22, 2005).
Rosenbaum, Jonathan. "*Miami Vice*." *Chicago Reader*, http://onfilm.chicagoreader.com/movies/capsules/30056_MIAMI_VICE (accessed August 22, 2006).
Routt, William D. "L'Evidence." *Continuum: The Australian Journal of Media & Culture* 5, no. 2 (1990), http://wwwmcc.murdoch.edu.au/ReadingRoom/5.2/Routt.html (accessed November 15, 2004).
Sragow, Michael. "All the Corporations' Men." *Salon.com* http://www.salon.com/ent/col/sraq/1999/11/04/mann (accessed November 11, 2004).
———. "Mann Among Men." *Salon.com* http://www.salon.com/bc/1999/02/02bc.html (accessed November 14, 2004).
Thoret, Jean-Baptiste. "The Aquarium Syndrome: On the Films of Michael Mann." *Senses of Cinema* http:www.sensesofcinema.com/contents/01/19/mann.html (accessed November 15, 2004).
Zacharek, Stephanie. "*Miami Vice*" (Film Review). *Salon.com*. http://www.salon.com/ent/movies/review/2006/07/28/miami_vice/index.np.html (accessed November 1, 2006).

Index

17 Days Down the Line, 23
60 Minutes, 131, 132
77 Sunset Strip, 30
2001: A Space Odyssey, 59, 114, 115

ABC (American Broadcasting Company), 25, 26, 169
Adamson, Chuck, 93, 112
The Agency, 169
Ali, 12, 13, 27, 28, 32, 50, 51, 56, 83, 90, 95, 106, 108, 112, 117, 151–66, 169, 170, 171, 177, 191, 194, 196, 199, 212
Ali, Muhammad, 2, 90, 151, 152, 191
All in the Family, 25, 30
All the President's Men, 134, 135
Allen, Woody, 41
Altman, Robert, 8–9, 10, 11, 187, 194, 195, 196
Anderson, Michael J., 176
Angel Heart, 53
Antonioni, Michelangelo, 56, 126, 184
L'Argent, 49
Armstrong, Gillian, 170
Arthur, Paul, 152, 163
Ashby, Hal, 41
Audioslave, 181
Auster, Al, 45
auteurism and authorship, 4–6, 11, 14–17, 153–54

Avary, Roger, 113
The Aviator, 98
L'avventura, 126

Bad Girls, 95
Balio, Tina, 95
Bardem, Javier, 180
Barker, Martin, 95
Bassett, Angela, 151
Bazin, André, 2
Beattie, Stuart, 172
Beebe, Dion, 170, 204, 205
Belushi, Jim, 42, 44
Bergman, Lowell, 131–132, 133
Berkeley, Xander, 111, 125
Bettelheim, Bruno, 64–65
Bingham, Howard, 159
biographical legend (as reading strategy), 4–7
Biopic genre, 3
Black Widow, 53
Blum, John Mortin, 107
Body Heat, 53, 54
Bonnie and Clyde, 195
Boorman, John, 59
Bordwell, David, 5, 7–10, 13, 14, 18n, 189
Bourke, Pieter, 142
Bram Stoker's Dracula, 98

Braveheart, 95, 96
Brenneman, Amy, 115, 119
Brenner, Marie, 132
Bresson, Robert, 13, 49
Brook, Michael, 116
Brophy, Philip, 116
Brown and Williamson Tobacco Company, 131, 132
Buckland, Warren, 10, 11, 12
Burton, LeVar, 164
Bush, Billy Green, 36
Byrne, Gabriel, 60

Caan, James, 41, 42, 43, 44, 46, 52, 53, 96, 100, 133
Cahiers du cinéma, 12
Caldwell, John Thornton, 29, 30, 31
Cameron, James, 184
Campion, Jane 170
Canby, Vincent, 44, 46
Cape Fear (1990), 98
Cassavetes, John, 41
Caton-Jones, Michael, 95
CBS (Columbia Broadcasting System), 131, 132, 169
Chandler, Raymond, 135
Charlotte Gray, 170
Chicago, 170
Cimino, Michael, 75
Clannad, 106–7
Coen brothers, 179
Collateral, 2, 13, 32, 56, 72, 73, 90, 108, 112, 117, 152, 164, 170–185, 187, 188, 191, 192, 195, 200, 201, 202, 203, 204, 205, 207
Combs, Richard, 1, 2, 90, 91, 100, 113, 114
Cook, David A., 9, 22, 184
Cooke, Sam, 160, 162, 163
Cool Hand Luke, 28
Cooper, James Fenimore, 94, 95
Coppola, Francis Ford, 98
Costner, Kevin, 95
costume film subgenre, 95

Cox, Brian, 76
crime genre, 3, 12, 13, 44, 79, 112, 122, 152, 171, 174, 187, 188, 197, 198, 202, 211, 212
Crime Story, 5, 41, 93, 111, 195–96
Crowe, Russell, 133, 141
Crowther, Bruce, 28
Cruise, Tom, 90, 171, 172, 174, 176, 181, 182, 183
Curtis, Clifford, 135

Dances with Wolves, 95
Dardenne, Jean-Pierre and Luc, 194
Dargis, Manohla, 2, 182, 194, 203
The Dark Crystal, 59
Dassin, Jules, 45
Davis, Miles, 178, 179
De Bankolé, Issach, 206
De Niro, Robert, 112, 115, 117, 118, 121, 122, 123
De Palma, Brian, 59, 190
Dead Birds, Dead Birds, 21
Dead Man, 95, 108
Defiant Ones, The, 28
Demme, Jonathan, 76
Denison, Anthony, 93
Dennehy, Brian, 36
The Departed, 98
Dickinson, Angie, 25
digital compositing effects, 115, 183–84
Dirty Harry, 23, 47, 122, 123
Dog Day Afternoon, 133
Donen, Stanley, 59
Donner, Richard, 59, 60, 95
Dr. Strangelove, or How I Learned to Stop Worrying and Love the Bomb, 113
Dragonslayer, 59
Dreyer, Carl-Theodor., 7, 8, 13
Drug Wars: The Camerena Story, 94
Dundee, Angelo, 167n19
Dunne, Paul, 107
Dylan, Bob, 164
Dzenis, Anna, 12, 21, 154, 155, 157

E.T.: The Extra-Terrestrial, 59, 65
Early, Gerald, 157
Eastwood, Clint, 59, 95, 122, 188
L'eclisse, 184
Ehrlich, Matthew C., 134
Eisenberg, Hallie Kate, 138
Eisenstein, Sergei, 45
Elliott, David, 157, 163
Elsaesser, Thomas, 10, 11, 12
L'Enfant, 194
Engel, Joel, 60
Eno, Brian, 116, 123, 124
Espositio, Giancarlo, 157
Excalibur, 59

fantasy genre, 59, 64, 65, 66
Far and Away, 95
Farber, Manny, 14
Farina, Dennis, 41, 52, 53, 76, 93
Farmer, Johnny, 164
Farrell, Colin, 197
Father Knows Best, 30
Feeney, F.X., 3
Ferrara, Abel, 11, 113
Fichtner, William, 118
film noir, 12, 30, 45, 53, 54, 171
Firestarter, 60
Fischl, Eric, 56
Flags of Our Fathers, 188
Ford, John, 3, 108, 117
Foxx, Jamie, 158, 159, 172, 182, 197, 202, 207
Fujimoto, Tak, 22

Gage, Kevin, 117
Gambon, Michael, 137
Gangs of New York, 98
    gangster genre, 12, 53, 55, 56, 198–99
Gast, Leon, 165
Gaye, Nona M., 165
Geronimo: An American Legend, 95, 151
Gerrard, Lisa, 116, 142, 143, 144, 147
Gershon, Gina, 133, 144–45

Gibbsville, 25
Gibson, Brian, 60, 151
Gibson, Mel, 95
Gilbert and George, 56
Gladiator, 51
The Glasshouse, 28
Glenn, Scott, 60
Godard, Jean-Luc, 15
Gone in Sixty Seconds, 170
Gonzalez, Ed, 194
Good Times, 27
Gooding, Jr., Cuba, 151
The Greatest, 151
Greist, Kim, 77, 105
Griffith, D.W., 209
Groove Armada, 176

Hackford, Taylor, 165
Hall, Albert, 160
Hall, Irma P., 179
Hall, Philip Baker, 140
Hanna, 111
Hannibal, 76
Hanson, Curtis, 133
Harkness, John, 96
Harrington, Laura, 111
Harris, Naomie, 197, 207
Harris, Thomas, 76, 77, 80
Hawkes, John, 200
Hawks, Howard, 3, 117
Hayden, Sterling, 173
Haysbert, Dennis, 113
Heat, 13, 24, 28, 41, 50, 51, 53, 56, 73, 90, 93, 94, 95, 100, 105, 106, 108, 111, 112–128, 131, 132, 134, 136, 152, 155, 158, 159, 164, 171, 172, 173, 179, 184, 187, 188, 191, 192, 195, 196, 197, 198, 199, 200, 201, 202, 203, 206, 207, 211
Henderson, Brian, 15
Henley, Barry Shabaka, 178
Henson, Jim, 59
Hero, 98
Hide in Plain Sight, 41

high-definition digital video, 169–70, 170–71, 171–72, 181, 184, 203–5
Hill Street Blues, 75
Hill, Walter, 95, 151
The Hire: Beat the Devil, 170
Hirsch, Foster, 122
Hitchcock, Alfred, 3, 63, 137, 182
Hockney, David, 56
Hoenig, Dov, 41, 68, 81, 121, 124
Hohimer, Frank, 42–43, 44, 57n4
Holy Smoke!, 170
The Home Invasions: Confessions of a Cat Burglar, 42–43, 60
Hooper, Tobe, 60
horror genre, 78, 81
Horwath, Alexander, 195
House of Flying Daggers, 98
Howard, Ron, 95
Hsiao-Hsien, Hou, 194
Hunger, The, 60

In the Cut, 170
Inland Empire, 194
The Insider, 4, 27, 28, 37, 50, 51, 56, 83, 90, 95, 100, 108, 112, 116, 131–148, 152, 155, 158, 165, 171, 175, 179, 192, 194, 195, 196, 197, 199, 200, 203, 207, 210, 211, 212
Insurrection, 22
Iron Butterfly, 88, 89

James, Nick, 113, 119, 120, 126, 127, 135
Janpuri, 22
Jarmusch, Jim, 95, 108
The Jeffersons, 30
The Jericho Mile, 4, 12, 21, 26–29, 31–38, 41, 46, 50, 51, 55, 60, 66, 72, 191
Jones, Kent, 49, 129n17
Journalism film genre, 134–35, 142
Judd, Ashley, 119
Julia, 30, 31
Jurassic Park, 183

Kael, Pauline, 196
Kaplan, Jonathan, 95
Kasdan, Lawrence, 53, 95
The Keep (film), 12, 59–73, 75, 78, 95, 99, 112, 116, 136
The Keep (novel), 63–64
Keita, Salif, 165
Kelly, Richard T., 183
The Killing, 93, 115, 173
Killing Zoe, 113
Kilmer, Val, 113, 117
King of New York, 113
King, Noel, 196
King, Stephen, 64
Kirkwood, Gene, 59
Koch, Jr., Howard, 59
Kramer, Stanley, 28
Krull, 59
Kubrick, Stanley, 45, 59, 62, 63, 64, 93, 113, 114
Kung Fu, 30, 31
Kurosawa, Akira, 53

L.A. Confidential, 133
L.A. Takedown, 94, 111–112, 189
LaBelle, Patti, 209
Lady in the Lake, 135
LadyHawke, 60
The Ladykillers, 179
The Last of the Mohicans (1936 film), 94, 107
The Last of the Mohicans (1992 film), 4, 13, 24, 90, 94–109, 111, 139, 166, 179, 201, 207
The Last of the Mohicans (novel), 94, 95, 107
Law and Order, 169
Law and Order: Special Victims Unit, 169
Lawson, Richard, 27
Lear, Norman, 30
Lee, Spike, 151, 190
Leigh, Mike, 22
Leitch, Thomas, 172

Lester, Mark L., 60
Letters from Iwo Jima, 188
Lewis, Daniel-Day, 90, 96, 106
Li, Gong, 105, 197
Ligeti, György, 115
Lindstrom, J.A., 112, 113
Lombardozzi, Domenick, 206
London Film School, 21, 22
The Loneliness of the Long Distance Runner, 28
The Long Goodbye (Altman), 8
The Longest Yard (1974), 28
Longo, Robert, 56
Lopez, Jennifer, 151
Lubezki, Emmanuel, 155, 159, 160, 161
Lumet, Sidney, 122, 133, 134

Malcolm X, 151
Man on Fire, 170
Manhunter, 13, 24, 27, 41, 50, 51, 53, 60, 72, 75, 76–91, 93, 95, 96, 97, 100, 105, 116, 119, 121, 122, 134, 136, 139, 142, 172, 179, 191, 192, 200, 201, 206, 207
Mann, Ami Canaan, 169
Manovich, Lev, 183
Marc, David, 25, 26
Marcuse, Herbert, 131
Marquez, Gabriel Garcia, 62, 63
Marsan, Eddie, 208
Marshall, Rob, 170
Martin, Adrian, 10–17, 44, 188
Maude, 30
   Maverick, 95
May, Jodhi, 102, 105
Mazar, Debi, 140
McAlister, Michael, 161
McArthur, Alex, 111
McCabe and Mrs. Miller, 187
McCarthy, Todd, 151
McCauley, Neil, 112
McKellen, Ian, 60
Mean Streets, 42
Means, Russell, 99, 107

Memoirs of a Geisha, 170
Men of Honor, 151
Miami Vice (film), 13, 24, 28, 41, 95, 96, 105, 106, 108, 112, 142, 152, 187, 188, 189, 191, 192, 194–212
Miami Vice (television series), 4, 31, 75–76, 93, 97, 111, 196
Million Dollar Baby, 188
Ming-Liang, Tsai, 129n17
mise-en-scène criticism, 4, 10–17, 96
Mitry, Jean, 114
Mizoguchi, Kenji, 15
Mizrahi, Moshé, 42
Moby, 116, 209, 210
The Mod Squad, 30
modernist cinema, 190–91
Montgomery, Robert, 135
Moonlighting, 94
Morris, Meaghan, 14
Murphy, Geoff, 95
music, *see* sound design and music
Myhre, John, 154
Mystic River, 188

Naremore, James, 53, 54, 63
Nava, Gregory, 151
NBC (National Broadcasting Company), 22, 93, 94, 169
Neale, Steve, 95, 113, 121
Nelson, Thomas Allen, 114
Nelson, Willie, 42
neo-noir, 12, 53, 57, 78, 79, 122, 171
Network, 134
New Hollywood cinema, 8, 10, 11, 187, 191, 194–97, 208, 212
Newman, Kim, 62
Nolan, Patrick J., 26, 27
Noonan, Tom, 76, 119
La Notte, 184

O'Connor, Carroll, 25
O'Connor, John J., 25, 93
O'Hara, John, 25
Olsen, Mark, 171

Olstead, Renee, 139
One Hundred Years of Solitude, 62
Ortiz, John, 197
Ozu, Yasujiro, 8, 13, 141

Pacino, Al, 93, 112, 117, 121, 122, 123, 133, 139, 145, 146, 159, 193, 207
Pakula, Alan J., 134
The Parallax View, 134
Parker, Alan, 53
Passengers, 116
Peckinpah, Sam, 95, 104, 108, 124, 194, 196
Peeping Tom, 87
Penn, Arthur, 194, 195, 196
Percy, Valerie, 43
Perkins, V.F., 12
Petersen, William, 76, 207
Phillips, Kendall R., 89
Pinkett-Smith, Jada, 175
Pinto, Antonio, 185
Piter, Stéphane, 74n15
Plank, Scott, 111
Plummer, Christopher, 139, 146
Police Story, 25
Police Woman, 25
politics (of Mann's cinema), 192–94
Poltergeist, 60
Poltergeist II, 60
The Pope of Greenwich Village, 59
Portman, Natalie, 117
Pouget, Ely, 111
Powell, Michael, 87
Prochnow, Jürgen, 60, 70
product placement, 186n17
Prosky, Robert, 42, 60

Quart, Leonard, 45
The Quick and the Dead, 95, 133

Rafelson, Bob, 53
Raimi, Sam, 95, 133
The Rainmaker, 98
Ramparts (magazine), 131
Ratner, Brett, 76, 77

Ray, Robert B., 9, 134
Rear Window, 182
Red Dragon (film), 76
Red Dragon (novel), 76, 77, 80
Redford, Robert, 113
Reininger, Gustave, 93
Reservoir Dogs, 113, 121
Rififi, 45
Ritt, Martin, 28
Rivele, Stephen J., 152
Rob Roy, 95, 96
Robbery Homicide Division, 169–70
Robbins, Matthew, 59
Robin Hood: Prince of Thieves, 95
Rochlin, Margy, 75
Rodriguez, Elizabeth, 197, 207
Roe, Bill, 170
Roëves, Maurice, 101
Rolling Stone (magazine), 75–76
The Rolling Stones, 31, 32
Rosenbaum, Jonathan, 1, 13, 179, 194, 203
Rosenberg, Stuart, 59
Roth, Eric, 133, 152
Rouch, Jean, 41–42
Routt, William D., 16
Rowan and Martin's Laugh-In, 30
Rubini, Michel, 81
Rudolph, Alan, 11
Ruffalo, Mark, 180

Santucci, John, 41
Saturn 3, 59
Scarface (1932), 173
Scarface (1983), 59
Schager, Nick, 194
Schindel, Barry, 169
Schweig, Eric, 99
Scorsese, Martin, 42, 98, 162, 190, 195
Scott, Randolph, 95
Scott, Ridley, 22, 51, 76
Scott, Tony, 60, 170
Selena, 151
Self, Robert T., 9
Sena, Dominic, 170

Serpico, 122, 123, 133
Sharrett, Christopher, 56, 57, 100, 108, 136, 187, 193, 196, 210
Shary, Timothy, 187, 188
The Shining (film), 62, 64
The Shining (novel), 64
Siegel, Don, 122
The Silence of the Lambs, 76
Silver, Ron, 158
Simpson, Philip L., 78, 79
Sizemore, Tom, 117, 169
Smith, Gavin, 68
Smith, Will, 2, 156, 159, 161
Sneakers, 113
Soderbergh, Steven, 190
sound design and music, 31–33, 49–53, 67–68, 69, 71–72, 82, 89, 116, 143–44, 147, 181, 184–85, 206, 209–10
Sounder, 28
Spelling, Aaron, 23, 26
Spielberg, Steven, 59, 65, 183
Spinotti, Dante, 77, 96, 97, 114, 115, 120, 123, 136, 140, 141, 143
Staiger, Janet, 6, 7, 13
Starsky and Hutch (television series), 23–25, 47
Statham, Jason, 174
Steensland, Mark, 3
Sterritt, David, 44
Stone, Oliver, 22, 152
Stowe, Madeleine, 101, 105, 106
Strauss, Peter, 26
Studi, Wes, 102, 151
Sudden Impact, 59
Superman, 59

Tangerine Dream, 42, 49, 50, 51, 52, 67–68, 72
Tarantino, Quentin, 113, 190
Tati, Jacques, 13
Taxi Driver, 195
Taylor, Paul, 75
The Terminator, 183
Terms of Endearment, 59

Theroux, Justin, 206
Thief, 12, 13. 24, 28, 37, 41–57, 59, 61, 62, 73, 78, 83, 90, 95, 96, 100, 106, 108, 113–14, 116, 120, 122, 132, 133, 139, 152, 158, 164, 171, 172, 177, 179, 191, 192, 195, 198, 199, 200, 201, 203, 207
Thompson, Clifford, 157
Thompson, Kristin, 61
Thompson, Robert J., 25, 26
Thomson, Alex, 67
Thomson, David, 14, 195–96
Thoret, Jean-Baptiste, 1, 133–34, 145
Thorin, Donald E., 41, 54
Three Times, 194
Tillman, Jr., George, 151
Titanic, 183, 184
Tobolowsky, Stephen, 145
Tolkien, J.R.R., 65
Tomashevsky, Boris, 5
Toney, James, 165
Tosar, Luis, 197

Unforgiven, 95
University of Wisconsin at Madison, 21, 131
The Uses of Enchantment: The Meaning and Importance of Fairy Tales, 65

Van Peebles, Mario, 156
Variety, 151
Veevers, Wally, 59
Vega$, 26
Venora, Diane, 105, 117, 138
Vertigo, 137
Vertov, Dziga, 45, 113, 136, 208
Voight, Jon, 118, 160

Waddington, Steve, 101
The Wall Street Journal, 132
Wallace, Mike, 132
Walt Disney Company, 29
Warshow, Robert, 55, 198
Washington, Denzel, 151
Watson, Alberta, 60

Weld, Tuesday, 42
Western genre, 95, 104
What's Love Got to Do With It, 151
When We Were Kings, 165
Wigand, Jeffrey S., 131–132
The Wild Bunch, 95, 108
Wildermuth, Mark E., 3, 5, 71
Wilkinson, Christopher, 152
Williams, Tony, 78, 79
Wilson, F. Paul, 60, 63–64
women (as subjects of Mann's films), 105–6, 207–8

Wood, Robin, 137
Wyatt Earp, 95

The X-Files, 170, 171

Yates, Peter, 59–60
Yerkovich, Anthony, 75, 76, 189
Yimou, Zhang, 98
Young Guns II, 95

Zacharek, Stephanie, 201

About the Author

Steven Rybin teaches in the School of Interdisciplinary Arts at Ohio University in Athens, Ohio, where he is also pursuing a doctoral degree in Film Studies and Aesthetics. His writing on film has previously appeared in the online journal Senses of Cinema.